D0764251

Rachel Roddy writes a weekly column for *Guardian Cook*. Her first book, *Five Quarters,* won the André Simon Food Book award and the Guild of Food Writers' First Book award. Rachel lives with her partner, Vincenzo, and son, Luca, near the food market in Testaccio, a distinctive working-class quarter of Rome, and spends part of the year in Vincenzo's family house in Gela, south-east Sicily.

racheleats.wordpress.com   @racheleats   @rachelaliceroddy

Rachel Roddy

Two Kitchens

Family Recipes from Sicily and Rome

With photography by
Nick Seaton and Rachel Roddy

CONTENTS

A new kitchen

Like the rest of the house, the kitchen blind had been closed for 15 years. I tugged the strap down hard. At first the blind jolted up but then, instead of continuing to roll up as a single sheet, the plastic sections collapsed back down one by one, as fast as an automatic rifle. Light streaked in, momentarily blinding me and illuminating both the room and the clouds of dust the blind had released. As it settled, the kitchen I had heard so much about revealed itself. It was my partner Vincenzo's grandparents' kitchen in Gela, on the south coast of Sicily, and the place he has always considered home. It was larger than I had imagined – six metres by four – with a low sink, a single arching tap above it and a curtain below, a small gas stove, a narrow work surface, and at one end a hatch through to a dining room of the same size. Two floors above me, Vincenzo and his cousin Elio were trying to get the motor for the water pump going on the flat roof, its wheezing attempts like a flat car battery, while my then-three-year-old son, Luca, ran around the house collecting more dust. This was in May 2015.

I had first visited Sicily ten years earlier, an impulsive trip with no luggage and no real plans other than a vague idea about finding a Caravaggio and a volcano. I began travelling clockwise around the circumference of the island, mostly by bus. It was March. It was warm and the air so full of spring I could almost taste it. The bus, skirting the coast, cut between rich blue sea and the island itself, expansive, muscular and profoundly green. I caught my breath. The journey felt more important than the stops: Barcellona Pozzo di Gotto, Lascari, Messina, Taormina, Catania, Syracuse, looping inland to Enna. In a museum in Messina I found the Caravaggio, two in fact, and later, in Catania, a city that seems carved out of volcanic lava, I took a chair lift and inadvisably walked up to the snowy peak of Etna. It was also in Catania that I discovered that almond granita and warm brioche is considered a normal and ordinary way to start the day. I also noticed a flat for sale near the fish market.

The idea of replacing my London flat with that one taunted me. It was fanciful thinking but, reflecting back twelve years later, it's clear that this was the moment when I knew I would stay in Italy, realization solidifying into resolve as I walked and walked. I didn't buy that flat; instead, I decided to go to Rome to learn some Italian. As it turned out, a part of Rome called Testaccio stuck a foot out and tripped me up with its easy charm. In a way, I found Sicily in Rome when I met Vincenzo, and we settled in to life in Testaccio, a quarter that feels more like living in a small provincial town than part of a capital city.

Living with a Sicilian, though, and one whose love of the food of home is deeply rooted, brought a rich culinary vein of tomatoes and oranges, ricotta and oregano, of dishes invested with the warmth of Sicily. Vincenzo's parents also lived in Rome and were quietly traditional in the way they ate, certain flavours as omnipresent as their lapses into Sicilian dialect. I became accustomed to flashes of Sicilian genius: wedges of lemon with everything, breadcrumbs on pasta, the perfume of saffron, pasta with sardines and aromatic wild fennel, swordfish and aubergine, orange and fennel salad, salted ricotta, pine nuts and raisins in places I might not expect; and to the fact that every important occasion was marked with a triumphantly Baroque cake called *cassata*, or custard topped with hundreds and thousands.

Ask someone to show you how to cook something and there's a good chance you will get more than just a recipe. Recipes live in stories: small everyday ones and much bigger ones. Vincenzo's mother, Carmela, passed on her recipes to me along with pieces of family history that I might never have discovered otherwise. Each dish felt like a portal into their life, both in Sicily and away from it, where recipes became a way of preserving, remembering, and being transported.

What food do you pack in your suitcase when you go away? Like many immigrants, the movement of food became central to my life when I moved away, a clear reminder of here and there. Each time I went back to the UK I would take back pieces of my new life: pasta, Parmesan, pecorino, peperoncino and guanciale. Then, on my return, I'd fill my suitcase with baking powder, marmalade, Yorkshire tea, Marmite, fruit cake, Lancashire cheese, Polo mints and leaf gelatine. Vincenzo's parents first left Gela when he was a boy, and the Sicilian food they took with them was a tangible link

to their home region. His grandmother, Sara, who stayed in Gela, may have missed her daughter and grandchildren, but at least she knew they had plenty of her *salsa* (tomato sauce).

For most Italians, Gela is now defined by two things: the mafia and the monstrous oil refinery that was built there in the 1960s. Vincenzo likes to tell a story about being at a dinner party where two Sicilians from Catania, on hearing a mention of Gela, laughed and said *devi andare a Gela, per vedere quant'è brutta* (you have to go to Gela just to see how ugly it is). Once or twice I have met a historian whose eyes have lit up at the thought of ancient Greek Gela, but guide books advise you to drive straight past.

Like a child being told not to do something, though, all this just fuelled my curiosity. I was curious to see Gela, to understand. At the same time, although we had lived in Rome for ten years, Sicily had deeply influenced the way we cooked and ate. Occasional visits had provided feasts of the flavours we both craved, but our day-to-day life was Roman. Sicily was always bubbling just below the surface, though, for Vincenzo, whose attachment to his place of birth, and to its food, is powerful, but for me too. Then: 'Why don't you go and spend some time in *nonna's* house?' his father, Bartolomeo, suggested one night after dinner. It turned out that the family had been waiting for us to ask, for someone to open the house and pull up the blinds.

In May 2015 we drove our heroic Fiat Panda from Rome to Naples, took the night boat to Palermo, then drove through the heart of the island to the opposite coast. From whichever direction you arrive, you see the oil refinery first, one of its chimneys striped like socks, and the city sprawls, the outskirts

modern and bloated. In the claustrophobic heart of the old town
you see layers of history: new houses built into the medieval city
wall, traces of Arab city planning. It is a place full of disrepair
and despair, but quietly beautiful and intriguing if you give it
time, and explore the back streets, hidden courtyards, churches
and shops. The family house is on via Mazzini, one of a grid
of streets in the old town. It was a shock the first time I saw it:
several of the houses were closed up, two others had simply
collapsed, and street cobbles burst up in little eruptions. The
house itself was stark. Once inside, though, it felt like a home,
although plain. I was still standing with a piece of the blind in my
hand when Vincenzo and Elio came back down from the roof.
What did I think of the house? Vincenzo asked. 'I like it very
much,' I said. 'I knew that,' he replied.

What makes a kitchen inviting? Technically, the kitchen in
Gela is too small, too low, too old and ill equipped (everyone
in the family had taken something), and yet it welcomes. I was

ready to look for clues and found some straight away in the set of yellow glass plates and bowls which is the long-lost twin of the one we have in Rome, a garage full of equipment for harvesting wheat and tomatoes, and bottles of Martini and Cinzano dating back to 1976. Then there were the two faded, ever-so-slightly sunken marks in front of the stove where *nonna* Sara had stood.

Before any cooking, though, there was shopping. Gela no longer has a central market, just a dispersed one that plays out on street corners, pavements, people's front doors and garages. As in many of the world's most abundant markets, the spectre of poverty hovers. Vegetables dense with flavour and character, the deeply coloured fruit of back-breaking labour, are sold by the kilogram and cost almost nothing. Later, in August, a searingly hot one, we find tomatoes, crates and crates of them, that taste so resolutely like tomatoes it is disconcerting, figs that taste like honey, and aubergines, some pendulous and black as night, others round and pale purple, which are dense and creamy. There are car boots full of peaches, metre-long *cucuzze*, great floppy bunches of squash greens with tendrils,

and onions the size of frisbees. By September there were grapes and more grapes, the kind that burst in your mouth and taste almost drunken. I felt drunk on it all. It all seemed ideal until Vincenzo's cousin reminded me that it isn't: between the good farmers, workers, middle men and opportunists, the good and the not-so-good-stuff, you need to know where to go.

We have now spent two long summers in Gela, and made several shorter visits, each time bringing back more recipes with us, which, alongside our Roman favourites, have become part of our lives. Gela continues to confound my romantic ideas about Sicily and Sicilian food, but at the same time pulls me in with its brilliance, its smells, habits and traditions. It feels important to note that although I hope I have respected the traditional ways of doing things and local formulas, these are very much my interpretations of Sicilian and Roman dishes – it is home cooking, which is by its nature anarchic, resourceful and personal. This is a recipe book that reflects the way I cook and eat: uncomplicated, direct and adaptable family food that reflects the season, is rich in vegetables and pulses, and suits our modest budget and the basic equipment we have in both kitchens. As an English food writer living between Rome and Sicily, I also have an eye on my English kitchen, and how the recipes translate there. When I can't find a kilogram of Sicilian tomatoes that cost almost nothing (which I can't in Rome or London), I adapt. One thing I don't compromise on is extra-virgin olive oil, the soul of almost all the food I cook. Quality oil, ideally Sicilian, pungent and slightly bitter, with the flavour of olives intact, has become a habit.

The two kitchens of the title are Rome and Gela. In a sense, though, we could have called the book 'many kitchens': there is my ever-present English one, and now your kitchen, or kitchens, as you make the recipes your own and bring your own experience to them, while making yourself, your friends or your family something good to eat.

VEGETABLES AND HERBS

Tomatoes
22

Aubergines
44

Peas
56

Broad beans
68

Cauliflower
82

Potatoes
94

Onions
106

Herbs
116

Tomatoes

'My grandfather was a tomato farmer.' There were other lines
too, about drumming, politics, pasta; a series of green lights
that kept the words flowing. There was a perfect Negroni too:
three fastidiously equal parts of gin, Campari and Martini, with
just the right amount of ice. It was cool, then warm, then sweet,
then bitter enough to burn the back of your throat. It was the
tomatoes that won me over, though. This, my first conversation
with Vincenzo, took place over the bar where he worked, a
row of bottles behind him. I had been living in Testaccio for
only a few months, working in a trattoria that thought it was
a restaurant next door to his bar. I had no intention of staying
more than a year before going back to Sicily to finish the journey
I had interrupted. Having already spent two months in Sicily,
everything about Vincenzo – his proportions, his colouring,
the rug of black hair, the curve of his nose – was familiar. The
conversation was led by music: New Orleans funk, jazz, ska…
I am no music nerd, but I know one when I see one, and can
keep my end up. Talking about music was easy, other subjects
less so. I persisted, fascinated by the island he came from,
which was all I wanted to talk about. I must have told him I
had interrupted my journey in Sicily at Enna, an ancient and
bleakly alluring town high in the the navel of the island. It was
at that point that he offered small pieces of information about
his home town of Gela on the south coast, and the fact that his
grandfather had farmed wheat and tomatoes there. It seems
ridiculous now to have found this so seductive; perhaps I was
being subconsciously calculating, the future food writer sensing
potential material. My enthusiam was also, in no small part,
thanks to the second Negroni glowing on the bar. He still teases
me about that first conversation, with its soundtrack of Dr. John
and Grant Green and my insistent questions about tomatoes.

When Vincenzo was growing up, tomatoes were everything
and everywhere. His grandfather Orazio, who had begun
farming at the age of ten, cultivated two varieties of tomatoes:

the round, deeply fluted fleshy variety known as *nostrani* (ours), and cherry tomatoes with thick skins and almost dry, acidic but sweet flesh that grew *al grappolo* (in bunches). Wheat was his most important harvest, and artichokes and broad beans were vital in the crop rotation, but tomatoes were at the heart of it all. There was an agricultural crescendo building up to tomato season in the summer months, when the sun and volcanic Sicilian soil joined forces to produce legendary quantities of tomatoes that seemed as much a part of Sicily as vines and olives, even though they are relative newcomers, having arrived in only the sixteenth century, and remaining a mere curiosity until the early nineteenth century. The fruits of these months culminated in the most important week and domestic ritual of the year, when families would put away tomatoes for the following year. Orazio wasn't just growing tomatoes for his own family, but for the extended family and neighbours, and everyone would await the news that the tomatoes were ready. Vincenzo's grandmother, *nonna* Sara, would dry empty beer and soda bottles in the sun for days in anticipation: these are the details I love. Then the crates of tomatoes would arrive, potential pressing against their thin skins, and the whole street turned into a production line as the race against ripeness began.

Vincenzo and his cousins have knee-high memories of the great wall of crates and a sea of bright red, of aluminium cauldrons that three of them could hide in, of the child-sized sieve and ladle, the crank of a vegetable mill the size of a man's arm. Much of the equipment is still in the garage, and is still monumental in its own way. Tomatoes were cooked, drained to get rid of watery juices, then milled to produce two sorts of *salsa* (sauce), one a smooth passata and another *a pezzetti* (in pieces), with a chuff of basil. Vincenzo's uncle Liborio, for whom this really was the way of his young life, has the sharpest memories about how, in the days before metal tops, his older brother put a cork in each bottle and then bound it with string before wrapping the bottle in newspaper to be reboiled. One bottle would always explode. There were fragments of stories about the *strattu* made from tomatoes dried in the sun on boards on the roof and worked with a dough scraper until they reduced to a thick, clay-like deep rusty red paste. Tomatoes preserved for the year meant exactly that: they would be eaten all year round, with *pasta e pomodoro* of some sort for nearly every meal. The sunburnt *strattu,* the concentration of summer in Sicily, was put into almost every dish.

There are tomatoes that are everything, and tomatoes that are not. I was born in 1972 in the middle of middle England, so I know all about the clichés of cardboard and cotton, disadvantaged tomatoes with no sense of sun or urgency about them. Like everything, though, tomatoes are relative. I also knew the best tomatoes in the world, the ones we grew against the sunny garden fence. They collected as much English sun and growbag goodness as they could, and we watched and poked and twisted until they came away in our hands, the flesh sweet and acidic. There were also the huge tomatoes my mum would bring back from the Athenian grocer in Bayswater, great heavy fleshy things that seemed plumped up. Possibly they were Dutch, but they were fleshy and blowsy and I thought they were delicious. I was given the job of peeling them, a kitchen task I still love, plunging them in hot water so that the skins split, then into cold water so the skins would slide off. My mum made

tomato sauce too, nothing like Sara's street-sized quantity, but a fair amount, and her resourcefulness was every bit as admirable. She brought out the best in tomatoes that were lacking, or used tinned plum tomatoes with a squirt of concentrate, a bit of red wine and lots of olive oil. There was often a pan of sauce burping away on the back of the stove, its taste a contradiction – both of home and somewhere else. To me it was the best sauce.

Tomatoes are all relative. Vincenzo and I met in Rome: in the middle, tomato-wise. For me, coming down from northern Europe, Roman tomatoes were a source of much joy. For Vincenzo, coming up from the south, Roman tomatoes were not a patch on Sicilian ones. I think there is a certain amount of *campanilismo* (loyalty to your belltower) here: the local Testaccio tomatoes may not be as good as those from further south, but they are still good, superb even during their true season, when Roman markets are splashed with red.

We visited Sicily many times, but it took us ten years to get to Gela. That first summer, the tomatoes didn't disappoint. Exactly as described, they were almost exaggerations of themselves, the local ones ridged and intensely flavoured, the San Marzanos long and slender, the cherries bursting with sweetness and acidity that catches the roof of your mouth. They were everywhere, the street corners throughout the city all stained red. A father and son pitched up at the end of our street, their car boot full of tomatoes, 1 euro per kilo. It all seemed like a Sicilian paradise – until I realized it wasn't, and felt foolish. Present-day Gela is a very different world from the one in which Orazio grew his tomatoes. The reality we discovered was like a crate of tomatoes in the back of the car on a very hot day: beautiful on the surface, but underneath a bit fizzy and fermenting, and at the very bottom weeping and absolutely rotten. It was obvious that something wasn't right, to find these fruits of backbreaking labour at such pitiful prices. As we drove around during that summer we found ourselves again and again among miles of greenhouses growing the seasonless produce – often all show and no substance – that customers now want all year round. We saw small armies of cheap labour coming to pick them, and vicious dogs that chased us away when we took a wrong turn. One day I talked to the father of a little boy Luca was playing with in the park, who had been a tomato farmer until it became impossible to survive. It was the industrial boom of the 1970s that emptied Sicilian agriculture of young men who wanted something different from the backbreaking labour of their fathers. But the subsequent slump, when the exploitative greed of middlemen and the mafia ruined the industry, left it all in a terrible mess. While we talked, our boys transformed the top of the slide into a pirate ship. Suddenly he stopped and stared and joked nervously: I wasn't a journalist, was I? I told him I was a writer, but only of recipes. The story of Sicilian tomatoes is the elephant in the room; after looking at it, we can move on to the stories of people still farming fairly, growing tomatoes in the sun and selling them for a decent price. We buy their tomatoes and eat them all summer long.

I can offer one piece of advice about sun-drying tomatoes on a Sicilian rooftop in August: check the weather forecast. And even if you do, be distrustful and keep an eye on the sky, as great grey clouds may arrive, swallow the blue and unload the first rain in months. Rain is a precious relief after days of sirocco, the hot, still wind that blows in from the Middle East, covering everything in its wake with a layer of fine yellow sand; but less so if you have balanced a tray of tomatoes outside between two chairs. I stood for some time, looking at the rain falling like a chain curtain, before remembering. Shit. I ran up the two long flights of stairs, my flip-flops doing exactly that, on to the flat roof to find most of the tomatoes floating in a puddle.

That experience during the first summer in Sicily seemed to sum things up. We knew that things had changed in Gela, that people didn't preserve tomatoes as they once had. What I wasn't prepared for was that, in a town where once almost everybody had done it, almost nobody did any more. And there was no one to ask. We were in Sara's house, but she wasn't there. Sara's sister had quietly lost her mind; Elio, Vincenzo's closest cousin, is a man of very few words; the other cousins were keen to tell stories, but details and explanations were missing. Our fruit and vegetable seller made suggestions, but not very helpful ones. One day I impulsively went up on the roof, put a piece of hardboard across two chairs and covered it with halves of cherry tomatoes. It was incredibly hot that first year, and at noon the sun would centre itself over the roof and give a fierce burning stare that bleached everything. The halves sweated and then,

almost before my eyes, starting looking crepey at the edges. By the end of the day the flesh had sunk completely and the seeds were like buttons on a military jacket. I ate two or three, like damp, intensely flavoured tomato leather. I would leave them for one more day. That was when it rained. I'm not sure why I didn't pick them up from the puddle; the rain stopped as soon as it started. But I didn't, and I didn't talk about it either; it all felt so pathetic, an appropriation of customs that were not mine, the rain pouring scorn on it all.

The following summer, just a few days into our stay, we were walking to the supermarket on via Ventura. There is a particularly pretty road lined with oleanders; on one pavement was a chair with a board on it, and on that were tomatoes opened up to the sun. A woman came out with her daughter and we asked. She showed me how to prepare the tomatoes, how to open them up, using your thumbs to brush away the excess seeds, and then later, as they dry, you do the same motion to retain the shape. A few days later, in Piazza Giacomo, I looked up at a balcony beside the church of San Giacomo to see a man cutting tomatoes in half and arranging them them on a board. You know how, once you've noticed a detail for the first time, it's then all you see? After that I saw trays of tomatoes everywhere: on high window ledges, on top of laundry racks, on a chair propping open a door. So the tradition was still alive, quietly, mostly among the older Gelese.

At Vincenzo's insistence we bought tomatoes from the car boot sale at the end of via Mazzini, round with deep frills and thin skins, and fleshy. Vincenzo washed the board and I washed the fruit, then began cutting. Elio arrived, sat down and started helping, opening the halves out with his massive thumbs, flicking away some of the excess seeds. Actions seem to jolt memories and soon they were both talking, remembering how Sara would assess a tomato, selecting the best ones for drying (as in life, the more perfect the specimen the better it will preserve); how they called them *chiappe* (bum cheeks) because the tomatoes weren't cut all the way through but stayed in pairs; how she salted them, then watched and watched until they were dense and dry with a faint juicy potential. There was no rain this year, and our tomatoes dried in two-and-half days. The five kilograms had become small, wrinkled, pliable rounds, a concentration of tomato and sun, and now fitted into one tub. They are now in Rome, to be snipped into pieces and plumped back to life in pasta sauce or stew. Next year we will make two batches.

Salsa
Simple tomato sauce

Serves 6

1.5kg ripe tomatoes

The onion version
1 small onion
6 tablespoons extra-virgin
   olive oil
1 tablespoon tomato purée
a pinch of red chilli flakes
   (optional)
a pinch of sugar (if necessary)
salt

The garlic version
2 garlic cloves
5 tablespoons extra-virgin
   olive oil
a sprig of basil
a pinch of sugar (if necessary)
salt

There are tomato recipes throughout the book, of course, but here I concentrate on the basics: sauce and salad. They aren't really recipes at all, but aren't many of the best things like that? Tomato sauce, like tomatoes themselves, is relative. Where are you making it? What time of year is it? Who and what is it for? Your aim, surely, is richly flavoured sauce. More than recipes, I like collecting advice about tomato sauce: how to coax the best out of it, when it needs enhancement, how long to cook it for, how a handful of unseasonal roasted cherry tomatoes helps midwinter tinned tomato sauce no end, as does a spoonful of tomato concentrate, or a pinch of sugar – it's true – to offset the acidity of tinned tomatoes. I am going to suggest three sauces: this very simple one with two variations, a sauce to make in big batches that is particularly useful in winter and England, and Uncle Liborio's summer sauce.

Many of the recipes ask for a simple, smooth tomato sauce, made with fresh or tinned, with just enough oil, salt, garlic or onion. This is the sauce you want for baked pasta, or pasta with aubergine and salted ricotta, or your own *arancine*. You could just use a bottle of passata at a push, but making your own is worth the effort. This is our standard sauce, pure-flavoured and uncomplicated. I usually opt for the garlic version, the cloves peeled and crushed with the back of a knife. Garlic's fiercely sunny perfume flatters the tomatoes, but don't let it burn or it becomes an acrid bully. The onion version is excellent too, just don't add too much onion: it's not ragù. Or maybe you want ragù; it's your sauce. The food mill, or mouli, is indispensable here, doing a job no other tool can, pressing every bit of goodness from (and also removing) the skin and seeds. In the absence of a food mill you can use a sieve or a stick blender, but use cautious blasts so it doesn't turn into foam.

Wash the tomatoes, cut them in half and put them in a heavy-based pan with a little water (they should still have the washing

water clinging to them) over a medium heat. Simmer for a few minutes, stirring attentively, until they give out enough liquid to stop them sticking. Remove from the heat. If you can see a lot of watery juices, drain them away, then pass them through the food mill in preparation for the next stage.

For the onion version, finely dice the onion. In a large, deep heavy-based frying pan or casserole dish, gently fry the onion in the oil until soft. Add the puréed tomatoes and simmer for 20–30 minutes, or until the sauce is rich and thick. Taste it after 15 minutes or so and decide if you want to add the purée. Add salt to taste, the chilli flakes if you wish and a pinch of sugar if the sauce is too acidic.

For the garlic version, peel the garlic cloves and, if you want a stronger flavour, press the cloves with the back of a knife until they split but remain whole. (If you want a mild garlic flavour, leave them peeled but whole). Put the olive oil, garlic, basil and puréed tomatoes in a heavy-based pan, bring to a gentle boil, then reduce the heat and simmer for 30 minutes, or until the sauce is rich and thick. Add salt to taste and a pinch of sugar if the sauce is too acidic, and remove the basil before serving.

My big-batch sauce

Makes about 2 litres

3 garlic cloves
100ml olive oil
750g fresh tomatoes, skinned
    and roughly chopped
2 x 800g tins plum tomatoes
red chilli flakes, to taste
sugar, to taste (optional)
salt

Everyone has their own recipe for tomato sauce, shaped by taste, influences and practice. This one is influenced by Sicilian *salsa*, the *sugo* that I've eaten here in Rome, and also by being back in England regularly and wanting a sauce that works when I can't get hold of a glut of gorgeous fresh tomatoes. Like so many Italian recipes, it is open to improvisation, so treat this as a template: use all tinned tomatoes in winter, more fresh in summer, tweak with salt, chilli and sugar. That said, I will be prescriptive about the quantity of olive oil: don't skimp. And buy the best tinned plum tomatoes you can, ideally San Marzano.

The other beauty of this sauce is that it keeps for a week in the fridge, and if at any point you think *basta* (enough) sauce, it freezes brilliantly. The last bit of advice is from my mother-in-law, Carmela: the sauce should cook at a gentle simmer that has you peering under the pan to see if the flame has gone out, until a red burp on the surface reassures you that all is well.

Crush the garlic with the back of a knife so that it splits but remains whole. In a large heavy-based pan over a medium-low heat, warm half the oil and the garlic. Fry it gently for a few minutes, until pale gold and fragrant; it must not brown. Remove the garlic, if you like. Add the fresh tomatoes, a good pinch of salt and the chilli. Simmer, uncovered, for 10 minutes.

Use kitchen scissors to roughly chop the tomatoes in their tins, then tip them into the pan with the rest of the olive oil. Bring the sauce to a simmer, reduce the heat to very low and let it simmer very gently, uncovered, for 45 minutes, occasionally squashing the tomatoes against the pan with a wooden spoon.

Take the pan off the heat, taste and adjust the seasoning (if the sauce seems a bit sharp you can add a teaspoon or so of sugar). If you like a smoother sauce, pass it through a food mill or blend with short, cautious blasts with a stick blender (not too fast, or it will turn into a pink foam).

Pomodoro a picchi pacchio
Liborio's tomato sauce

Serves 4–6

1kg ripe tomatoes
2 garlic cloves
a large sprig of basil
6 tablespoons extra-virgin
 olive oil
salt

This is a sauce for high summer, when the doors and windows are open and you're cooking in a vest. Once you have taken the skins off, summer tomatoes can be crushed or squished by hand. It's the combination of the rich, slightly concentrated juices and the oil that makes this chunky sauce so good. Rip the basil with your fingers and serve with a pasta shape that catches the sauce, such as penne, casarecce or rigatoni. The name *picchi pacchio* (or *picchi pacchiu* or *pic pac*) seems to be used for various sauces, but in my family it means a chunky tomato sauce like this one, perhaps because *picchio* in Sicilian suggests a female, so the name means something *buono* (good) and inviting, which this is.

Peel the tomatoes by plunging them into boiling water for 60 seconds, then use a slotted spoon to lift them out (save the water for cooking the pasta) into a large bowl of cold water, at which point the skins should peel away easily. Squash the tomatoes with your hands or chop them roughly, catching the juices.

If you want a milder flavour, crush the garlic cloves with the back of a knife so that they split but remain whole; otherwise, slice them thinly. Rip the basil into pieces. In a large, deep, heavy-based frying pan or casserole, warm the olive oil and garlic. Once the garlic is fragrant, remove it if you wish, then add the tomatoes, basil and a pinch of salt and simmer for 10–20 minutes, or until the sauce is thick and rich.

Fagioli al pomodoro
Beans with tomato

Serves 4

1kg fresh borlotti beans in their
    pods, or 300g dried borlotti
    beans soaked overnight, or
    2 x 400g tins borlotti beans
1 small onion
1 small celery stalk
3 tablespoons olive oil or lard
500g best-quality plum
    tomatoes, milled or crushed
a handful of fresh basil
salt and freshly ground
    black pepper

Beans and tomatoes make a good couple. When they are in season, fresh borlotti work wonderfully; dried ones are different but just as good, as are tinned. The sauce should be rich and slighly jammy, so go slow. I am tempted to say you must wait a day, as it is undeniably better after a rest, but a few hours will do. The other day I served this with crumbled salted ricotta, more olive oil and focaccia, and it was a gorgeous lunch.

If you are using dried beans, soak them in plenty of cold water for at least 8 hours or overnight. Drain the beans and put them in a heavy-based pan, cover with at least 5cm water, bring to the boil, then reduce the heat to a simmer. Cook the beans for 1 hour, then begin checking for doneness. Once the beans are tender, remove from the heat and leave them in their cooking water.

If you are using fresh beans, shell them, then boil them in salted water for about 25 minutes, or until tender.

Finely chop the onion and celery. Put the olive oil, onion and celery in a deep sauté pan with the oil and cook over a medium-low heat until soft and translucent.

Mill, crush or purée the tomatoes with a stick blender until they are smooth and add them to the pan. Stir, season with salt and pepper and simmer for 15 minutes. Drain the beans and add them to the pan (you can also add a little of the cooking liquid to thin them slightly, or use it for soup), stir and cook for another 10 minutes. Check the seasoning and tear in the basil. Allow the beans to sit for 10 minutes (or a few hours) before serving.

These are even better the next day, maybe even better the day after that. If your kitchen is cool you can leave them overnight in the coolest corner and then reheat them gently the next day. If you keep them longer than a day, store them in the fridge but remember to pull them out an hour or so before you want to gently reheat and then eat them.

Baked tomatoes with anchovies, garlic and breadcrumbs

Serves 4

extra-virgin olive oil
700g tomatoes, ideally
    small plum-sized ones
1–2 plump garlic cloves
8–12 anchovy fillets
100g soft breadcrumbs,
    from day-old bread
salt

A Sicilian rooftop is all very well, but a domestic oven can do an equally good job of baking tomatoes until they are wrinkled and their flavour is rich and concentrated. Exactly how long you cook your tray of tomatoes for depends on both the tomatoes (and how much water they contain) and what you want to serve them with. If they are to eat with fish or roast chicken they need to be quite soft and fleshy, so that they create an almost-sauce. If you're serving them as part of an antipasti with olives, salami and cheese, or to be mixed with little gem lettuce – which is a most tasty and satisfying salad – you can cook them for longer, until they are drier and the crumbs are really crisp.

Preheat the oven to 180°C/160°C fan/gas mark 4. Grease a baking tray with olive oil, then halve the tomatoes lengthways and sit them cut-side up in the tray. They should be quite snug. Slice the garlic very thinly and cut the anchovy fillets in four. Push a sliver of garlic and a piece of anchovy deep into the fleshy pulp of each half tomato. Scatter the breadcrumbs over the tomatoes. Sprinkle with salt and zig-zag generously with olive oil.

Bake the tomatoes for 20–30 minutes, or until they are very soft and bubbling at the edges and the breadcrumbs are golden and crisp on top. You need to keep an eye on them.

Insalata di pomodoro
Tomato salad

Serves 4

2 shallots
6 tablespoons extra-virgin
    olive oil
1 tablespoon good-quality
    red wine vinegar or sherry
    vinegar
3 large, fleshy, ripe but firm
    tomatoes
salt

When it is tomato time and they are full-flavoured and cheap we eat them straight, sliced, halved, quartered or diced with salt and extra-virgin olive oil, probably with some ripped basil, tomatoes' soulmate. Occasionally I hide them under a blanket of ricotta. Then there is this salad, the one we ate growing up, in which the dressing makes up for what the tomatoes lacked. When made with good fleshy tomatoes, such as beefsteak or *cuore di bue,* and shallots that are chopped very finely, it is a smashing salad. My dad makes the dressing in a jar, shaking it until it thuds (the water helps with emulsifying). This is also nice with tinned tuna, ideally fleshy chunks of *ventresca* (belly tuna).

Make the dressing by chopping the shallots very finely, putting them in a bowl and whisking them with the olive oil and vinegar, along with 1 tablespoon water and a good pinch of salt. If you want to peel the tomatoes, do so, then slice them and arrange them in overlapping slices on a large plate. Pour over the dressing, making sure the shallots are well distributed. Serve.

Insalata con l'acqua
Tomato, cucumber, onion and bread salad

Serves 4

600g ripe but firm tomatoes
2 small cucumbers
1 large red onion
4 tablespoons good-quality
    red wine vinegar
100g capers packed in salt
600g two-day-old sourdough
    bread
a handful of basil leaves
a pinch of dried oregano
6 tablespoons extra-virgin
    olive oil
salt

The name means salad with water. It is is rather like panzanella, so a resourceful, high-summer salad that makes the best of the fleshy tomatoes, the plentiful juice of which, along with olive oil, brings old bread back to life. For this Sicilian version, water is added, just a little, to help soften the bread further. For someone like me, who has always thought water is the enemy of salad, this seemed odd. But it is only a little water, and if the ingredients are full of flavour and the bread robust – two-day-old country bread or sourdough work well – it is wonderful, the water mingling with the olive oil, vinegar, tomato juices, capers and onion into a dressing. In Gela one night I made this for Vincenzo's father, who hadn't eaten it since he was a boy, and who then insisted I make it every night for the rest of his stay, using extra bread to mop up the dressing.

Roughly chop the tomatoes, catching the juices. Peel the cucumbers and quarter them lengthways – you can cut away the seeds if you wish – then cut them into 2cm pieces. Slice the onion thinly and sit it in a bowl of cold water with 2 tablespoons red wine vinegar for 15 minutes or so. Rinse the salt from the capers and tear the bread into pieces.

In a large, shallow serving bowl, make a layer of bread, then cover it with the tomatoes, cucumber, drained onion and capers. Tear over the basil and sprinkle with oregano. In a bowl or jar, whisk or shake together 50ml water with the remaining vinegar and salt, then add the olive oil and shake again until it emulsifies. Pour it over the salad. Toss well, allow it to sit for 5 minutes, then toss again and serve.

Aubergines

My Sicilian father-in-law, Bartolomeo, tells a story about aubergines. As autumn teetered on the verge of winter, the whole family would leave their unheated apartments and go down to the ground floor, where the bakery was. His mother Lilla ran it capably, an extraordinary feat for a widowed woman in her late husband's town – a town in which the mafia was so tightly woven into the fabric of the place it was inseparable from it. The adults of the family, along with friends and neighbours, would pull chairs close to the huge *forno al vapore* (steam oven), one of the first of its kind in Sicily and still generously giving out residual heat from the day's baking. While the adults talked the children would play, delighting in the warmth. At some point Lilla would take aubergines and make incisions in the deep-purple skin just large enough for the flesh to accept a small clove of garlic. She would then put the aubergines in the oven, possibly alongside a tray of whole onions still in their skins or scrubbed potatoes. An hour or so later they would be pulled from the oven, the aubergines collapsed into wrinkles, the charred skin flaking away. The fleshy insides, soft and slightly smoky rags rich with garlic, were eaten with bread or the roast flesh of the potatoes before everyone made their way home, or up to bed.

I have often heard it said that aubergines are to Sicilians what potatoes are to the Irish. Which is fitting, considering they are relatives, both belonging to the deadly nightshade family that also includes tomatoes and peppers. This deadly relationship explains why, even though they had arrived in Europe with Arab traders in the Middle Ages, aubergines were considered inedible, dangerous even. The Italian name, *melanzane*, comes from the Latin *mala insana*: insane apples. By the eighteenth century, like tomatoes, aubergines were very at home in the southern Italian soil, and had become a defining ingredient.

Vincenzo's family call aubergines *milunciani*, which has slipped into *melanzane* over their years in Rome. His grandfather didn't grow aubergines, but their neighbours did. Like everything grown or made, aubergines were currency to be exchanged for olive oil, cheese or anything else they didn't produce themselves. There were several varieties: long, lustrous inky-black ones called *nostrano* (our own kind), spherical ones the colour of lavender called *tunisine* and middling ones streaked with purple and white. All varieties can be good, but when choosing aubergines make sure they are heavy, with skin that's bright, firm, glowing and offering resistance: it should bounce back when you press it. Aubergines are a yin-yang vegetable, the dark skin slicing open to reveal pale, sweetly spongy flesh that tastes not so much of the earth or the sun as the tang of the sea. Which brings us to salting them, and whether to or not.

I have come to the conclusion that salting is a personal thing: some cooks and chefs that I admire do, and some don't. Traditionally, salting was a way of eliminating water by breaking down the cells – thank you, Harold McGee – in order to draw out the bitterness and at the same time temper the aubergine's legendary sponge-like ability to soak up oil as it cooks. A neat side effect of salting is that the aubergine is also well seasoned. Nowadays, with bitterness bred out of most varieties, salting is about eliminating water. However, I have found that if you press unsalted slices in a cloth until they are really dry, then fry them in a good few inches of oil, they absorb it, yes, but then release some of it back once they are golden, and so in the end they absorb more or less the same amount of oil as salted slices would. This, though, is very unscientific and entirely personal, and a good friend disagrees with me vehemently. The best way is to experiment – but isn't it always? Although I don't generally salt, I did discover a nifty salting system, which is to lay the slices or cubes in a colander, sprinkle with some coarse salt (the rule of thumb is 1 tablespoon salt for 1 kilo aubergines), then cover with a plate, put something heavy like a big pan of water on top and wait for the puddle. After an hour, shake off the salt (some people rinse and squeeze), then pat dry and fry. I always fry in olive oil, the soul of good Sicilian cooking. Any discussion about aubergines in Sicily, though, must begin with caponata.

Caponata
Sweet-and-sour aubergine stew

Serves 6

1kg aubergines
extra-virgin olive oil, or
 whatever oil you prefer
 to fry in
4 celery stalks
75g capers, ideally packed in salt
150g olives (use your favourite
 type; I like black Gaeta olives)
1 large red onion
200ml tomato sauce
 (see page 32 or 36) or
 good-quality passata
75g raisins (optional)
50g pine nuts (optional)
50g sugar
50–75ml red wine vinegar
a small handful of basil leaves
 (optional)

Every morning of the week except Sunday, Vincenzo's grandmother Sara would wake at five o'clock to put the coffee on. By the time it was ready, her husband, Orazio, would have woken, washed and dressed as he always did, in black trousers. He would drink his coffee and eat a piece of bread before picking up a package and going downstairs. Until the early 1960s, the basement was a stable for his mule, Giuseppina, and later – once his eldest son, Totò, learned to drive – a home for the tractor that would take them both to the land they rented on the edge of the province. They would arrive in the field at about 6 o'clock and work until 10 o'clock, at which point he would open the package, which contained bread, tuna and caponata that Sara had made, and a litre of his own wine.

Like her grandmother and mother before her, Sara made great quantities of caponata, the quintessential sweet-and-sour Sicilian stew. It's a dish that makes absolute sense in Sicily: the abundance of aubergines, the home-made tomato sauce that families still put aside each year, plentiful celery, olives and capers, the sweet-and-sour presence of sugar and vinegar about flavour as well as conserving. Like any dish made according to a family recipe shaped by necessity, there are as many versions as cooks.

I make caponata often, both in Rome and London; it translates well anywhere. Like so much traditional Italian cooking, the key is choosing the right ingredients and practice: tasting and trying again and again, adjusting the quantities to your own taste, until you have a version you really like. It's important to fry the aubergines in plenty of hot oil (I use extra-virgin olive oil); the cubes should dance around the pan until golden. The finished dish needs to rest for at least an hour, ideally three. It's even better the next day, and keeps well in the fridge for up to four. Traditionally it would have been kept for much longer, and thus contained far more vinegar; it was bottled and put aside for the winter, more like a relish or pickle. In my modern version, inspired by Sara and my friend (and food writer) Fabrizia Lanza, the ingredients are distinct but united by a sauce rich with, but not overwhelmed by, tomato. I particularly like caponata as part of a picnic-style lunch with tuna, bread and wine. It has an affinity with roast meat, particularly lamb. It's also good stirred into pasta or as the filling for a savoury tart.

Cut the aubergines into 1–2cm cubes. Heat about 5cm oil in a small, deep, heavy-based frying pan until hot. Fry the aubergines in batches – do not crowd the pan – until golden brown, then drain on kitchen paper, sprinkle with salt and set aside. The oil can be strained and used to fry again.

Trim the celery stalks of any tough ends or strings and cut in half. Bring a small pan of water to the boil, add the celery and cook until tender but still with bite – usually about 5 minutes. Drain. Once cool enough to handle, chop the celery into 1cm chunks and set aside. If the capers are salted, soak them for a couple of minutes, then drain them. If they are in brine or vinegar, drain and rinse them. Pit the olives.

Slice the onion thickly. In a large, deep frying pan, warm 4 tablespoons oil over a medium-low heat, add the onion and cook until soft and translucent. Add the celery, stir and cook for a minute or two. Add the tomato sauce and cook for another 2 minutes before adding the capers, olives, raisins and pine nuts and stirring again.

Make a well in the middle of the pan and add the sugar and the vinegar to it, allowing the sugar to dissolve in the heat. Stir and cook for a minute or two, tasting to see if it needs more sugar or vinegar. Turn off the heat, add the aubergines and rip the basil into the pan. Stir the mixture gently so that the aubergine remains in nice distinct pieces. Leave to sit for at least 2 hours, or better still several, turning gently once or twice.

Melanzane al forno
Baked aubergines

Serves 4–6

1kg small, slim aubergines
the same number of garlic
    cloves as aubergines
extra-virgin olive oil
salt

This is our version of Lilla's bakery-oven aubergines. They are delicious eaten like Vincenzo's family did next to the oven, peeling away the blistered flesh, then squashing the smoky, sweet-like-butter flesh and finishing with a squeeze of lemon. I think of this as a deconstructed baba ganoush, and it also goes well with roast or grilled lamb. A couple of halves are good on green salad leaves with some crumbled salty cheese. Aubergines prepared this way can be curled up in a jar and covered with olive oil to preserve them. They can then be served as an antipasto, possibly with a little vinegar to cut through the oil and make the flavour keener. If your oven is big enough, why not bake some red peppers or whole onions too, for a Sicilian feast?

Preheat the oven to 190°C/170°C fan/gas mark 5. Wash and dry the aubergines and thinly slice the garlic. Cut each aubergine in two lengthways and cut a criss-cross pattern on the cut side of each half, deep enough to push a slice of garlic in, but taking care not to pierce the skin. Push a slice of garlic into some of the cuts; how many depends on how big the aubergine is.

Arrange the aubergines cut-side up in a baking tray, sprinkle with salt and zig-zag with oil. Bake for 30–50 minutes (again depending on size), or until the halves are very soft, wrinkled and golden at the edges.

Pasta con le melanzane
Pasta with aubergine

Serves 4

2 large aubergines
olive or groundnut oil, for frying
1kg fresh tomatoes or 500g
    passata
2 garlic cloves
a small handful of basil
1 teaspoon sugar (if you need it)
500g pasta, such as spaghetti,
    rigatoni, casarecce, mezze
    maniche or penne
200g salted ricotta, grated
salt

In Catania this is called *pasta alla Norma* in honour of the operatic masterpiece by Catania's favourite son, Vincenzo Bellini. Others call it *spaghetti alla coppola* (spaghetti with a hat on). My Vincenzo calls it *pasta con le melanzane,* so I do too. It is a favourite (along with all the other favourites), especially in the summer, when it is made with vegetables that are full of sun. It can be a winter dish too, with tinned tomatoes and an unseasonal aubergine. It was a good moment last year when I made this with one of the jars of tomatoes I had bottled the previous summer. I was aware, a bit embarrassed even, of my meagre output compared with *nonna* Sara's extraordinary bottlings. Vincenzo, however, is moved by my efforts. This is his history, taken from one kitchen to another, a single taste that calls up the memory of his grandmother and Gela. Tradition demands spaghetti for Norma, but we often use thick tubes of ridged rigatoni.

Peel strips from the aubergine so that they are striped, then cut them into 5mm slices. If you're going to salt them, do it now; otherwise just dry them with a clean tea towel. Heat about 5cm oil in a frying pan and fry the slices, turning them halfway, until

they are golden brown on both sides, then drain very well on kitchen paper. Set the slices aside, ideally near the stove so they keep warm-ish.

Meanwhile, bring a large pan of water to the boil. If using fresh ones, peel the tomatoes by plunging them into boiling water for 1 minute, then lift them out with a slotted spoon and cool under cold water, at which point the skins should slip away. Roughly chop the tomatoes, removing the seeds if you wish (I don't). Crush the garlic cloves with the back of a knife so that they split but remain whole. Warm some more oil in a frying pan and add the garlic. Once the garlic is fragrant and lightly gold, remove it from the pan, add the fresh tomatoes (or passata) and cook until they collapse into a sauce. At this point you can pass the tomatoes through a food mill back into the pan, or if you're happy with the texture, simply tear in most of the basil, add the sugar if you think the sauce is too sharp, and a good pinch of salt.

Bring the pan of tomato water back to the boil, add salt, stir well and add the pasta. Cook it until al dente, then drain it. Mix the pasta with the sauce and a handful of salted ricotta, then divide it between bowls, top with several slices of aubergine, a little more salted ricotta and a couple more basil leaves. Pass around the remaining aubergine slices and cheese so that people can help themselves.

Parmigiana di melanzane
Aubergine parmigiana

Serves 6

3 large aubergines

olive or groundnut oil, for frying

5 hard-boiled eggs

250g provola or mozzarella

500g tomatoes or passata

1 garlic clove

3 tablespoons extra-virgin olive
    oil, plus extra for brushing

a small handful of basil

1 teaspoon sugar (if you need it)

fine breadcrumbs, for lining the
    dish

60g caciocavallo or Parmesan,
    grated

In Rome we have *tavole calde* ('hot tables'), which are functional, canteen-like places with counters you slide a tray along and tables you don't linger at, unless of course you linger. In Sicily there are the *friggitorie* (frying places), which, true to their name, serve up *fritti* (fried things). In Gela this is mostly *arancine*, the tennis-ball-sized spheres of rice filled with ragù and peas, or peas and béchamel (see page 59). There might also be trays of the crusty-topped baked things with tomatoes, basil and cheese that southern Italians can make so well, most notably baked pasta and aubergine parmigiana. This is a Sicilian version of the much-loved dish, which is possibly named after *palmigiana*, the pattern of overlapping slats in a window shutter. Even if this isn't true, it's a nice image, not least because I have one such shutter here in Rome and it catches my eye when I am standing at the stove. In Sicily, caciocavallo cheese might have been used instead of Parmesan. Some may roll their eyes at the addition of hard-boiled eggs; Sicilians, who love to hide them away in pies and bakes, probably won't. Feel free to leave them out.

Cut the aubergines into 5mm-thick slices. If you're going to salt them, do it now; otherwise just dry them with a clean tea towel. Heat about 5cm oil in a frying pan and fry the slices, turning them halfway, until golden brown on both sides, then drain well on kitchen paper. Set aside, ideally near the stove so that they keep warm-ish. Peel and slice the eggs. Slice the provola or mozzarella cheese.

If you are using fresh tomatoes, peel them by plunging them into boiling water for 1 minute, then lift them out with a slotted spoon and cool under cold water, at which point the skins should slip away. Roughly chop the tomatoes, removing the seeds if you wish (I don't). Crush the garlic with the back of a knife so that it splits but remains whole. Warm the olive oil in a frying pan and add the garlic. Once the garlic is fragrant and lightly

gold, remove it from the pan, add the tomatoes (or passata) and cook until they collapse into a sauce. At this point you can pass the tomatoes through a food mill back into the pan, or if you're happy with the texture, simply tear in some of the basil and add the sugar if you think the sauce is too sharp, and a pinch of salt.

Preheat the oven to 170°C/150°C fan/gas mark 3. Brush a small ovenproof dish or roasting tin with the olive oil and dust it with breadcrumbs. Make a layer of aubergine, then a layer of sliced egg and cheese, cover it with some tomato sauce and add a little torn basil and a sprinkling of grated cheese. Repeat this layering, finishing with a layer of aubergine, a thin layer of sauce and dusting of grated cheese and breadcrumbs. Bake for 30 minutes, or until the top is golden and crusty and the edges are bubbling. Allow it to sit for at least 1 hour before serving. It's even better the next day.

Cotolette di melanzane
Aubergine fritters

Serves 4

2 large aubergines
plain flour, for dusting
2 eggs, lightly beaten
fine breadcrumbs, for coating
50g Parmesan, grated
a handful of flat-leaf parsley,
    finely chopped
olive oil, or your preferred oil
    for frying
lemon wedges, to serve
salt and freshly ground
    black pepper

Slices dipped first in egg, then in seasoned breadcrumbs and fried until golden: I wonder if this is the best way to eat aubergines, the crisp, rough coat giving way to tenderness within. The pleasure of eating them hot makes the risk of burning your tongue worthwhile, so rush them to the table with napkins and big wedge-grins of lemon. You could serve these before a meal as an antipasto. They are also good as a main course, with a spoonful of thick tomato sauce or a crisp salad.

Peel strips from the aubergines so that they are striped, then cut them into 5mm slices. If you are going to salt them, do it now, otherwise simply pat them dry with a clean tea towel.

Prepare three plates for dipping: put the flour on one, the eggs on another and a mixture of breadcrumbs, Parmesan, parsley and salt and pepper on the third. Over a lively heat, heat enough oil to thinly cover the bottom in a deep frying pan. Meanwhile, have ready a plate lined with kitchen paper for blotting and a warmed serving plate. Working one at a time, dip each slice in first the flour, then the egg, then the seasoned breadcrumbs, put in the hot oil and fry, turning halfway so that the slice is burnished gold on each side. Drain on the kitchen paper and serve hot with wedges of lemon.

Peas

Rome, in April. After a month of showers during mad March, April feels grand. The sun warms arms, wisteria drips from the buildings like bunches of tiny grapes, the trees along via Galvani put on their blossoms and arch towards the sky, and the peas have arrived at Testaccio market. They are not strictly local; they were grown by Filippo on his land near Scauri, more or less halfway between Rome and Naples. Filippo is one of the few farmers who still brings his own produce to Testaccio market each day, an 85km drive along via Appia, one of Rome's consular roads, which brings him almost all the way into the centre of the city. 'I picked them last night' is a line I have learned to take with a pinch of salt in Rome, but with Filippo I know it to be true. I have stood next to him as he harvests fruit and vegetables, watched his slight, strong body and his hands, wide and thick, move at such speed that everything blurs. I watch the same hands shake crates of peas into place on his stall in the middle of the market. Taste them, he says, *tenerissimi*, the tenderest. He is right, to a point: the first pod contains small, sweet peas, like tender, buttery grass. The second pod I open is full of cannonballs.

It was the cannonballs – coarse and mealy field peas – that the ancient Romans depended on. Dried until grey, they were a vital winter sustenance and could be simmered into a nourishing and sensible mushy pea soup seasoned with herbs and spices, which I imagine was rather like an English pease pudding. Even when fresh, this sturdy field pea was a worker. It seems it was Italian gardeners of the late Renaissance who developed the sturdy field pea into the tender garden pea we know now.

Everybody loves peas. There is nothing like fresh ones, eaten alone straight from the pod, or pea shoots, whose tendrils seem like spring unfurling. Gardeners will tell you it is their privilege alone, and that peas are never the same at the supermarket, shop, or even market. I can tell you there is great deal of joy to be had from peas in pods from all those places. I also love frozen peas, and always have a bag in the freezer – in fact, peas, along with ice cubes, broad beans and Parmesan rinds, justify the existence of my freezer. It is true that frozen peas are like caricatures of peas – a bit too perfect, a bit too sweet – but they are peas, and therefore good and endlessly useful. *Risi e bisi* (rice and peas) is probably most often the reason I pull the bag out; or I might put a handful in soup, or serve them with mashed potatoes, or add them to a stew of peas, potatoes and onions, which is a great favourite inspired by the buttered and minted potatoes and peas of my childhood, as well as the olive oil-rich spring vegetable stews of artichokes, peas, broad beans and onions from Rome and Sicily, *vignarola* and *frittedda*.

Sicily, in July. The night boat from Naples docks in Palermo at half past six. Luca and I come off with the foot passengers, then wait on the quayside while Vincenzo goes down into the bowels of the boat to collect the car. It is usually about 7 o'clock by the time the Fiat Panda comes scuttling down the corrugated ramp and we jump in. It is always a palaver to get out of the port, the huge articulated lorries swinging impossibly, and the narrow exit, already a bottleneck, is always crowded with officials and not-so-officials. We ping out and scoot around the relatively quiet port road until we get to Piazza Acquasanta, in the corner of which is Bar Turistico. Apart from us, the bar has never felt in the least bit touristy, just locals and port workers coming in for their breakfast. Next to the small curved bar, the glass-fronted counter is half filled with sweet things, like *cartocci fritti* (fried dough whirls) and *iris fritta* (ricotta-filled dough balls dusted with sugar), and half with savoury: a sandwich of prosciutto and hot béchamel, a blob of which may well end up in your lap, a fat pizza called *sfincione* and a line of *arancine*. Vincenzo doesn't eat meat, but makes exceptions for Sicilian sausages cooked on the rooftop *brace* (grill) and *arancine al ragù*: a deep-fried ball of rice with a heart of meat ragù, which includes – and for me this is the magical bit, the proof that their presence stirs joy – peas, tiny green rounds in the middle of an orange. We sit up on the stools near the door and eat our breakfast, looking out over the road towards the sea.

Arancine
Little oranges

Makes 12

600g Italian risotto rice

6 eggs

50g Parmesan or caciocavallo, grated

1 small onion

1 celery stalk

4 tablespoons extra-virgin olive oil

250g minced or hand-chopped beef

1 tablespoon tomato purée

125ml red wine

1 bay leaf

250ml tomato sauce (see page 32 or 36) or passata

200g podded fresh or frozen peas

125g plain flour

225g fine dried breadcrumbs

olive, sunflower or groundnut oil, for frying

salt and freshly ground black pepper

Although *arancine* means 'little oranges', in Bar Turistico they are more like cricket balls, and heavy. In Catania they are called *arancini* and are shaped like tall cones; in Gela we can find both balls and cones. Rather like fish and chips in England, I have never thought to make *arancine* at home in Gela. We walk down the narrow pavement on via Matteotti and turn into the small piazza where there is a *friggitoria* (frying place) called Abruzzese with tables near a statue. On summer evenings, once the air has cooled a little, famiIes come for *arancine*, slices of a bread pie called *impanata*, chickpea fritters, cold beers and *limonata*, then sit for hours, parents talking, children running around the statue as near as they can to the edge until one of them falls off. In our kitchen in Rome, though, I do make *arancine* from time to time. It is a project, and there is the frying! Invite a crowd (in our case a small one), enlist a helper, fling the doors open and have lots of cold beers at the ready.

This is more or less the recipe taught me by Margherita, Cinzia, Tatiana and Maria Grazia, the kitchen volunteers at the church in Gela, who prepare the rice and ragù with peas to make 100 *arancine* every Thursday, then mould and fry them on Friday to sell after the weekly performance by the youth theatre. It really is worth making the rice or the ragù the day before, both to reduce the workload and potential mess, and because both benefit from a rest.

Cook the rice in lightly salted boiling water until tender, which usually takes about 17 minutes. Drain the rice well, then tip it into a wide bowl, add 2 of the eggs and the grated cheese, season with salt and pepper, stir well and allow to cool.

Finely chop the onion and celery. Warm the olive oil in a frying pan over a medium-low heat, add the onion and celery and cook until soft. Add the beef and cook until it has lost all its red and is brown and crumbly. Add the tomato purée and wine and allow to bubble for a few minutes, then add the bay and tomato sauce and simmer gently for 50 minutes. Add the peas and simmer for another 5 minutes or so, or until the peas are tender. Allow the ragù to cool.

When the rice and ragù are cool, begin assembling. Take a large handful of rice in your cupped left hand and press it with your thumb to flatten and make a cup shape with a dent in the centre. Fill the dent with a tablespoon of ragù, then shape the rice over it to make a ball about 5cm across. Use both hands to shape it into a ball with no filling showing.

Lightly beat the remaining eggs. Set up three bowls: one with flour, one with egg and one with breadcrumbs. Get out a wire cooling rack. Working one ball at a time, roll it first in flour, then in egg, then in breadcrumbs, then sit it on cooling rack while you do the same with the rest of the mixture.

Preheat the oven to a low setting. Heat a pan of frying oil – enough to completely cover the balls – to 190°C. Deep fry the arancine a few at a time until they are dark golden brown and crisp. Lift them out of the oil with a slotted spoon on to a baking tray. If you wish, put them in a low oven to rest and dry for a few minutes before serving.

Cipolle, piselli e patate in umido
Onions, peas and potatoes

Serves 4

1 large white onion or
    10 spring onions
butter or olive oil, or a mixture,
    for frying
1 large potato or several new
    ones (about 600g in total)
about 100ml wine or water
400g podded fresh or frozen
    peas
a handful of mint or fennel
    fronds
salt and freshly ground
    black pepper

A steamy braise is probably the best way to describe this. Like the *minestra* opposite, you stagger the ingredients into the pan. Onions, peas and potatoes are a good trio; start by softening the onion in olive oil, then add the potatoes and cover the pan, which creates steamy juices in which the ingredients are cooked, and are in turn absorbed back into the final dish. Add mint at the end and serve with rice or a slice of sheep's cheese or a poached egg on top, or anchovy breadcrumbs.

Slice the onions thinly and put them in the pan with the oil or butter, then heat from cold over a low heat until the onion is starting to soften; this will take about 5-6 minutes. Peel and slice the potato and add it to the pan with a pinch of salt, then stir until each slice is glistening with fat. Add the wine or water, cover and let everything cook, half steaming and half braising. After 15 minutes, add the peas, cover and cook for another couple of minutes, then uncover and finish cooking until the peas are tender. You may need to add a little more water. Finish with the mint or fennel fronds.

Minestra di primavera
Spring or green soup

Serves 4

3 spring onions
1 celery stalk with leaves
6 tablespoons extra-virgin
   olive oil
200g green beans
1 medium potato
50ml white wine
a Parmesan rind,
   if you have one
1 small courgette
300g podded fresh or
   frozen peas
300g podded fresh or
   frozen broad beans
a handful of spinach
10 basil leaves
toasted bread and pesto,
   to serve (optional)
salt and freshly ground
   black pepper

A very green spring soup. I can't help but think of this as a ball that starts off small with a soffritto of aromatic vegetables in olive oil, and then as it rolls along at a simmer it collects layers: first the sturdy ones (potatoes and green beans), then the courgette, then peas and broad beans and finally, during the last roll, the spinach and basil. This means that each vegetable is given the right amount of cooking and remains bright, tender and green. You can prepare all the vegetables at the beginning, but the roll of additions also means you can do it as you go, especially with the radio on and the windows open to let in the breeze.

I have given a list of ingredients, but only as a starting point to get the ball rolling. You can substitute according to what you have, and to your taste. The template works well for all seasons, the soup changing form and colour from month to month. You could finish it with some ripped basil or a spoonful of pesto.

Finely chop the onions and celery. In a large heavy-based pan, warm the oil over a medium-low heat, add the onions and celery with a pinch of salt and cook until soft and fragrant. Meanwhile, top and tail the green beans and chop them into short pieces. Peel and chop the potato and add it to the pan, stirring so that each piece is coated with oil. Add the green beans, then a splash of wine and let everything sizzle. Add 1.2 litres cold water and the Parmesan rind. Bring to a gentle boil, then reduce to a simmer.

After 20 minutes, dice the courgettes and add them to the pan. Pod the peas and broad beans. If the broad beans are large and have tough outer coats, remove them by plunging the beans into hot water for 1 minute, then immediately into cold water. Pinch off their opaque coats. Add the peas and beans to the pan and cook until tender, which will not take very long. In the final minutes of cooking time, tear the spinach and basil and add them. Taste and add salt and pepper to your taste. Serve alone, or over toasted bread, with a blob of pesto on top if you wish.

Cuttlefish with peas

Serves 4

1kg cuttlefish, cleaned
1.2kg fresh peas in their pods,
    or 500g frozen ones
1 small onion
5 tablespoons extra-virgin
    olive oil
2 anchovy fillets
100ml tomato passata, or
    1 tablespoon tomato purée
    dissolved in 100ml water
250ml dry white wine
a few sprigs of flat-leaf parsley,
    finely chopped
100g rice (optional)
salt and freshly ground
    black pepper

'The reason I add tomato,' Mauro, my Roman fish seller, explains, 'is so that I have a good broth. Once you have served up, you add a couple of handfuls of rice to the broth remaining in the pan and cook it until the rice is tender,' he says, kissing his pinched fingers. 'The next day you can make a risotto with the ink. Nothing is wasted!' Then he wraps the cuttlefish in a piece of white waxed paper, the ink sacs in another, and puts both into a plastic bag, which he spins, knots and hands over.

Also known as ink fish, a cuttlefish has a small sac inside its head filled with a thick black-brown substance that is released when the fish needs to cloud the scene to make an escape. They need to be cleaned carefully, which is little messy, but not difficult. First you rub away the thin skin and speckled frill from the bee-shaped body, then use a sharp knife to cut it open from head to tail. Pull away the stiff white cuttlebone and the membrane, lift out the innards and – very carefully – the ink sac. Keep the tentacles above the eyes, but discard the rest of the head. Rinse everything carefully and cut the body into strips.

This recipe is very similar to an even more traditional dish, *palombo e piselli* (dogfish and peas), and both are still eaten in Rome, traditionally on a Friday. The combination of tender cuttlefish and the sweetness of the peas with just enough broth is a very good one. You don't need to add the tomato, or the rice in the remaining broth, but they are very nice. Toasted bread rubbed with garlic is good, too.

Rinse and dry the cuttlefish. If they are large, cut them into thick strips, otherwise leave them whole. Pod the peas, if using fresh ones, and finely chop the onion.

Warm the olive oil over a medium-low heat in a large, deep frying or sauté pan, add the anchovies and prod them with a wooden spoon until they disintegrate. Add the onion and fry gently until it is soft and fragrant, then add the tomato and cook

for a few minutes more. Add the cuttlefish, stir, then add the white wine, cover the pan and cook for 20–30 minutes, adding the peas after 10 minutes. The exact timing will depend on the size and cut of the cuttlefish. The pan should not dry out, and you want broth, so add a little more wine or water if necessary. Taste and season with salt and pepper to taste, then finish with the parsley. If you are using rice, you need a fair bit of broth, which you can lengthen with more water or wine. Simply add the rice to the broth after taking out the cuttlefish, add a pinch of salt if you think it needs it and simmer, stirring, until the rice is cooked.

Risi e bisi
Rice and peas

Serves 4

1kg tender, fresh peas in their
  pods, or 300g frozen peas
1.5 litres light chicken, veal,
  vegetable stock, water, or
  stock made by boiling the
  pea pods
1 small onion, or 2 spring onions
  with greens
50g pancetta or unsmoked
  bacon (optional)
30g butter
2 tablespoons extra-virgin
  olive oil
250g risotto rice, ideally vialone
  nano or arborio
50g grated Parmesan, or to taste
finely chopped flat-leaf parsley,
  to taste (optional)
salt and freshly ground
  black pepper

If you have found peas in their pods, and have managed to get them home without eating them all, you might like to make a pea-pod stock for your rice and peas. This is just the pods boiled in water until you have a green, faintly sweet stock, which seems to get even more deeply flavoured as you cook it and it becomes the colour of a pea-green boat. Rice and peas, *risi e bisi*, is rather like like risotto, but possibly nearer a thick soup. This is Vincenzo and Luca's favourite thing to make with fresh peas, which is a joy of a dish, but it is also good with the trusty bag pulled from the freezer.

Shell the peas, if using fresh. If you are making a pea-pod stock, put the pods in a large pan, cover with 1.7 litres cold water, bring to a gentle boil, then reduce the heat to a simmer and cook for 20 minutes. Strain the stock, measure out 1.5 litres and keep it warm. If using other stock or water, warm it through.

Finely chop the onion, the pancetta too if you are using it. In a large, deep frying or sauté pan, warm the butter and olive oil over a medium-low heat, then add the onion and pancetta and fry gently until both are soft and fragrant. If you're not using pancetta, add a pinch of salt too. Add the peas, cover with some of the warm stock or water and simmer for a few minutes, depending on how tender the peas are.

Add the rice, stir, then add the rest of the stock. Season with salt and plenty of pepper, then cook gently over a medium-low heat, stirring every now and then until the rice is tender, which will take about 16 minutes; keep tasting to check. The final consistency should be somewhere between a soup and a risotto, so quite fluid. Add a little warm water if necessary. Finish with plenty of grated cheese and the parsley, if you are using it.

Broad beans

In Rome, *fave* (broad beans) are harbingers of spring. The first pods, slender with slight curves, appear in March. So too do the signs, dutifully sellotaped to the doors and windows of *trattorie*, market stalls and shops, usually something along the lines of *ci sono fave in questo locale* (there are broad beans here). For quite some time I thought this was advertising, fresh *fave* being something to boast about, after all. It is, however, a sober caution: favism is a potentially fatal sensitivity to broad beans that occurs in some people of Mediterranean ancestry. It is an ancient affliction. It wasn't just that the Pythagoreans believed the beans contained the remains of human souls, and that the pods were a pathway to Hades for the dead – some of them actually suffered from favism, which is why Pythagorus is remembered not only for this theory, but also for banning the beans. These days the affliction is very rare, so although the signs are still very much a warning, they are in a way an invitation too, for there are *fave* here.

The first young beans are often offered exactly as they come, in their pods, with pecorino, Rome's beloved sheep's milk cheese. The habit is as much about shared ritual as taste. Everyone takes a pod, then unzips it with their thumb to reveal a velvet lining and the line of four or five small, pale, flattish green beans. The beans, when tiny, are extremely tender, taste grassy and sweetly waxy and combine curiously well with craggy pieces of salty cheese (feta and young salted ricotta also work well). We often have *fave e pecorino* as part of an antipasti lunch alongside toasted bread rubbed with olive oil, salami, olives, tomato salad and something slightly mysterious – small whole artichokes perhaps – under oil. The habit of *fave e pecorino* continues until the first of May, Workers' Day, when it is traditional to escape the city for a day trip and picnic. Drawings and paintings of this *scampagnata*, or scamper to the country, show great spreads of beans, cheese, salami and casks of local wine. These days the picnic is just as likely to include tuna and pasta salad, crisps, houmous and a six pack, but the beans and pecorino are still there, a reminder of another time. Back in the *trattorie*, and homes, broad beans play an important role in *vignarola*, a spring vegetable stew, in which their distinctive, creamy bitterness is a great complement to the sweet peas, velvety artichokes, lettuce and fatty guanciale (cured pork cheek). Vignarola might have been cooked for hours, until incredibly soft and a dark, military green, or quickly to make a bright, vital stew. Lovers of the dark stew, which is more traditional, often turn their nose up at the bright one. Lovers of the bright one sniff at the old-fashioned. I don't find one better than the other, just different, and make both at home depending on how old they are. In Sicily, a similar stew of broad beans, beans, artichokes and onions is called *frittedda* and is eaten alone with bread, as a side dish or stirred into pasta or a frittata.

The many ages of beans: that is the point with *fave*. Sweetness and youth are what makes the raw beans precious, so we have to move, and eat faster than vegetable biology. As the season progresses you may still find tender ones, but the pods get

gradually darker and longer, their curves bolder, the ends blacker and the beans larger and more white than green. As I write this during the last days of June, most stallholders shake their heads when I ask for *fave*. When I do find them, they seem almost exaggerated versions of themselves and the beans inside are huge, with great thick coats that need pinching off. This is the challenge for the cook: to know where exactly the beans are on the scale of tender to starchy. How thick are the coats, and do they need removing? Only you can decide, and you need to taste. In the past, anything more than a baby bean and I whipped off the white coats like an anxious mother. Now I quite like the flavour that comes with age and the slight bitterness of the coat – in the pasta dish below, for example. At a certain point, although no mid-life crisis, I prise off the coats. Podding and peeling beans is a task best done in company, ideally that of a real person, or otherwise music. The best way to peel beans is to plunge them into boiling water and then straight into cold, at which point the coats will pop off, possibly sending the bean across the room, when you squeeze them. The bright-green inner bean is an undeniable delight, even more so when stewed with onion and tossed with good olive oil and piled on toast, or stirred though fresh egg pasta, whole or pounded to a vivid green paste along with a spoonful of ricotta and a splash of pasta-cooking water.

And when you can't get fresh broad beans, which is most of the time, there are frozen ones. Hooray for frozen broad beans, which I like almost as much as I like frozen peas. True, their flavour is slightly compromised, but only a little, and the podding is already done. What's more, I think the freezing process does something to the skin: you only need to defrost them a little, nick the coat with your nail and then pinch it off, if you want to. Frozen beans are usually small, so the coats are still edible. Beans that have been frozen need only a little cooking to bring out their sweetness. With the exception of the ritualistic podding and eating with cheese, any recipe that calls for fresh broad beans can be made with frozen ones, if you can extract the bag from its icy position between the mystery soup and the ox tongue you're never going to cook, that is.

Frittata di fave e cipolla
Broad bean and onion frittata

Serves 4–6

1 large white onion,
    or 5–6 spring onions
5 tablespoons olive oil
200g broad beans, coats
    removed
6 large eggs
a handful of chopped dill or
    fennel fronds (optional)
100g sheep's or cow's milk
    ricotta, or 50g grated
    Parmesan (optional)
salt and freshly ground
    black pepper

In Italy, if you change the subject or turn a discussion in your favour you may be told not to *girare la frittata* (don't flip the frittata). It is a phrase I am very familiar with, as apparently I am very good at flipping situations. The origin of the expression is – like so many turns of phrase – the kitchen, and the belief you should never flip a frittata, just cook it on one side. I understand this reasoning, and a well-made omelette or an unflipped, barely set frittata, really almost custardy on top, is a tender thing. However, many people, me included, do invert the just-set frittata on to a plate and put it back in the pan briefly, which seals it. Finishing it under the grill is also an option, but that does make the eggs quite sturdy. Flipping or no flipping, frittata with broad beans, the bright green tiddlywink-like rounds suspended in deep yellow, looks lovely and is delicious. You could add some Parmesan or ricotta. The idea for this recipe came from my friend Rosa Malignaggi.

Thinly slice the onion. In a medium cast-iron or non-stick frying pan, warm the olive oil, add the onion and fry gently until very soft. Add the broad beans and cook for 2 minutes.

Beat the eggs in a large bowl and season with salt and pepper. Pour them over the vegetables or – if you are afraid of the egg sticking, or you are using a cast-iron pan – scrape the vegetables into the egg bowl, wipe the pan clean, smear it with butter, then pour it all back in the pan, stirring until the eggs begin to cook. Scatter over the herbs and then the cheese, if using.

Let the frittata cook over a low heat. As the edges start to set, use a spatula to ease them away from the pan sides. Once the frittata is golden underneath, mostly set but with a wobbly top, which takes about 8 minutes, you can either serve as is or, if you want it firmer, finish it in the oven, or invert it on to a plate and return it briefly to the pan to cook the other side. Let it sit for a few minutes before serving.

Fave e patate all'agro
Broad beans, potatoes and lemon

Here is an idea: boil a couple of large waxy potatoes in their skins in well-salted water until easily pierced with a knife. While they cool, plunge 300g podded fresh or frozen beans into boiling water for a minute, drain, plunge them into cold water and then pop away the outer coats. Once the potatoes are cool enough to handle, peel and cut them into rough chunks. Whisk together 6 tablespoons olive oil, the juice of 1 lemon and a pinch of salt, add some ripped mint, dill or fennel fronds and whisk again. Put the potatoes and beans in a bowl, pour over the dressing, toss and serve. The term *all'agro* means sour, which comes from the lemon, which is then tempered by the olive oil. It goes beautifully with grilled lamb chops, grilled cheese or grilled fish.

Sugo con le fave
Pasta with fresh broad bean sauce

Serves 4

5 spring onions
a handful of flat-leaf parsley
50g pancetta, guanciale or
   bacon
1 tablespoon extra-virgin
   olive oil
400g podded broad beans
500g pasta (farfalle, fusilli
   or casarecce work well)
50g freshly grated pecorino
   or Parmesan, or a spoonful
   of ricotta
salt and freshly ground
   black pepper

This is a recipe by one of the greatest Italian food writers and historians, Oretta Zanini di Vita. Its charm lies in its distinctive flavour and the beautiful light green colour of the sauce. The broad beans are cooked in a mixture of oil and water, during which time much of the water evaporates, leaving only an oily vegetable essence. The pancetta or guanciale (cured pork cheek) is essential; if you don't eat it, I suggest making something else. Oretta is very specific that beans should not be double peeled for this: the slight bitterness – Romans love bitter – is important to her. You can, of course, peel them, and your work will be repaid by a very bright green sauce (which I like), and you won't need to cook them for quite as long. For an even softer, creamier dish, use ricotta instead of Parmesan or pecorino.

Finely chop the onions and parsley and dice the pancetta. In a heavy-based pan or earthenware dish, gently fry the onion, parsley and pancetta in the olive oil until the onion is soft and the pancetta has rendered its fat. Add the broad beans and 300ml boiling water and a pinch of salt – how big a pinch will depend on the saltiness of the pancetta. Bring to a gentle boil, then reduce the heat to a simmer and cook for 10–12 minutes or so, until very soft and surrounded by just a little oily liquid. Remove half the beans from the pan and pass them through a food mill, or reduce them to a purée with a stick blender, then return them to the pan.

Meanwhile, bring a large pan of water to the boil, add salt, stir and add the pasta. Cook until al dente. Once cooked, drain the pasta and add it to the beans in the pan. Alternatively, mix the two in a warmed serving bowl, adding a handful of cheese as you mix. Divide between bowls, passing more cheese around for those who want it.

Insalata di fave, finocchio e menta
Broad bean, fennel and mint salad

Serves 4

150g small and tender shelled
  broad beans (about 500g
  beans in their pods)
1 large or 2 small bulbs of fennel
a handful of mint
5 tablespoons olive oil
juice of 1 orange
a pinch of dried oregano
  (optional)
prosciutto or feta, to serve
  (optional)
salt and freshly ground
  black pepper

A bright delight of a salad and combination of flavours: sweetly waxy beans, aromatic fennel and pungent mint, all sweetened slightly by orange. Unless the beans are tiny, I think they really need peeling here. The addition of prosciutto or feta and focaccia (see page 354) turns a salad into lunch.

Plunge the broad beans into boiling water briefly, then straight into cold water. Remove their white coats. Trim the fennel, removing the tougher outer layer (use it for stock) and setting aside any feathery fronds, then slice it as thinly as possible. Tear the mint into little pieces with your fingers.

In a small bowl, whisk together the olive oil, orange juice, salt and oregano, if you are using it. In a serving bowl, mix the beans, fennel and mint with the dressing. If you are adding prosciutto or cheese a flatter dish is better, so that you can arrange it on top.

Dried broad beans

Wheat, tomatoes, artichokes and cotton may have been his main crops, but for Vincenzo's grandfather Orazio broad beans (*fave*) were the workers. Crops needed rotating and soil replenishing with the broad beans that transport nitrogen from the air into the soil via their root, making them an excellent fertilizer. As a result, broad beans were plentiful, eaten fresh when small and young and then, as they got older and starchier, traded with shepherds for cheese, sold, or dried for the winter.

If the beans are dried with their jackets, they need soaking, then cooking for an hour or two, and they retain some shape. When the jackets are removed the beans split, and look like creamy white, slightly melted buttons, or tiny bits of bone. Split broad beans don't need soaking and cook to tender collapse in 30 minutes or so, which is one of the reasons I love them so much. When simmered back to life, dried broad beans have something of the chickpea, the cannellini and the chestnut about them, with slight bitterness from the tannins. The amount of water is key: add less and the purée is stiff and can be enriched with olive oil, garlic and lemon and eaten as a dip. Add more water and you have a soft, soupy consistency, which is what you want for *maccu di fave* (see page 80), a sustenance dish that has been eaten all over the south since antiquity.

I was once reprimanded for my apparent glorification of *cucina povera*, of poverty I have never known (which is true), but surely we should celebrate and eat dried broad beans, which are important for the environment, plentiful, cheap, nutritious and soul-satisfyingly good. I use them more and more in the kitchen: a handful in soups, where they give body and thickness but don't dominate, or in houmous-style dips, which I eat with salad or spread rather thickly on toast.

Maccu di San Giuseppe
A sort-of Saint Joseph's soup

Serves 4–6

200g dried chickpeas
200g dried broad beans
100g lentils
100g split peas
1 large onion
3 ripe tomatoes
2 celery stalks
1 small bulb fennel
400g greens, such as chard,
    borage or spinach
6 tablespoons extra-virgin
    olive oil, plus extra for frying
3 thick slices of bread,
    cut into cubes

San Giuseppe (St Joseph) or Fathers' Day falls on 19 March in Italy. San Giuseppe is an important patron saint, a protector of the poor and curer of illnesses, and his saint day falls two days before the start of spring, so his is a twofold celebration. In farming families like Vincenzo's, this was done by making *maccu di San Giuseppe* from the final leavings of last year's harvest, in their case wheat grains, broad beans, lentils maybe.

To be too presciptive about the ingredients would be to miss the point: you use whatever you have in the cupboard. You cook your dried beans in abundant water, add vegetables along the way and enrich it at the end with extra-virgin olive oil, which is a bit like making soup backwards. Traditionally, terracotta cooking pots were used because it was all people had, but the habit has remained because the terracotta neutralizes acidity, which softens the flavour.

Soak the chickpeas and broad beans in plenty of cold water for at least 8 hours or overnight, adding the lentils and split peas for the last hour of soaking. Drain and rinse.

Put all the pulses in a large heavy-based pan or earthenware cooking pot, cover with 2 litres cold water and bring slowly to the boil, skimming off any foam. Reduce the heat to a simmer and cook for at least 2 hours, or until the pulses are very soft.

Meanwhile, dice the onion along with the tomatoes and celery and trim the fennel and greens of any tough stems or leaves, then chop them roughly. After the pulses have been cooking for 1 hour, add the onion, celery, tomatoes, fennel, greens and a generous pinch of salt and cook for another hour.

During the last 5 minutes of cooking, when the pulses are very soft and the vegetables tender, taste to check the seasoning and add salt if needed. Add the olive oil and several grinds of black pepper. Heat some more olive oil in a pan, fry the cubes of bread until golden and scatter them on top of the soup to serve.

Maccu di fave
Dried broad bean purée

Serves 4–6

450g dried peeled broad beans
extra-virgin olive oil, to serve
salt

To serve
200g short pasta, ideally ditalini
1 small onion or several spring
    onions, chopped
1 tomato, roughly chopped
4 tablespoons olive oil

To serve with greens
500g greens, such as cicoria
    or puntarelle, or a mix of
    spinach, rocket, chard and
    dandelion
1 fat garlic clove
4 tablespoons olive oil

Maccu, which sounds as much like a dance move as it does lunch, is what I make most often with dried broad beans. Usually I serve it with greens that have been boiled and cooked again briefly in olive oil and garlic, or sometimes with pasta, finishing both with extra-virgin olive oil. The contrast of the soft purée and tangle of greens is simple and so good.

The *maccu* may seem like soup as the beans cook, but they continue to absorb liquid, the consistency changing from soft to stiff in no time. Keep an eye out, taste, observe, and add more water and salt as you see fit.

Soak the broad beans in water overnight, then drain. Put the beans in a heavy-based pan, cover with 2 litres cold water and add a pinch of salt. Bring to a gentle boil, reduce the heat to a simmer and cook, stirring occasionally, for 1½ hours, or until completely tender and collapsing into a pale purée. For an even smoother purée, blast it a couple of times with a stick blender.

To serve with pasta, add 300ml boiling water, then the pasta and another pinch of salt, and cook, stirring constantly, until just tender, adding a little more boiling water if necessary. Meanwhile, sauté the onion and tomato in the olive oil until soft, then add them to the beans and pasta. Divide between bowls and zig zag with a little more of your nicest extra-virgin olive oil.

To serve with greens, wash the greens thoroughly, then blanch them for a few minutes in a large pan of well-salted boiling water. Drain the beans. Gently crush the garlic with the back of a knife and heat the olive oil in a frying pan over a low heat. Add the garlic and cook until it is just turning golden and fragrant, then remove it. Chop the greens, add them to the pan and cook for a few minutes, stirring, so each leaf is coated with garlic oil. Remove the pan from the heat. Put the *maccu* in bowls and serve with a pile of greens on top of each one.

Cauliflower

We drove past Rosa's several times during our first trip to Gela in May. The pale blue wooden door, propped open by crates filled with spring vegetables, had caught my eye. On one occasion a traffic jam meant we stopped almost in front, and a woman, who I now know to be Rosa, was standing on the step with her hands in the pocket of a grubby white apron, behind her a droop of blue-and-white striped fabric. I was struck by the pleasing simplicity of it all and asked Vincenzo if it was a shop, market stall, or simply someone's house, and whether he remembered it from when he was a boy. He didn't, but then it was on the other side of town – which, I would later find out, is all of eight minutes on foot. As for the nature of the place, he said it was all three: a shop, a stall and someone's house. This was one of my first glimpses of Gela's dispersed market, which plays out all over the city, on corners, in side streets and in people's homes.

Of course, there was always a chance it might turn out to be a disappointment. It wasn't. During our first long summer stay three months later, I would walk to Rosa's every day. The building, which like many in Gela is a stark concrete block with a garage or storeroom on the ground floor – is mitigated by the wooden door, bleached and blistered by the sun, and the vegetables grown by Rosa's husband Giuseppe on his farm land about 5km outside the city. In a nice bit of symmetry, it is almost precisely where Vincenzo's grandfather once farmed. The blue-and-white fabric that had caught my eye turned out to be a curtain that divides the garage in two, and Luca, my curious then-four-year-old, for whom a closed curtain is an invitation, was the first to discover a blue Fiat Punto on the other side.

Rosa herself is plump and lovely and invites proximity and confidence. I choose to hug few people, but almost immediately Rosa became one of the few. Hers is an all-enveloping hug, one of confidence and comfort. Almost immediately I found myself explaining our situation and what were doing in Gela, which she thought was *bellissimo* and called her daughter straight away

to tell her. Rosa was concerned that I might be disappointed with the vegetables, as Giuseppe only has what he grows, and said I might need to go somewhere else for other things. In that moment, I was sure that I wouldn't.

From the start, Rosa took her position seriously and over the summer made sure she kept back the right things for us. She called me when Giuseppe was bringing peaches and figs so ripe and fresh they were still warm from the day's sun and had a drop of nectar where they were pulled from the tree. By the time August faded into September we had found a rhythm, with me timing visits to coincide with Giuseppe's arrival with that day's harvest, and Rosa more or less predicting what I would buy: the last of the cherry tomatoes, the peak of the violet-coloured *tunisine* aubergines, the first of the late figs. During our last week, as the heat was broken by soft breezes of autumn, Giuseppe picked his first cauliflower, a tiny white thing, cupped by huge fringe of green leaves. By the time we returned to Gela for a long weekend in November, the shop had completely changed colour, with no more hot splatters of red and purple: now it was leafy and green, filled with wrinkled cabbages whose leaves looked like something out of a porcelain factory, dark green Sicilian broccoli with its small florets and fleshy ribs, and piles of cauliflowers, some a familiar mass of creamy-white whorls, some lime green, others an extraordinary violet colour. These were the cauliflowers of Vincenzo's childhood, great curdled things that taste creamy and almost sweet.

I've always liked cauliflower, even more so these last few years because it is one of the vegetables that is equally good in all three kitchens: ours in Gela and Rome and my mum's in Dorset. These recipes have their roots in all three places and feel at home in all of them. When choosing a cauliflower, look for one that smells and looks good, with tight and creamy whorls. I may be repeating myself by noting Jane Grigson's advice, but it is such good advice: if the cauliflower looks at you with a vigorous air, buy it; if it looks in need of a good night's sleep, leave it where it is. The leaves are the real clue to freshness: they should be tenderly green with white ribs, and firm: standing to attention rather than floppy. When fresh, the leaves are every bit as delicious as the cauliflower itself, and are a key element in both the first recipe, a quintessential Sicilian one: *pasta chi vrocculi arriminati* (cauliflower goes under multiple, and confusing, names in Italian), and the last, a most English one: cauliflower cheese.

Pasta chi vrocculi arriminati
Pasta with cauliflower, anchovies, saffron, pine nuts and raisins

Serves 4

1 head cauliflower (about 1kg)

1 small onion

50g raisins

6 tablespoons extra-virgin
   olive oil

a pinch of red chilli flakes

6 anchovy fillets packed in oil

50g pine nuts

a pinch of saffron
   (about 12 strands)

500g dried pasta, such as
   bucatini, casarecce,
   penne or busiate

salt

Arriminati means both mixed and seasoned, and is the ideal word to describe this dish of pasta mixed with cauliflower that has been deeply seasoned with the good Sicilian combination of anchovies, pine nuts, raisins and saffron. It's a good example of a dish in which the anchovies are anything but fishy and intrusive: instead, they melt into the background, providing a deep savouriness that works nicely with the sweetness of the raisins and brings out the creaminess of the cauliflower. But try telling that to my sister: she loathes anchovies and can detect them a mile off. The chilli is not traditional, but I like its heat and liveliness. A version of this dish was one of the first things Vincenzo's mother, Carmela, cooked for me.

As a variation, instead of the pine nuts, raisins and saffron, try capers and black olives; the cooking method is exactly the same. I also like this variation without pasta as a vegetable dish, alone or with a hard-boiled egg or a piece of poached cod or, better still, salt cod.

Bring a large pan of water to the boil. Trim the cauliflower, discarding any tough outer leaves and cutting away fibrous parts of the stem, then cut it into florets, cutting any tender leaves into reasonable pieces, and wash them. Once the water boils, add salt, stir, then add the cauliflower and cook until it can be pierced with a fork but is still firm, not soggy – this usually takes about 6 minutes.

Meanwhile, thinly slice the onion and soften the raisins in a little hot water. Warm the olive oil in a large, deep frying or sauté pan over a low heat. Add the onion and fry gently until soft, then add the chilli and anchovies. Continue frying very gently, nudging the anchovies with a wooden spoon until they break up and melt into the soft onion.

Use a slotted spoon to lift the cooked cauliflower from the pan into the frying pan, stir and continue cooking for a couple more

minutes. Drain and squeeze the raisins, then add them to the pan along with the pine nuts and saffron. Taste and add salt if necessary. Remove from the heat.

Bring the cauliflower-cooking water back to a fast boil, add the pasta and cook, stirring every now and then, until al dente. Use a slotted spoon to lift out the pasta, and the water that clings to it, into the frying pan. Return it to the heat and cook for another minute or so, stirring so the flavours come together. Serve immediately.

Cauliflower cakes

Serves 4

500g potatoes, ideally 2 or 3
    roughly the same size
1 head cauliflower (about 1kg)
150g fresh ricotta, or 100g
    grated salted ricotta,
    pecorino or Parmesan
100g fine breadcrumbs,
    plus more for dusting
1 heaped tablespoon salted
    capers, rinsed and roughly
    chopped
2 large eggs, lightly beaten
flour, for dusting
olive oil and butter, for frying
salt and freshly ground
    black pepper

The capers are essential here, their salty, briny nip razzing up the soft beige cakes. I sometimes also add some very finely chopped anchovies and substitute parsnip for some of the potatoes. I shape these in the same way as traditional fish cakes, i.e. nice thick rounds, but there is no reason why you couldn't make smaller cakes. Go slow in the pan; you want them to have a real crust. I like them with a green salad, ideally one with peppery leaves such as rocket or watercress.

Scrub the potatoes, but don't peel them. Put them in a pan, cover with cold water, bring to the boil and cook until tender. Drain. Once they're cool enough to handle, peel them.

Trim the cauliflower, discarding any tough outer leaves and cutting away the fibrous parts of the stem, then cut into florets and wash them. Reserve any tender leaves for something else. Boil the cauliflower in plenty of fast-boiling, well-salted water until tender, but not soggy. Drain thoroughly.

Put the cauliflower in a large bowl and mash it. Pass the potato through a food mill or potato ricer into the bowl, or mash it with a fork. Add the cheese, breadcrumbs, capers and 1 egg, season with salt and black pepper, then use your hands to bring the mixture together into a soft mass.

Line a tray with baking parchment. Dust the work surface and your hands with fine breadcrumbs, then shape the cakes by taking balls of mixture, rolling them between your palms and flattening them into cakes around 2.5cm high and 7cm across. Dip them in flour, then into the remaining egg, then coat them in breadcrumbs. Put them on the tray until you're ready to cook.

In a frying pan, heat some olive oil and a knob of butter. Once hot, add the cakes 2 or 3 at a time, depending on how big the pan is (don't crowd it). Once a nice golden crust has formed on one side, turn the cakes and fry on the other side. Drain quickly on kitchen paper, then serve immediately.

Cotolette di cavolfiore
Cauliflower wedges with breadcrumb or polenta crust

Serves 4

1 large cauliflower (about 1kg)
2 eggs
flour, for dusting
100g coarse breadcrumbs
    or polenta
olive or vegetable oil, for frying
lemon wedges, to serve
salt and freshly ground
    black pepper

The key to these is getting a lovely, deep-golden crust on both sides, then serving them while still very hot. The salt and lemon are important too, brightening and sharpening. Orange and fennel salad (see page 166) is a good addition, as is some sort of chutney.

Trim the cauliflower, discarding any tough leaves but keeping the tender inner ones. Cut a deep cross into the base. Bring a large pan of well-salted water to a fast boil and add the cauliflower, stem side down. Cook at a steady boil for 20 minutes or so, or until the cauliflower is tender to the point of a knife. Drain. Once cool enough to handle, cut the head into 2.5cm wedges.

Lightly beat the eggs. Prepare 3 plates: one with flour, one with the eggs and one with the breadcrumbs or polenta with some black pepper. Pour enough oil into a deep frying pan to come 2cm up the sides, and heat it until hot.

Dip a cauliflower wedge in first the flour, then the egg, then the crumbs or polenta and lower it into the oil. Fill, but don't crowd, the pan with more wedges. Once a deep golden crust has formed, turn it and cook the other side. Use a slotted spoon to remove the wedges, first on to some kitchen towel to blot, then on to a warm serving dish. Sprinkle with salt and serve straight away.

Cauliflower cheese with Parmesan and white beans

*Serves 4 as a main
and 6 as a side dish*

700ml whole milk
1 bay leaf
1 small onion, studded with
   3 cloves
1 large cauliflower (about 1kg)
50g butter, plus extra for dotting
50g plain flour
75g Parmesan or Cheddar,
   grated
1 x 400g tin cannellini beans,
   drained
breadcrumbs (I use soft
   fresh ones), for topping
salt and freshly ground
   black pepper

A splendid thing, I think. Vincenzo doesn't agree with me at all, which means that for the sake of table harmony, I make it less often than I would like. This is a dish in which my English and Italian kitchens come together happily, the very English Jane Grigson recipe I have been eating all my life adapted in my Roman cooking world. The Parmesan lends its sharp saltiness to the sauce and the white beans, soft and nutty, add another note. Cauliflower cheese is also a lovely celebration of the cauliflower leaves, which are all too often just trimmed away and discarded. Sweet and fleshy, the leaves provide another welcome texture to the final dish. My dad loves a spoonful of mango chutney with cauliflower cheese, and has passed the habit on to me.

Preheat the oven to 200°C/180°C fan/gas mark 6. In a small pan, bring the milk, bay leaf and onion slowly to the boil. As soon as the milk starts to rise in the pan, take it off the heat and leave it to sit and infuse for 15 minutes.

Bring a large pan of salted water to the boil. Trim the cauliflower, discarding any tough outer leaves and cutting away fibrous parts of the stem, then cut it into florets with the tender leaves still attached. Once the water boils, add salt, stir, then add the cauliflower and boil until it can be pierced with a fork but is still firm, not soggy. This usually takes about 6 minutes. Drain.

Melt the butter in a heavy pan, stir in the flour and cook to a roux (a sticky paste that comes away from the sides of the pan) for 2 minutes, without letting it brown. Remove the bay leaf and onion and then, over a very low heat, pour the flavoured milk gradually into the roux, whisking constantly. Raise the heat a little and bring the sauce to simmering point, whisking until the sauce thickens to the consistency of thick double cream. Turn down the heat and let the sauce simmer gently for 20 minutes. Stir in all but a small handful of the cheese, taste and season with salt and pepper.

Arrange the florets in a baking dish, scatter over the drained beans, pour over the cheese sauce and dust the surface with breadcrumbs, the remaining cheese and a few dots of butter. Bake for 20 minutes or so, or until the surface is blistered and golden and the sauce is bubbling at the edges.

Potatoes

When I was growing up in Harpenden, a nice but dreary town north of London, it wasn't uncommon to come into my parents' old kitchen, which was large, to find several people standing in a line very close to each other against the cast-iron, four-oven Aga. It was pillarbox red, a colour no longer manufactured. It was always on and always hot. Even on warmish days when the windows were open, people made a beeline for it, hands behind backs on the rail handcuff-style, bottoms sticking out slightly to press up against the warmth. There was really only room for three, but the usual customs about personal space were forgotten; once you had taken up position it was hard to leave, especially during the dark of winter. I would sometimes lie on top of it to do my homework with a pillow stuffed between the two lids and another on the plate-warming end. Jeans dried on the rail in front of it until they were as stiff as cardboard, wet books were left on it until they opened out like accordions, shoes were dried out in the coolest oven. It really was the burning red heart of the house.

Of course, the constant heat meant almost constant cooking. But the thick cast iron that kept our bottoms warm also kept cooking smells in. There was absolutely no sign that something was cooking until you opened the door to a cloud of smoke or – if you left it long enough – the cremated remains of something in the bottom of a pan, or lumps of charcoal that had once been potatoes. Best of all was forgetting a potato, then remembering in the nick of time and running down the stairs just in time to catch it, the skin hard and slightly ashen, the insides like fudge. I would press butter into the flesh and eat it against the Aga. When I was a teenager, a potato thrown into the oven was easy comfort food, and the smell of baking potato is a sharp stab of nostalgia; its taste, too, is a deeply familiar kind of sustenance. My dad thinks this is because I have Irish roots, the Roddys not so far back having been the Reedys, many of whom fled Ireland during the potato famine.

Even today, when I need comfort or don't know what to cook, the answer is usually either eggs or potatoes. During Roman and Sicilian summers, when it gets too hot to turn on the cooker after 11 o'clock, I boil long, waxy potatoes whole in the morning, which is about as organized as I get. Once cool, they are peeled and left naked, ready to be eaten whenever, usually in slices with butter or olive oil, too much salt and plenty of black pepper. At certain moments there is nothing better.

Vincenzo agrees, although his Proustian nostalgia is – another cliché – for the potatoes cooked by his grandmother Sara. Ask someone to describe a nostalgic dish and they often go into minute detail. Sara was notoriously frugal with olive oil because it was precious stuff, and a famously hasty cutter. Vincenzo can mime her caution with the olive oil pourer, her erratic slicing. She was also famous for never rushing: everything was cooked slowly and purposefully, which the two faded and slightly sunken patches in the speckled travertine floor in front of her stove seem to prove. Her potatoes were fried slowly until they were a muddle of fat soft bits and very thin crisp bits. I tried hard to recreate them in Gela, using the same pan, the same stove, the same oil and potatoes from the same land, and they were fine, but not Sara's.

Choosing potatoes is not easy. Ask advice, or find a good all-rounder if that makes it easier. For me, this is Desiree in the UK and the long, yellow, slightly waxy potatoes from Viterbo in Rome. Rather than looking for a particular variety for each dish, I focus more on the time of year, which also informs the way I cook potatoes: their progress from new to old mirrors our own seasonal appetites beautifully. In spring, new-season crops, bright and waxy, are for salads and for tossing with spring greens. Boiling continues through the summer as chunks of potato soak up the oily juices of deep red stews. As autumn taps its toe in the wings, holding out your cardigan, and the potatoes mature, I start roasting. Then, as cardigans are put under coats, mashing too – more insistently as the winter progresses. As the new year starts, when the sugar has converted to starch and potatoes are considered old, it is time for soups in which the potatoes collapse and thicken.

If I am cooking potatoes for a salad or to add to a stew or savoury tart, I scrub them, then boil them whole and unpeeled. This means they retain their shape better (the skin holds everything together) and don't get waterlogged. As they cool,

the skin curls and is easy to peel away. Buy potatoes from a farmers' market if you can, and look for those still with their protective coat of mud, as washing before storing is detrimental. If you can, buy and store a big bagful. I keep my modest sackful in the darkest corner of the kitchen where Vincenzo can trip over them, and dream of the day when we have a cellar.

Potato, onion and caper salad

Serves 4

2 large potatoes (about 800g)
2–3 tablespoons red wine
    vinegar
1 large red onion
60g capers packed in salt
6 tablespoons extra-virgin
    olive oil
2 tablespoons freshly squeezed
    lemon juice or 1 tablespoon
    red wine vinegar
a small handful of flat-leaf
    parsley, mint or dill, chopped
salt

Amiable and sturdy, with a soft, neutral flavour, potatoes don't just stand up to strong flavours, they embrace them. This is where a fair number of my pre-boiled potatoes end up. The combination of the sweet, slightly sharp onion and the spritely, salty bite of capers is great. This is also good with some tuna or hard-boiled eggs, or both, in which case you might add some black olives as well, the baked ones that are wrinkled and black as night.

Scrub, but don't peel the potatoes. In a large pan, cover the potatoes with cold water, add salt, bring to the boil, then cook at a lively simmer until tender to the point of a knife. Drain and leave to cool.

Slice the onion into slender moons, soak them in a bowl of cold water with the red wine vinegar for 15 minutes, then drain. Rinse the capers thoroughly. Whisk together a dressing of extra-virgin olive oil, lemon juice or vinegar and a pinch of salt.

Once the potatoes are cool enough to handle, peel them. Slice them roughly, put them in a bowl and scatter over the onion, capers and herbs. Pour over the dressing, toss gently (hands are best) and serve.

Potatoes and greens

Serves 4

2 large potatoes (about 800g)
300g mixed greens, such as
   spinach, radish leaves, chard,
   rocket, watercress or sorrel
2 garlic cloves
1 small dried red chilli or a pinch
   of red chilli flakes
6 tablespoons extra-virgin
   olive oil
salt and freshly ground
   black pepper

I am a fan of greens, particularly slightly bitter ones, cooked twice: first boiled and then sautéed in olive oil with garlic and chilli. In Rome this process is called *ripassata* (re-passed), or *strascinata* (dragged), which is a good description, reminding you that the greens really do need to be dragged around the pan so as to catch lots of flavour. In Sicily I starting adding chopped boiled potatoes, maybe a little oregano, to the greens and it has become a favourite. I like a combination of greens and the different textures and levels of bitterness: spinach, chard, radish leaves, sorrel, watercress. In Sicily we picked some *cavoliceddi*, a wild cousin of the mustard family whose intensely bitter flavour was stunning with the potatoes. This is no time for parsimony: everything should glisten with olive oil. Some lemon juice makes it even more sharply appetizing. Serve alone, or with salty cheese, hard-boiled eggs, lamb chops or roast chicken.

Scrub, but don't peel the potatoes. In a large pan, cover the potatoes with cold water, add salt, bring to the boil, then cook at a lively simmer until tender to the point of a knife. Lift from the water with a slotted spoon and leave to cool in a colander. Once they are cool enough to handle, peel and chop them into large chunks.

Wash the greens thoroughly, then boil them for a few minutes in the potato water or another large pan of salted boiling water. Drain well.

Meanwhile, crush the garlic cloves with the back of a knife so that they split but remain whole. Chop the greens roughly. In a frying pan over a low heat, sauté the garlic and chilli in the olive oil until it is just turning golden and fragrant. Remove the garlic. Add the greens and cook for a few minutes, stirring so that each leaf is coated with oil. Add the potatoes, season with salt and pepper, stir and serve.

Patate a sfincione
Potato, tomato and oregano bake

Serves 4

2 large potatoes (about 800g)
1 large white or red onion
4 large tomatoes
extra-virgin olive oil, for
    drizzling
6 tablespoons pecorino,
    Parmesan or caciocavallo,
    grated (optional)
a pinch of dried oregano
200ml vegetable stock
6 tablespoons breadcrumbs
salt and freshly ground
    black pepper

There is some debate as to whether the roots of the word *sfincione* are Arab or Greek, but either way it means 'sponge-like' and is the name for Palermo's most famous deep, soft pizza topped with tomato, onions, anchovies, cheese, oregano and breadcrumbs. We could understand *patate a sfincione,* which is no doubt inspired by that Palermitan pizza, as 'soft potatoes'; or perhaps 'tender' is a better word, as they collapse, along with the tomato and onion, into a tender bake. It is sort of Sicilian *pommes boulangère,* which means 'cooked in the bakers' oven', since this was also traditionally cooked in the days before people had ovens at home.

Its deliciousness depends very much on the contrast of the soft, well-seasoned inside and the golden crusty surface. To ensure this contrast you need to make sure of three things; that the *sfincione* is deep enough, say 4cm; that there is enough liquid, from very juicy tomatoes and the addition of some white wine or stock; and that the topping has a good balance of breadcrumbs and cheese and enough olive oil. In Sicily they use fine dried breadcrumbs, but I prefer semi-soft fresh ones so that they crisp as they toast. I make this in an oval ovenproof dish or my faithful aluminium cake/pie/everyman tin, which is 6cm deep and 26cm across.

Preheat the oven to 200°C/180°C fan/gas mark 6. Slice the potatoes and onions thinly. Slice the tomatoes thinly, catching the juices. Rub a roasting tin or ovenproof dish with oil and make a layer of potatoes, then onions, then tomatoes and juices. Zig-zag with a little oil and sprinkle with cheese and oregano. Now repeat this process until all the ingredients are finished; ideally the last layer will be potatoes. Pour over the stock. Finish with a thick layer of breadcrumbs mixed with cheese and zig-zag with olive oil. Bake for 1–1¼ hours. Leave to settle for a bit before serving.

Gattò di patate e melanzane
Potato and aubergine cake

Serves 6–8

1.5kg potatoes, ideally
    several evenly sized
    medium-large ones
2 large aubergines
olive oil, for frying
120g Parmesan, grated
100g butter
4 eggs, lightly beaten
100g salami, diced (optional)
50ml whole milk
300g mozzarella, smoked
    cheese such as provola,
    or a mixture of the two
fine breadcrumbs, for sprinkling
salt and freshly ground
    black pepper

This is based on a recipe for *gattò di patate* from my Neapolitan almost-neighbour Daniela del Balzo. To your potatoes you add good things: butter, Parmesan and 4 eggs. Mix everything to a cream. You then press a layer of this mixture into a buttered and breadcrumb-dusted tin, cover that with a layer of mozzarella, smoked cheese and the aubergine before finishing with another layer of potato, which you sprinkle with breadcrumbs, dot with butter and bake.

The quantities below are for a big *gattò*, which is perfect food for a crowd, or you could share this amount between two dishes: one to eat, one for the freezer. If you do make a big one, rest assured that it is delicious the next day. I warm a little butter in a frying pan, then re-heat it slice by slice, which gives a nice crust. As an accompaniment, I think greens or broccoli *ripassati* are good. I have, of course, put a fried egg on top of a slice, because what isn't better with an egg on top? How this dish brings on comforting waves of cheesy, buttery potato nostalgia for me. An ideal family dish for a weekday supper.

Scrub, but don't peel the potatoes. In a large pan, cover the potatoes with cold water, add salt, bring to the boil, then cook at a lively simmer until they are tender to the point of a knife. Drain.

Slice the aubergine into 5mm slices lengthways, then salt them if you wish (see page 46). Fry them in olive oil until golden brown on each side, or brush them with oil and cook them on a ridged grill pan. Remove and drain on kitchen paper.

Preheat the oven to 180°C/160°C fan/gas mark 4. Once the potatoes are cool enough to handle, peel them, then pass them through a potato ricer or food mill, or mash them in a large bowl. Add the grated cheese, half the butter, the eggs, the salami if you are using it and the milk. Season with salt, pepper and a pinch of grated nutmeg and mix well.

Use half the remaining butter to grease a large ovenproof dish (I use my enamel 28 x 36cm baking dish), then dust it with fine breadcrumbs. Press half the potato mixture into the bottom of the dish. Layer the slices of aubergine on top. Dice or thinly slice the cheese and make a layer of both on top of the potato. Cover the cheese with the rest of the potato mixture, pressing the top down firmly. Sprinkle the top lightly with breadcrumbs and dot with the last of the butter. Bake for 40–50 minutes, or until the top is golden and crusty. Allow to sit for 10 minutes before serving in generous squares. Remember it is still very good the next day.

Onions

Prendi una cipolla e lo taglia fina, fina. Take an onion and chop it finely, finely. So often have I been told to begin like this that I had earmarked it as a possible book title, or first line at least. Then I was given a copy of Martino Ragusa's classic book *Giovedì Gnocchi, Sabato Trippa* (Thursday Gnocchi, Saturday Tripe), a useful and occasionally hilarious book of recipes and advice. He had already used it as his first line, brilliantly, although in Italian, which I suppose makes it still available.

So you do. You take an onion from the bowl or basket or cupboard, a movement so familiar it is a kind of kitchen warm-up. Without thinking, you weigh it up, cupping it like a bowler before a spin: 100g, 200g, not that it matters, really. Still not thinking, you turn it over and a crisp layer of skin comes away and floats to the ground. Are you good at cutting onions? I wish I was better at it, and promise myself that one day I will take a course, and that afterwards I will keep my knives sharp so that the sound of them hitting the chopping board is like gunfire. Until then, my blades are a little dull and my cutting is average. I do know you cut through the root first, then peel away the skin carefully so as to remove just the thinnest layer, then you place the onion on its side and make two horizontal cuts, before lifting your fingers to form a bridge and chopping *fina, fina.* You might also be chopping celery, carrot, garlic or parsley stems, but the onion is the foundation, crisp, sweetly pungent and full of potential, which comes at a cost. I am sure the tears are worse if you wear contact lenses. Depending on how old the onions are, my suffering ranges from watery eyes to a flood of tears, which inevitably means I rub my eyes with my oniony fist. Then I really am in trouble and have to leave the room.

When we drive to the town of Scoglitti during our summer visits to Gela, parked along the way are vans full of onions from a small town called Giarratana. *Cipolle di Giarratana* are distinctively round and squat. Most are the size of a large orange that has been sat on, others as large as a fat frisbee. They have

paper-thin, very pale yellow skin and pure white flesh that is mild, milky and sweet: it is easy to imagine that someone might eat one like an apple. Cooked, these onions turn golden and sweet, which makes them ideal for the sweet-and-sour onion dishes the Sicilians are so fond of. Rosa and Giuseppe, our vegetable sellers in Gela, have a similar local white onion, and a yellow and a red, and at least twice a week in summer a man with a van full of red onions drives under our window shouting *cipudda, cipudda*! We often buy a case, since unlike other more perishable vegetables, onions are easy, tenacious sorts that only need hanging up to dry, and will then keep us going for a while.

An abundance of onions means an abundance of ways to use them. As foundations, but also as an ingredient in their own right: roasted whole, stuffed, stewed and as the main player in salads. When I asked Rosa which onion was best for which dish, she said the yellow ones for sauces, the white ones for stewing, roasting and stuffing, and the red ones for salads, but then turned all her advice on its head by saying that the only rules are the ones you make up yourself. Rosa, like Vincenzo's mother Carmela, likes to remind me that soaking slices of onion in cold water with a little vinegar will take the edge off their pungency. Also, that rubbing a cut onion on your joints will keep them in good nick, and that a cut onion on a window ledge will keep out the ants.

Much has been written, both scientific and lyrical, about the transformation of onions and other alliums when they meet heat. Crisp and pungent softening into silky and sweet but still resolutely savoury, the harmonious flavours and moisture are indispensable as a foundation to countless dishes, which is why so many recipes begin with that line. In this book there are more than 40, many of which are Sicilian. *Pazienza* is another thing I have been told: it takes time for the onion to transform, release its liquid and become more like fabric than a vegetable. Not that you really need to think: you have done this hundreds of time before. But it pays to look closely every now and then, to watch the transformation as the moons or squares relax and soften. It is a very democratic act, this starting point, and beyond it we are pulled in different directions: staying pale and soft; turning darker and more caramelized; the addition of herbs, spices or vegetables. But at the start we are all the same, an onion in a pan.

Cipollo al forno
Roasted onions

Serves 8

8 white or red onions, about
    300g each (the flatter the
    bottoms the better)
extra-virgin olive oil, to taste
red wine vinegar, to taste
salt

The smell of scorched onion skins, as Simon Hopkinson says, is 'one of the greatest kitchen smells of all time.' It is one of the greatest smells of the railway arches in Catania, too. You smell it before you see them, no mean feat considering that you're on the fringes of the infamous fish market. Pass under the bridge and to your left are table-sized *brace* (grills), great black menacing things filled with red-hot charcoal. Go as near as the heat will allow and you will see the whole onions on top like squashed cricket balls, their skins scorched and black, great fleshy peppers with flashes of red under the charred skins, and possibly aubergines too. I can't help remembering a self-appointed barbecue expert once telling me that you must not char anything when grilling. There's no such advice here. In Gela too, the bakeries use the residual heat from a day's baking to roast trays of onions and peppers, which sit outside the bakery to cool and entice customers, which they do. You buy one, two, six to take home. Roasted onions are gorgeous.

Even though you don't have direct heat and smoky char, an ordinary domestic oven does a surprisingly good job of toasting the outside while the inside melts. Peeling them is a messy business that you may want to do in the kitchen, or maybe just put them on the table and let everyone get on it with. The insides, soft, silky and dressed with olive oil, red wine vinegar and salt and pepper, are excellent with most grilled meat and fish, especially sausages, lamb and mackerel.

Preheat the oven to 200°C/180°C fan/gas mark 6. Put the unpeeled onions on a baking tray and roast them until golden, almost dark, and incredibly soft within. This usually takes about 1 hour. Take out of the oven and allow to sit for 20 minutes. Bring them to the table like this and let everyone get on with it, or peel off the outer layer so you are left with the soft heart, which you can dress with a little salt, olive oil and vinegar.

Involtini di cipolline
Spring onions wrapped in pancetta

Serves 4–6

olive oil, for brushing
12–16 spring onions
12–16 thin slices of pancetta
freshly ground black pepper

The smell of roasting onions is one thing, that of roasting bacon another, and here they are together. We cook these on a small charcoal grill so that the fat drips and hisses on the hot coals and the onions char. The smell is glorious. You need to wrap the pancetta tightly and leave the bulb exposed.

Heat a ridged grill pan and brush it with oil. Pull away any very damaged outer layers from the spring onions, then wrap them in a spiral of pancetta, leaving the fat bulb poking out. Cook, turning them as needed, until the pancetta is crisp and toasted and the bulb is charred. Eat straight away, with black pepper if you wish.

Cipolle ripiene
Stuffed onions

Serves 4

8 onions, about 300g each
    (the flatter the bottoms
    the better)
olive oil
200g dried breadcrumbs
100g pecorino, grated
grated zest of 1 unwaxed lemon
50g raisins, soaked in warm
    water for 10 minutes to
    plump up (optional)
50g pine nuts
a pinch of dried oregano
freshly ground black pepper

Come round to collect the aubergines at 3 o'clock, Rosa told me, so you can also taste my stuffed onions and write about them for your book. I walked over at one of the hottest points of the day, the sun high and fierce, so nobody else was about, and shouted up at her window. Next thing she was at the door, with the five aubergines I needed to make a parmigiana, and a tray of her onions. If you think about it, onions are the ideal vegetable for stuffing, since the layers, once softened by boiling, separate easily and provide a neat cavity. You chop the onion you have removed and mix it with breadcrumbs, cheese and herbs – the quintessential Sicilian stuffing that we meet again and again, and which can be adjusted to your taste – then stuff the mixture into the hollow cavity and bake them, in tomato sauce if you wish. The last one, squashed into bread or simply eaten standing by the fridge the next day, is the most delicious.

Peel the onions carefully, making sure not to cut away too much of the base, as they need to stay together. Bring a pan of salted water to a gentle boil and cook the onions for 10 minutes, or until just tender – test them with the point of a knife. Lift from the water with a slotted spoon and leave to cool. Once they are cool enough to handle, use a fork to pull out the centre of each onion, leaving two thick layers to stuff.

Preheat the oven to 180°C/160°C fan/gas mark 4. Chop the centres of the onions and fry them in a little olive oil. Add the breadcrumbs, cheese, lemon zest, raisins, pine nuts and oregano and season with salt and pepper. You want a firm but damp stuffing that holds together when you squeeze it.

Lightly oil an ovenproof dish that will accommodate the onions snugly. Fill each one with stuffing, pressing it into the corners. Grate over a little more cheese, zig-zag with olive oil and bake for 20 minutes.

Cipollata
Sweet-and-sour onions

Serves 6–8

1kg onions
6 tablespoons extra-virgin
    olive oil
3 tablespoons red wine vinegar
3 tablespoons sugar
salt

Cipollata is a dish somewhere between a relish, a side dish and a salad. It has the qualities of all three but won't commit, which is what makes it so delicious and useful. It has the soft, companionable, sticky sweet-and-sour nature of a chutney or relish, but it isn't cooked to death, so it retains some texture and takes up enough room to be considered a vegetable side dish. Then there is the slight crunch and verve, which gives it the feeling of salad.

Like its Roman cousin *cipolline in agrodolce* (sweet-and-sour pearl onions), Sicilian *cipollata* is good with many things: as an antipasti with salami and cheese, especially aged sheep's cheese; as a great accompaniment to fish pan fried or baked with a breadcrumb crust, which it sharpens and brightens rather like a lemon; and in sandwiches of all sorts. The method took me by surprise to begin with, but it works: you start by cooking the onions in water, which evaporates away to leave the onion soft, at which point you add the oil, vinegar and sugar, which you adjust to taste. Thanks to the double preserving forces of sugar and vinegar, it keeps for over a week in a jar with a lid in the fridge.

Halve and slice the onions (not too thinly), then put them in a large, deep frying pan or casserole dish and cover with 250ml water. Set the pan over a medium-low heat and cook, stirring, until the water has evaporated. Add the olive oil and a pinch of salt and fry the onions, stirring more or less constantly, until they are very soft and pale but still have integrity – this is not onion jam. This will take about 15 minutes. Add the vinegar and sugar and cook for 5 minutes longer, taste and adjust the flavours if you like, then remove from the heat and allow to cool.

Tunnina ca'cipuddata
Tuna with sweet and sour onions

Serves 4

6 tablespoons extra-virgin
    olive oil
800g fresh tuna, cut into
    1cm-thick slices
4 onions, preferably white
    or golden
60ml red wine vinegar
2 tablespoons sugar
a small handful of fresh mint
salt

Born out of the need to conserve without a fridge, you can find sweet-and-sour fish dishes all over Italy, such as Rome's salt cod with tomato and vinegar and Venice's sardines with sweet-and sour-onions. Here, a sort of *cipollata* is paired with fresh tuna, which is a superb, most appetizing combination. It is a recipe from Lilla, Vincenzo's paternal grandmother, who comes from Messina, the corner of Sicily nearest Italy's toe. Lilla sometimes made it with sardines. Vincenzo's father, when recounting this recipe, told me that it was better the next day four times. At home we have it with bread, but rice, couscous or plain boiled potatoes (ideally waxy ones the colour of butter) with olive oil and parsley would work well.

In a large frying pan over a medium-low heat, warm 3 tablespoons olive oil. Fry the tuna slices swiftly on both sides until they are just cooked through and lightly coloured. Lift them on to a plate and set aside.

Halve and slice the onions to about 2mm thick. Return the pan to the heat, add the remaining olive oil and then the onions. Fry the onions gently until they are soft and translucent, but still have some texture. Add the vinegar and sugar and cook for a few minutes longer.

Arrange the tuna in a shallow serving bowl, spread the onions over the top and rip over the mint. Wait for at least an hour, or up to a day, before eating. Room temperature is best.

Herbs

What was better then

Than to crush a leaf or herb
Between your palms

Then wave it slowly, soothingly
Past your nose and mouth

And breathe?

From Seamus Heaney, 'A Herbal', *Human Chain* (2010)

Carmela, my mother-in-law, looked at me, disbelieving. I might as well have told her that I didn't own a toothbrush or an iron, or that my kitchen didn't have a stove or a knife. She chose not to believe me. 'You must have oregano,' she said, looking up at the shelf of jars and bottles, pressing her hands together and shaking them in a sort of reprimanding prayer. 'You must, it is vital, *la morte sua*, it will be nothing without it.' The rolls of beef simmering in tomato sauce next to us seemed to burp in agreement. I am well practised at the dash for something forgotten. I have long legs and can take the stairs three at a time (or at least I could back then), be at the nearest shop in a minute, and then – if there is no queue – back with a pint of milk, a dozen eggs or small jar of oregano in three. And I was. 'It will do,' Carmela said, as she pulled off the plastic seal, flicked open the lid, shook some leaves into her cupped hand and breathed in before throwing them over the beef.

Sicilians adopted the name from the Greeks: *oros ganos*, joy of the mountains. As for the Greeks, who weave oregano into bridal crowns as well as their cooking, oregano is a defining flavour for Sicilians. Several varieties grow wild all over the island, on mountains and hillsides, and by the ruined house we drive past on our way to Scoglitti. The plant is a foot or so high, with woody stems, tiny spade-shaped olive-green leaves and, when it blooms, a lacy umbrella of white or pale purple flowers. The scent loads the air, aromatic and musty, like camphor and mint, reminding us they belong to the same family. It should be picked when it is flowering, and therefore still soft; left in the sun, it will dry enough to scratch your legs. On several occasions I have smelt it before I could find it, because I didn't really know what I was looking for among the leggy thistles and foliage. Oregano is collected almost religiously by those who know where to find it, and is bound with string and hung in big bunches (cut and dried in the truest sense), then used by everyone, sprinkled liberally in and on to food, giving it character and a fine partner, *la morte sua*: the death of it, but in the best possible way.

It turns out that oregano is the death of the far end of via Mazzini in Gela, too. This year we arrived in early July, and the man who parks his car there – his wife in the front and the things he has collected in the boot – had fresh green almonds in their velvet coats, crates of *pere facce bedde* (pears with beautiful faces), which were the size of figs and smudged with blush, and bunches of wild oregano. He suggested hanging them upside-down in a dry, shady room; I hung mine on a washing line strung across the top room. The woody stems and almost velvety leaves and flowers dry quickly into a crisp crackle, which is what you want, oregano being one of the few herbs that seems to concentrate its scent as it dries. In the last few days of our stay I set to work pulling the leaves and flowers off the stems. It was a particularly hot day and this, combined with the fierce scent, took me back to the day when I got lost in the John Lewis perfume department, aged eight. I decided I would finish it another day. A few days later I popped out for a matter of minutes, and when I got back the scent accosted me at the front door. Vincenzo's uncle Liborio, like his mother before him, had rubbed the oregano stems over newspaper before wrapping it in a bundle for us to take back to Rome. It is now in a jar sitting on the shelf: a bit of Gela in Rome. It reminds me of a Sicilian friend who now lives in the US and packs bunches of oregano in his suitcase. His clothes smell of it for weeks, and when he adds a pinch to a simmering pan, the warm, stony, herb-scented hillside of his childhood rises up before him. When he eats he feels happy and sad in equal measure; it seems no coincidence that the smell of oregano is sometimes described as melancholy.

Free and plentiful, Sicilian oregano is a different beast from the ancient jars of dusty powdered stuff I've had in my kitchen over the years, dreary potfuls that were already middle-aged on the shelf. If you have some that has been hanging around too long, bin it, buy a new, smaller jar and give it a use-by date yourself (of no more than a year). Better still, buy a bunch of Sicilian or Greek oregano stems, which don't cost the earth if you can find them. If you live in large country house, or a house with an airy larder, it is nice to hang it on the wall and roll off the leaves and flowers as you need them. In a small Roman kitchen next to a busy road, the bunch gets sooty and musty pretty quickly, so I lay some newspaper on the table and rub the leaves and flowers off the stems before storing them in a jar. Be gentle: you want the pieces to remain as large as possible. The more finely powdered the herb, the more the aroma gets lost.

Since oregano is scattered throughout my Sicilian-inspired cooking, it is also scattered throughout this book, in starring roles or working quietly and faithfully away in the background. I sometimes think of herbs as character actors, each one with a distinct personality that can change a scene completely: lifting it, bringing depth, giving the star turn something to spar with. Having been the woman who had none in her kitchen, I am now dedicated to oregano's warm, aromatic and slightly bitter flavour, and find myself using it more and more – even in ostensibly Roman dishes too, which traditionally would have used rosemary. An important thing to note is that the flavour of oregano is communicated by stewing rather than frying. Oregano and rosemary are often interchangeable, although, like music, they pull dishes in different directions. Rosemary, with its piney, woody scent, is virile and almost muscular and adds a very different note from the sweet mustiness of oregano. A good example is Roman lamb braised 'hunters' style', which is made with garlic, white wine and rosemary, sharpened perhaps with a little vinegar. An almost identical family recipe from Gela uses oregano. Yet another version, from my friend Fabrizia Lanza in central Sicily, and given below, partners lamb with mint. It is not only delicious, but also a reassuringly familiar dish for me, the Englishwoman who grew up with lamb and mint sauce for Sunday lunch.

Mint sauce aside, I have learned to cook with mint in Rome, where wild mint, *mentuccia*, with its gangly stems and little fragrant leaves, grows in the cracks in the pavement. Historically this *mentuccia* was collected, but these days comes along with cigarette butts and traffic fumes, so I buy wild mint plants, which I use with artichokes, sweet-and-sour courgettes and pumpkin.

From early spring to mid autumn there are great bunches of basil at the market, and therefore on my draining board in a jam jar. And if I don't need a bunch, a lanky stalk often appears in the top of my bag, along with a posy of parsley, a carrot, a stick of celery – the *odori* (aromas) that are the foundations of so many dishes. But basil, the quintessential summer herb, is best in bunches, or better still plants, even if they are small and in a plastic pot, the bright green fleshy leaves filling the kitchen with their warm scent, like spicy, slightly minty grass. I always think basil seems innocent from a distance, but shove your nose in or rip a leaf and the scent is hot, fierce even. Basil is the herb I use in the largest quantities, great bunches pounded into pesto, thrown by the handful into late summer stews, tucked between the red and the white in the mozzarella and tomato salad that we eat whenever we can.

Bay is my herb equivalent of jeans. It isn't my favourite – although I like it very much – but it is the herb I use all the time. We used to have a small bay tree on our narrow balcony. It was near enough for me to stick my hand out the door, tug a couple off, pass them under the tap, crumple them and throw them into the pan in a single move. It resisted two scorching Roman summers but then, halfway through the second winter, begrimed by traffic and blown and battered in a corner, it gave up. Now I have to rely on a leggy tree round the back of Monte Testaccio, grabbing a handful every now and then and using the leaves fresh at first, and then as they dry, their colour fading from forest to olive green.

The almost-leathery fresh bay leaves contain essential oils: pull a fresh one from a shrub, crush it, wave it before your nose and inhale, and the scent is almost hot, pungent like pine or eucalyptus. The effect in cooking is softened, but it still gives persistent savoury notes. The food writer and vegetable expert Deborah Madison calls the effect of bay in cooking grounding, sobering; it is my friend, the bay base line. Many people prefer dried bay leaves, in which the bitterness has lessened. These are more fragrant and sweetly spicy, like cinnamon and nutmeg, to which they are related. Crush a dried leaf so that it crumbles and you will see. I use fresh and dried interchangeably in the onion, celery and carrot soffritto that is at the foundation of so many soups and stews and ragùs, milky sauces and baked potato dishes, anything with lentils and beans (we eat a lot of lentils and beans), or sandwiched between fish and meat. Like any seasoning, precise amounts of herbs are difficult to give, as there are just too many variations – not least, personal taste.

Sammurigghiu
Olive oil, lemon and oregano sauce

Sicily in a sauce, or should I say marinade; *salmoriglio* is the more common Italian spelling. The smell when you make this is absolutely glorious: the grassy hum of olive oil, the bright eye-watering freshness of lemon, the sunny perfume of just-cut garlic, the musty sweetness of oregano. The smell gets stronger as you warm the sauce. I use this as a marinade for fish, especially swordfish, for lamb, chicken and vegetables of all sorts.

Suggestions for proportions: 100ml extra-virgin olive oil, the juice of 2 lemons, 2 teaspoons dried oregano and a fat clove of garlic that you have peeled and chopped very finely. All you do is mix them together. If you make it in a bain marie, or a heatproof bowl balanced over a pan of simmering water, and whisk vigorously, it will thicken and the fragrance will be released while you do so. You can still get a nice rich sauce, without heat, though, simply by whisking it all together.

Pane, ricotta, origano, olive e olio
Bread, ricotta, oregano, olives and olive oil

In Gela we buy small round semolina-flour rolls from the bakery. They tear open easily to reveal a soft, dense crumb. Often they are still so warm that a puff of steam escapes; if they aren't we reheat them in the oven, or on the grill on the roof, if it is going. The ricotta goes on first, then some oregano, the olives, some salt, and then to finish a zig-zag of olive oil.

Formaggio all'argentiera
Silversmiths' cheese

Serves 2

1 garlic clove

2 tablespoons extra-virgin
   olive oil

2 x 1cm thick slices of cheese,
   such as caciocavallo,
   tuma or provolone

1–2 tablespoons red wine
   vinegar

2 tablespoons chopped fresh
   oregano, or 1 tablespoon
   dried

a pinch of sugar

There are several wistful Sicilian recipes that come from a time when people had little and wished for much. *Pasta con le sarde al mare* (pasta with sardines at sea), for example, is almost identical to *pasta con le sarde*, only without the sardines, which are still, unfortunately, swimming around. There are recipes that mimic, such as a fat omelette padded out with breadcrumbs and rolled up to resemble a fish, called *pisci d'uovo* (fish made of eggs). Then there is *formaggio all'argentiera*, so named because the silversmith, ashamed that he had no rabbit to eat, found that cooking cheese with oregano and vinegar gave out a similar, almost meaty scent and thus confounded his neighbours, and perhaps his stomach. I have no idea if this is true, but the smell is quite something. The beauty is the just-melting cheese, crisping into craggy edges, so get it from pan to plate quickly, or simply bring the pan to the table, bread and wine at the ready.

Gently crush the garlic clove with the back of a knife so that it splits but doesn't break. Warm the olive oil in a heavy-based frying pan over a medium-low heat, add the garlic and fry gently until fragrant and just turning gold, then remove it. Add the cheese to the pan and fry until lightly golden and melting at the edges, then turn it over and fry the other side. Remove the pan from the heat, sprinkle with the vinegar, oregano and sugar, then turn the heat down to low and return the pan to it for 3–5 minutes, until the cheese is really soft and gently crisping at the edges.

Cianfotta
Mixed summer vegetables and herbs

Serves 4–6

500g sweet peppers
1 large potato, about 400g
1 large aubergine, about 400g
2 ripe tomatoes
2 large onions
1 plump garlic clove
6 tablespoons extra-virgin
olive oil
a large pinch of dried oregano
100g black olives, such as
Gaeta or taggiasca
a small bunch of dill or wild
fennel
a small bunch of flat-leaf parsley
a small bunch of basil
salt and freshly ground
black pepper

Rather like ratatouille, *cianfotta* is a soft stew of summer vegetables, with the addition of masses of herbs. Unlike ratatouille, all the ingredients are added at the same time, then left (bar the odd stir) so that heat and time work their alchemy and everything comes together into a mellow whole, soft, oily and rich. It shows how herbs work differently: oregano, a modest amount, is added early and works at the foundations, penetrating the vegetables as the dish bubbles away. Basil and parsley, lots of them, are added at the end so they are still vital, more of a lovely green vegetable than a token garnish. *Cianfotta* is good with rice or salted ricotta, or with feta, the soft and chalky cheese softening in the warm layers of oily vegetables.

Prepare the vegetables by cutting the red peppers into strips about 1cm wide and 5cm long, peeling and dicing the potato into 1cm cubes, and dicing the aubergine into the same size cubes. If you want, you can peel the tomatoes by covering them with boiling water for 1 minute, then plunging them into cold water, at which point the skins should slip away easily. Chop the tomatoes roughly. Thinly slice the onions and gently crush the garlic with the back of a knife so that it splits but remains whole.

Warm the olive oil along with the garlic and onions in a large heavy-based pan over a medium-low heat, and cook gently until soft and fragrant. Add the vegetables, a pinch of salt and the oregano, stir, then cover and cook for 40 minutes, lifting the lid and stirring often, adding the olives after about 15 minutes. You can now leave it to simmer until the vegetables are very tender.

The final stew should be rich and thick, with just enough liquid to keep it soft. If there is still quite a lot of liquid, increase the heat and let it evaporate away. Meanwhile, chop the dill, parsley and basil. Once the consistency is good, add the herbs to the pan and cook, uncovered, for 1–2 minutes longer. Serve warm, not hot.

Spezzatino di agnello all menta
Braised lamb with mint

Serves 6

1.5kg boneless shoulder
    or leg of lamb
1 large red onion
6 tablespoons extra-virgin
    olive oil
1 tablespoon tomato purée
250ml white wine
a pinch of saffron (optional)
a large bunch of mint
salt and freshly ground
    black pepper

This is another recipe inspired by my friend Fabrizia. Lamb and mint make good bedfellows, although I thought the recipe quite curious when I first read it. It works, though, the lamb simmering into tenderness in white wine and just a little tomato. The mint, and lots of it, brings a great pungent rush right at the end. It really is worth ripping the mint rather than chopping, as metal does make the mint discolour. That said, it will fade in the heat anyway. Season boldly; the salt and pepper are crucial. Rice makes a good companion.

Cut the lamb into 5cm cubes and thinly slice the onion. In a large heavy-based pan with a lid, warm the olive oil over a medium-low heat, add the onion and a small pinch of salt and fry gently until soft and translucent. Add the lamb and cook, stirring, until it has browned on all sides. Stir the tomato purée into the wine until it has dissolved, then add it to the pan and let everything sizzle for a couple of minutes.

Steep the saffron, if using, in 250ml warm water, add it to the pan along with a pinch of salt and allow to come to a gentle boil. Reduce the heat to a simmer, cover and cook for 40 minutes. Adjust the lid so the pan is partly uncovered and cook for 20 minutes more, stirring every now and then, by which time the lamb should be very tender and the sauce thickened. Pull the leaves off the mint, rip them roughly and add to the pan. Taste and season with salt and pepper.

Green sauce

Makes a large jar

3 salted anchovies, rinsed and
    deboned, or 6 anchovies
    preserved in oil
1 fat garlic clove
a handful of capers, rinsed
a handful of mint leaves
a handful of flat-leaf parsley
    leaves
a handful of basil leaves
a strip of lemon zest
6 chives, chopped
extra-virgin olive oil, to taste
lemon juice, to taste

A very green, very good, very sociable sauce. You can decide how thick or thin you want it to be by adding more or less olive oil and vinegar. A spoonful of thickish sauce is splendid with white fish or plainly roasted chicken, or spread on toast even. A thinner sauce can be used to dress hard-boiled eggs and vegetables, especially warm potatoes and green beans, sprouting broccoli or spring greens, and also salad leaves.

By hand, use a sharp knife to chop the anchovies, garlic, capers, herbs and lemon zest very finely, then scrape them into a bowl. Add enough olive oil to make a nice spoonable consistency and add lemon juice to taste.

Semifreddo di menta e cioccolato
Mint and chocolate semifreddo

Serves 6–8

500ml cream
5 bushy stems of mint
4 large eggs
100g caster sugar
60g dark chocolate

Baskin Robbins, the ice cream shop on the Finchley Road, was where I discovered mint choc-chip ice cream in the early 1980s – where I first delighted in the tiny fragments of chocolate, almost sharp in the frozen cream, the mint (artificial I'm sure) making everything seem even colder, like big gulps of very cold air. I was once told by a master ice-cream maker that mint choc-chip wasn't really a flavour, and I felt rather foolish. But then one day my local gelateria made *cioccolata con la menta*, which just shows that it's all about what you call it. In the absence of an ice-cream machine, this is my domestic version, which looks rather elegant, like a speckled log. The taste, too is elegant, as well as childish. When I eat it I am 10 and back on the Finchley Road.

Put the cream in a bowl, add 3 sprigs of mint and leave to infuse for at least 3 hours or, better still, overnight in the fridge. Line a large loaf tin with baking parchment. I use two pieces and leave a nice overhang in order to make lifting out easy.

Strain the cream, discard the mint, then whip the cream until it is thick. Separate the eggs, putting the whites in one bowl and the yolks in another. Add the sugar to the yolks and beat until smooth and fluffy. Whisk the whites until they stand in stiff peaks.

Strip the leaves from the remaining sprigs of mint and chop them finely. Chop the chocolate roughly but finely. Using a large metal spoon, fold the yolk and sugar mixture into the cream, then the egg whites. Gently fold in the mint and chocolate.

Pour the mixture into the lined tin and put the tin in the freezer for at least 8 hours, or better still, 12. To serve, lift the semifreddo out of the tin, invert it on to a suitable plate and gently pull away the paper.

La nociata
Honey, walnut and bay leaf sweets

Makes 35–45

500g shelled walnuts
500g runny honey
70 fresh bay leaves

I see Augusto, the owner of our local trattoria La Torricella, almost every day at the market, usually on his bike, his helmet a sort of crown. We still eat there more or less every week, sitting at a table outside from April to early October, and inside the rest of the year. We still have the fried anchovies, then *spaghetti alle vongole*. If Luca is with us, he has *gelato alla crema* with tiny wild strawberries (which aren't really wild), but otherwise the end is short, dark espresso and one of Augusto's biscotti, or if we are fortunate a curious thing called *nociata*, a sticky walnut-and-honey sweet sandwiched between two bay leaves. Of course, you throw the bay leaves away, but the scent it leaves on the lozenge of honeyed nuts is rather extraordinary. *Nociata* is traditional in Lazio and was traditionally made for Christmas. The sweets keep well for weeks in an airtight tin.

Chop the walnuts finely. Pour the honey into small pan and warm it over a low heat until it bubbles at the edges and has taken on a reddish colour, which takes about 3 minutes. Add the chopped walnuts to the pan and cook, stirring, for about 12 minutes, until the mixture is thick. Pour the mixture out on to a wet marble surface and roll it out with a wet rolling pin to a thickness of about 5mm. Alternatively, pour the mixture on to a large piece of greaseproof paper, then fold the paper over the top and use your hands or a rolling pin to roll it into a thickness of about 5mm. While it's still warm, cut the *nociata* into small oblongs or diamonds and sandwich them between two bay leaves.

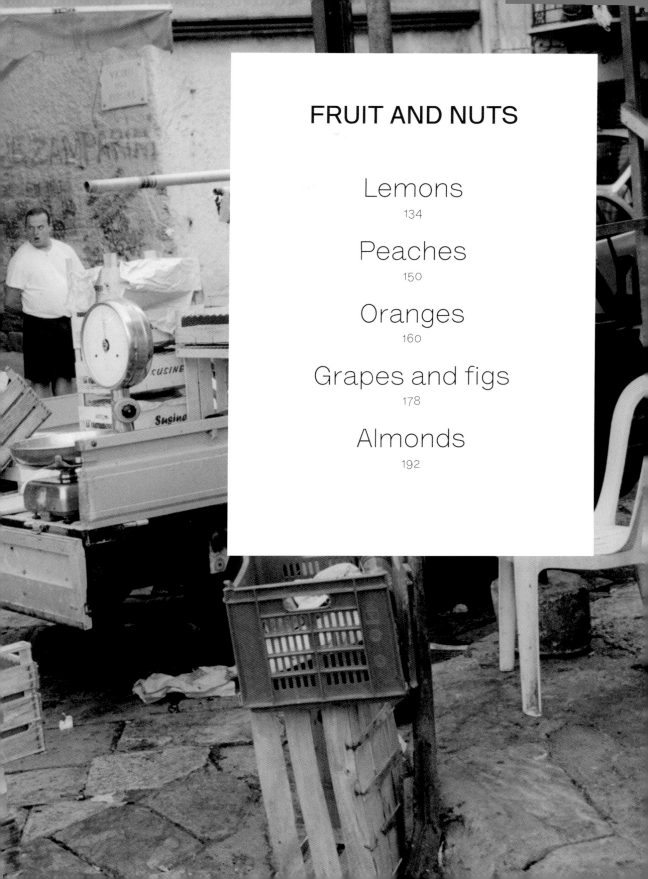

FRUIT AND NUTS

Lemons

Peaches

Oranges

Grapes and figs

Almonds

Lemons

Even after 12 years in Italy, I still get a ridiculous amount of pleasure from seeing actual lemons on actual lemon trees. On the nearby Aventine Hill, a leafy, largely residential part of Rome that rises next to Testaccio, there are dozens and dozens of lemon, orange, bitter orange and kumquat trees in the gardens of villas, in walled convent courtyards and lining the small parks. My favourite lemon tree, though, is in my friend Cinzia's garden. It is about 12 feet tall, so it pokes over the top of her garden wall, with wide, arching branches that are trimmed *alla tazzina* (like a cup), the best way for the tree to collect light. Its top branches almost reach through the door into her first-floor kitchen, which means Cinzia only has to reach from the top of the steps to pick a lemon.

Have you ever reached between the pale green leaves and picked a lemon from a tree? The scent as you twist it from the branch is sweet-smelling and somehow hot, bright and insistently alive. Like a child irresistibly drawn to a finger-sized hole, I find it almost impossible not to dig my nails into the skin of a lemon to unleash another wave. Cinzia's tree is a *limone di quattro stagioni* (a four-seasons lemon), so it is always bearing fruit. Yesterday, 2 May, we stood at the top of the steps after an afternoon of rain looking down on the tree, the air thick with its intoxicating fragrance. We could see this year's white blossoms, some of which were so open you could see the nascent green buds of fruit alongside the remains of last year's. By the time the first of this year's fruit is ready, Cinzia will have finished the huge, older, knobbly, deep warm-yellow fruit. As always, I was sent home with a dozen lemons in a bag that bounced against my leg as I walked back down the hill.

Lemons in Rome are one thing; those in Sicily are another. Like so many things, lemons were introduced to Sicily by the Arabs, whose farming and irrigation techniques changed the landscape of the island. In a tenth-century Arab treatise on farming, lemons are mentioned as part of ornamental gardens, and possibly they were used that way in Sicily too. In time, though, lemons became an essential part of the landscape, as much a part of Sicily and its food as the sunshine they personify. Lemon juice is used in drinks, ices, on vegetables and on meat and fish, giving moisture and sharpness, and is used to balance the sweetness of other fruit, or simply eaten as fruit. Vincenzo has inherited his grandfather's ability to eat a whole lemon like you or I would eat an apple, maybe peeled with a knife, maybe not. This is less surprising when you consider that Sicilian lemons are of a particular type. They have pale yellow skin over a thick layer of spongy pith which is more like aubergine flesh than the bitter-tasting white parts I am used to, and although sharp, it is fleshy, bright and edible, especially with a bit of salt. I can't, though. His mother, Carmela, also shudders. She prefers to do as her grandfather did: take a cup, rip small pieces of bread into it, cut very thin quarter-slices of lemon and add them to the cup, squeeze over the juice, add hot water, salt and pepper, and wait and wait. She makes this bread and lemon soup when she is jaded and needs cleansing and soothing. My granny Alice had a way with lemon quarters too, tipping them from the jars that came from Schweppes into every gin and tonic she served in her pub. Of course we tried them, then puckered. Alice also put empty halves on her elbows, to soften and bleach them. Aged eight, I was utterly confused as to why you would do this. At nearly 44 I understand.

Like sunshine in the kitchen, lemons – whether pulled from a tree or tipped from a yellow net bag – are beautiful, glorious and endlessly useful too, as a star ingredient, a quick dab of perfume, a seasoning or a quiet volunteer working away in the background. Lemon juice acts in much the same way as salt, bringing out flavours. It's the equivalent of a sound engineer, adjusting the balance, lifting, deepening, sharpening, brightening, filling out, making things taste more like themselves. When something is missing in a braise, stew, fruit pudding, soup or fruit purée, lemon is often the answer, pulling the dish together. A dish of lentils and hard-boiled eggs, for example, is transformed by a squeeze of lemon. You might not know it's there, but you would miss it if it wasn't. Lemon juice can also partially cook meat, fish, even vegetables, and its zest – as essential as the oils it contains – adds heat and intense fragrance.

When choosing lemons, look out for unwaxed ones with bright, unwrinkled skin; they should feel heavy in your hand. They're always available, but late November to March is when they are at their best, which is excellent timing if you think about it: brightness and eternal freshness at the time of year we need it most. I like my box grater for zesting. For squeezing I use an old-fashioned plastic two-piece, with a cone top over a collecting dish. The secret is making sure the lemon is at room temperature and rolling it around on the work surface like a ball before you squeeze it.

Spaghetti aglio, olio al limone
Spaghetti with garlic, oil and lemon

Serves 4

2 large unwaxed lemons
a large handful of flat-leaf
    parsley
500g spaghetti
1–2 garlic cloves
    (depending on taste)
1 small dried chilli or a pinch
    of red chilli flakes
6 tablespoons olive oil

Two kitchens meet in this great Roman standby *spaghetti ajo, ojo e peperoncino* (spaghetti with olive oil, garlic and chilli), as it is known in Roman dialect, which is given a Sicilian lift with some lemon zest. It's a dish I crave when I haven't had it for a while, especially in the dark days of winter, when all the steady, starchy sustenance needs a slap. It is a simple meal, but full of flavour; the bright, clean oil, the pungent garlic, throat-tickling heat of the chilli, grassy parsley (a fleck of which gets stuck in your teeth) and the volatile aromatic oil in the lemon zest. Quantities for something like this are, of course, personal; you might decide to leave out the chilli, or double the garlic.

Grate the zest from the lemons and very finely chop the parsley, then mix the two together and set aside. Bring a large pan of salted water to a fast boil, add salt, stir and add the spaghetti. Cook until al dente.

Meanwhile, very finely chop the garlic and chilli. In a large frying pan, very gently warm the olive oil, garlic and chilli over a low heat until fragrant, but do not let it burn. Once cooked, drain the spaghetti, or better still use a sieve or tongs to lift the spaghetti and a just a little residual cooking water into the frying pan. Stir, add the lemon zest and parsley, a pinch of salt and, if you like, a squeeze of lemon, then stir again, divide between plates and eat immediately.

Tagliatelle con limone e Parmigiano
Tagliatelle with lemon and Parmesan

Serves 2

220g dried or 350g fresh
tagliatelle or linguine
75ml extra-virgin olive oil
grated zest and juice of 1 small
unwaxed lemon
100g Parmesan, grated, plus
more for sprinkling

If you whisk lemon juice with plenty of olive oil and lots of freshly grated Parmesan you create a thick, grainy, deeply flavoured lemon and cheese sauce that you toss with hot pasta. The flavours work beautifully together; the sharp, lip-puckering acidity of the lemon is tempered by the Parmesan and the olive oil lends it a silky, glossy texture. All the ingredients come together into a surprising sauce that clings to each strand of pasta and manages to be both soothing and vital at the same time.

It is important to whisk the ingredients together in a warm bowl, especially on a cold day. The modest heat helps the ingredients come together. The hot pasta continues what the warm bowl started and brings out the heady scent of the lemon juice, zest and the salty sweetness of the Parmesan. I have also added rocket and basil to this, which worked well.

Bring a large pan of salted water to a fast boil. If you are using dried pasta that takes about 8 minutes to cook, add that to the water now. If you are using fresh pasta, which only takes 2–3 minutes to cook, start making the sauce first.

Warm a large bowl under a hot running tap, then dry it. Add the olive oil, some of the lemon juice and a pinch of zest and beat briefly with a little whisk until it emulsifies. Now add the Parmesan, beat again, taste and add more lemon if you want it. Taste and whisk again until you have a thick, grainy cream. Taste again; you probably won't need salt with all the Parmesan but if you feel the need, add some. Once the pasta is ready, drain it and quickly toss it in the bowl with the lemon and Parmesan sauce. Divide the pasta between two warmed serving bowls, and add more grated Parmesan if you like.

Coniglio in agrodolce
Sweet-and-sour rabbit

Serves 4

2 ripe tomatoes, or 200g
   tinned ones, drained
1 garlic clove
a pinch of dried oregano
   (optional)
6 tablespoons extra-virgin
   olive oil
1 small rabbit, cleaned and
   cut into 8–10 pieces
juice of 1 large lemon
   (about 60ml)
2 tablespoons sugar
a handful of black or green
   olives (optional)
salt and freshly ground
   black pepper

I think of this as a Sicilian variation on one of my favourite Roman dishes, *coniglio alla cacciatora* (rabbit hunters' style), using oregano instead of rosemary and lemon juice instead of vinegar for a typically Sicilian sweet-and-sour dish. It's a good example of how lemon can give a fragrant depth to a dish, also serving to tenderize the meat and help it come away from the bone.

When I first read the instructions for this very simple dish I was surprised by the early addition of tomato. It works well, though; the flavour of the tomato is absorbed by the rabbit as it browns, but then mellowed by the time the lemon is added and takes centre stage. You may well think that nothing good is going to come of this – it feels odd to brown meat with tomatoes already in the pan; there seems so much water, and then even more liquid when the lemon is added. Have faith: the liquid cooks down, and by the time the dish is ready the meat should be tender and surrounded by a slightly thickened sour (*agro*) and sweet (*dolce*) sauce. The juice of a whole lemon may sound a lot, which it is, and the dish is better for it. However, if you do shudder you can always add more sugar.

If using fresh tomatoes, plunge them into boiling water for 1 minute, then into cold water, at which point the skins should slip away. Chop the tomatoes and peel and lightly crush the garlic.

In a large, high-sided frying pan or casserole dish with a lid, cook the tomatoes, garlic and oregano until most of the liquid has evaporated, then add the olive oil and fry the rabbit pieces until they are lightly coloured all over – keep stirring so the tomato doesn't burn. Add 200ml water, season with salt and pepper, cover and cook over a medium-low heat for 45 minutes. Squeeze the lemon and dissolve the sugar in the juice, then add it to the pan and cook, uncovered, over a lively flame for another 15 minutes, tasting and watching. Add the olives at the end. Serve with bread to mop up the juices.

Granita di limone
Lemon granita

Serves 4–6

80ml sugar syrup
   (see method)
4 unwaxed lemons

Writing this in February has me wondering who on earth is going to bother with the palaver of it all, the grating and sliding the plastic box in and out of the freezer? We will, of course, once the heat has us moving slowly around the kitchen, our bare feet enjoying the cold tiles and faces welcoming the wave of cold air that comes from the open freezer door. One summer in Umbria, my brother Ben and I spent entire afternoons between the pool and the freezer, waiting for the moment when the granita was perfect, the glassy sweet-sharp crystals like snow. Lemon granita is best served in a little glass.

When I make sugar syrup I make usually make a large quantity in the ratio 2:1 sugar to water. Warm the water in a pan over a low heat – it must not boil or even get to a lively simmer – add half the sugar and stir until it dissolves, then add the other half and stir until there are no granules left. I usually make more than I need and keep the rest in a bottle in the fridge. A dash of vodka helps it last longer.

To make the granita, grate the zest from 2 of the lemons, then squeeze all 4 of them. Measure the juice and make it up to 900ml with water, then add the sugar syrup and the zest. If you have an ice-cream machine, pour the mixture in and follow the instructions to make a granita. Otherwise, tip the mixture into a shallow plastic freezerproof container and slide into the freezer. After 1 hour, as the mixture is starting to freeze, stir it with a fork and slide it back in. Repeat this every 30 minutes, stirring and scraping the mixture down from the sides with a fork as it starts to get harder. The idea is to end up with an icy slush, which takes about 4 hours. If the granita freezes over completely you can blitz it into glassy crystals in a food processor.

Lemon cream

Makes 8

3 juicy unwaxed lemons
275g caster sugar
6 eggs
250g mascarpone or
   300ml double cream

From a jolt of ice to a cream that isn't frozen. I can't decide when I like to eat my little pot more: about 15 minutes after it has come out of the oven, when it is still warm and the centre is still runny, or about an hour later when it is cool and set but still very soft and tender, or the next day after a night in the fridge, when it is deeply set, thick and fudgy.

Grate the zest from the lemons into a bowl, then squeeze them and add their juice to the bowl. Add the sugar and eggs to the bowl and whisk until everything is nicely incorporated (no need to whisk until thick). Stir in the cream or mascarpone, then cover the bowl with clingfilm and leave it in the fridge until you need it – ideally for 2 days.

When you are ready to bake, preheat the oven to 150°C/130°C fan/gas mark 2 and boil the kettle. Put eight small ramekins or ovenproof pots into a roasting tin. Divide the lemon mixture evenly between them.

Pour hot, but not boiling, water into the roasting tin until it comes halfway up the sides of the pots, then bake for 25 minutes, or until they are just set but still have a bit of wobble and runniness about them. They will set more as they cool.

Allow to cool for about 15 minutes before serving, or they will sit happily for a few hours. If you are making them a day in advance, keep them in the fridge but take them out a good 30 minutes before you serve them, so that they are cool rather than cold.

Sbriciolata alla crema di limoni
Lemon pudding

Makes 8–12 slices

For the crumbs
300g plain flour
120g caster sugar
8–10g baking powder
a pinch of salt
100g cold butter,
    plus extra for greasing
1 large egg

For the cream
4 unwaxed lemons
500ml whole milk
6 egg yolks
150g caster sugar
35g plain flour
35g potato starch or cornflour

This is Cinzia's recipe for *sbriciolata alla crema di limoni*, the literal translation of which is 'crumbs around a lemon cream,' which really is the best description since none of the other possibilities are quite right. The lemon cream is typically southern Italian, and therefore thickened with a little flour, which gives it an old-fashioned and homely feel, especially if you are used to more elegant, butter-rich lemon curds.

Preheat the oven to 180°C/160°C fan/gas mark 4 and grease and dust with flour a 28cm shallow cake or tart tin. Pare the zest of 3 lemons in strips and squeeze the juice. Warm the milk and zest in a small pan. Leave to sit for 1 hour, then lift out the zest.

Meanwhile, make the crumbs. In a large bowl, mix the flour, sugar, baking powder and salt. Dice the butter and add it along with the lightly beaten egg, then use cold fingertips to rub the butter and egg into the flour until the mixture resembles fat breadcrumbs. Sprinkle half the crumbs over the base of the prepared tin to make a nice, even layer that covers the base. Bake on the bottom shelf for a few minutes, or until the crumbs are firm and very pale gold. Remove and leave to cool.

In another large bowl, whisk the yolks and sugar to a thick cream, then sift over the flour and starch and mix until smooth. Whisk in about 150ml lemon juice. Warm the milk a little, then, whisking constantly, add it to the egg and flour mixture in a thin stream. Return the mixture to the pan and cook over a low heat, whisking, for about 15 minutes, until it coats the back of the spoon. Grate the zest of the final lemon into the cream.

Spread the cream over the crumb base, leaving a 1cm border. Cover it with the rest of the crumbs. Bake for 25 minutes, or until the crumbs are firm and golden. It must be absolutely cool if you want to turn it out, and even then you must do so very carefully by inverting it on to a plate, then on to another plate so that the golden crust faces up. It is nice at room temperature or chilled.

Taralli al limone
Sicilian lemon knot biscuits

Makes about 24

250g plain flour
100g lard or butter, diced
100g granulated sugar
1 heaped teaspoon cream
    of tartar
2 unwaxed lemons
a pinch of salt
1 large egg
125ml lukewarm milk
200g icing sugar

The etymology of the word *taralli* is not clear, but possibly comes from the Latin *torrere*, which means to dry up, parch, roast or bake. The most famous *taralli* are those from Puglia, which are small savoury ring-knots of unleavened dough, just the thing to *stuzzicare* (tease the appetite) as you drink your aperitivo.

Then there are sweet *taralli* made from lemon-scented dough, which are baked and dipped in lemon icing. The loop-knot takes practice. Your first one will be terrible, the next three lopsided, but by about number ten you will be feeling confident, and as you knot the last five you will have got the size and the knack of gently tugging the end through the hole down to a tee. Lard makes for a light and delicate pastry that flakes, while butter makes for a richer, denser biscuit. You can leave them uniced, in which case they keep longer.

Sift the flour into a large bowl. Add the diced lard or butter and, using your fingertips, rub it into the flour until the mixture resembles fine breadcrumbs. Add the sugar, cream of tartar, grated zest of both lemons and the salt. In a small bowl, beat together the egg and lukewarm milk and then add them, bit by bit, to the flour mixture until it comes together into a soft dough. Knead the dough vigorously until it is soft and smooth-ish and just a little bit tacky – but not sticky.

Preheat the oven to 180°C/160°C fan/gas mark 4. Line 2 baking trays with baking parchment. Working on a lightly floured surface, take lumps of dough and roll them into 1.5cm-thick ropes, then cut the ropes into 12cm lengths. Shape each length into a knot – you are almost tying the ends together – and transfer them to the baking tray. Bake until golden brown, which will take about 20 minutes.

Make a glaze by adding lemon juice slowly to the icing sugar until the consistency is thick enough to coat the biscuits. Dip the top of each knot in the glaze, then transfer to a wire rack to cool.

Peaches

The woman has been staring at me ever since I joined the small crowd gathered around the car boot sale in via Roma, Gela. The set-up is standard: a car parked at the entrance to a side street so that the boot, which is full of fruit, opens directly on to a busy road. A floral beach umbrella is wedged into the boot to give shade to more crates of fruit on the pavement, and near them an upended crate provides a surface for the balance scale. The contents of the boot tell you the time of year almost as accurately as a calendar: today, the last of the peaches, deeply coloured and smudged with white or yellowy-pink blush, and the first of the grapes, so it's mid July.

The staring woman has been served, but she is still talking to another customer, her eyes on me all the while. When her companion leaves she finally articulates what her eyes have been saying. *Non sei di queste parti?* (You aren't from round here?) Her words are as unequivocal as her stare: a statement, but also a demand, albeit one that feels more necessary than threatening. Maybe that's because I have a well-practised answer. I explain that I am English but my partner is from Gela, that we live in Rome but spend time in the family house here. I know the next question, which she bounces back like a ball. What is the family name? 'Caristia,' I tell her. By now the man on the other side of the boot has joined in. 'Which one?' he asks, circling his hand in a movement that reminds me of swirling wine in a glass. I remember the other family name, Maganuco, which I know is less common but is also the name of a street, the ultimate sign of belonging. At this they start reciting the names of family members: *Sara, Maria...* I know how this works now. Having established who I am, or rather who I am associated with, I need to be placed in a street or, better still, a house. I tell them via Mazzini and the woman is not sure where that is, but the peach seller, who has now joined in, does. Name and house established, the situation is entirely different, as if we all know where we stand. 'We have brought Sara back,' I add, 'her ashes,' at which they all look horrified and cross themselves repeatedly. The woman says something about shivering and graves. It was the mention of Vincenzo's grandmother Sara (whose ashes are currently sitting in the corner of our living room) that prompted me to offer more than I needed. Did I think it would ingratiate me further? At home later, Vincenzo, bewildered as to why I would talk about ashes while buying peaches, explains that since most Sicilians are buried rather than cremated, I had touched on something disturbing. I had sensed this at the time and apologized, and they had understood: I was English, so clearly a heathen. It took a minute, but then we were back to an understanding, and peaches. I bought three kilograms of white peaches and another three of yellow.

In season, there are peach stalls all over the city. When I first came to Gela it seemed like a sort of peach utopia, until I learned that it wasn't. Like tomatoes, peaches are big business (for some), especially around the inland town of Riesi, where the other side of the D'Aleo family live. Over the years, the peaches have been selected and trained on an industrial scale and are often picked from the tree early in order to make them more transportable. Perversely, some of these find their way to Gela. Provocative beauties they may be, blushing with perfect curves and bottom-like creases, but they never really come to any good. The man on via Roma clearly has the fruits of intensive farming, but they are good. Best of all, though, are the peaches from the farmer who occasionally parks a lorryful by the school, which are small and have uneven creases and birthmarks that could be considered defects. Even with these, whose flesh is like perfumed honey, it is all about timing and temperature: peach watch. You wait until the point of ripeness, until they look and, more importantly, smell right. A peach should smell like a peach. When, alone in the kitchen, you find an absolutely perfect one, there is only one thing to do, and that is to eat it leaning against the sink.

Between the via Roma peach man and the farmer, we have an embarrassment of peaches over the summer. *Peach watch my arse*, they seem to say as they topple from ripe to rotten in an afternoon. Even with seven of us in the house, we can't keep up with the race against ripeness. I ask advice at the peach boot sales, hoping for some innovative ideas to use them up, but

everyone says the same thing: eat them, drop them in wine or make jam. Then one woman suggests pickling them, or rather steeping them in vinegar, the mere thought of which jolts me in the best way. Of course!

To peel or not to peel? Sicilians do, which is as much to do with their suspicions about what the skin might conceal than anything else. I like the tickling fuzz and see the texture of the skin as an essential contrast to the lush flesh. Then there is the cracking of the pit to find the kernel, a minuscule dose of cyanide compound to remind us that even at the sweetest times there's always a touch of bitterness at the heart.

Prosciutto or burrata with peaches

Serves 4

4 ripe but firm peaches
8 thin slices of prosciutto
or 1 burrata, at room
    temperature

Along with figs or melon, peaches make excellent companions for prosciutto, the sweet, firm flesh complementing the tender, mildly salted ham, which should be sliced as thinly as possible. A different but equally good partner is burrata, a kind of mozzarella bag filled with *ritagli* (scraps) of mozzarella in cream, both of which spill out like riches when you open it.

If you want to peel the peaches, do so by plunging them in boiling water for 1 minute, then cooling them in cold water, at which point the skins should slip away. Cut the peaches in half, remove the stones, then cut them into quarters. On a nice big plate, arrange the peach quarters around the whole burrata, or drape the prosciutto slices around the peach quarters.

Pesche sott'aceto
Pickled peaches

Makes 500g

8 peaches
freshly squeezed juice of
   3 lemons
good-quality red wine vinegar
extra-virgin olive oil

Of course. A sweet, sharp, racy companion for a rich, fatty meat like roast or grilled pork, the sweetness complementing the sourness and – like a friend being brutally honest – cutting through the fat. As with most of of my preserving, I prefer doing it on a small scale because it is what I can cope with. You could, of course, pickle many more.

Preheat the oven to 160°C/140°C fan/gas mark 3. Wash the peaches, cut them in half and remove the stones. Squeeze the lemon juice into a bowl and put the peach halves into it for 4 hours, turning them every now and then. Meanwhile, wash a 500g jar and lid and place it in the oven for 10 minutes so that it is sterilized. Drain the peach halves, arrange them in the jar and fill the jar with red wine vinegar, making sure they are covered. Finish with a 1cm layer of olive oil, then seal the jar well and leave it for at least 1 month before opening.

Pesche al vino
Peaches in wine

Let me be clear: I am not talking about a Bellini (the cocktail made from puréed peach and Prosecco), a gunky affair that I have never liked. A ripe peach, though, whose honeyed sweetness is already a bit boozy, peeled, chopped and then dropped into the remains of your glass of red wine, so that the pieces get slightly drunk and stain your lips, is delicious.

Peaches poached with rosé and honey

Serves 6

6 ripe-but-firm peaches
150g sugar
150g honey
400ml rosé wine
2 bay leaves

When peaches are less than perfect, maybe a little too firm (and you have a suspicion they may never ripen), the answer is to give them a helping hand and cook them. By poaching them in a mixture of rosé wine, sugar, honey and bay, you are giving them all the warmth and honeyed sweetness they lack. Once the peaches are poached, the skins should come away easily. They look lovely sitting shimmering on the plate.

Halve the peaches and remove the stones. In a large saucepan, mix the sugar, honey, wine and bay and 200ml water and bring to a gentle simmer. Add the peaches to the pan. Increase the heat and bring to a gentle boil, then reduce to a simmer and cook, turning the peaches occasionally, until they are tender, which will take 5–8 minutes, depending on the size and ripeness of the peaches. Using a slotted spoon, transfer them to a big plate or baking tray. Once they are cool enough to handle, slip off the skins.

Remove the bay leaves from the poaching liquid and put it back on the heat. Bring to the boil and reduce it until it forms a light syrup that coats the back of a spoon. Remove from the heat and allow it to cool, then pour it over the peaches to serve.

Marmellata di pesche
Peach jam

Makes about three 450g jars

1.5kg ripe peaches
900g sugar
freshly squeezed juice of
    1 lemon
1 vanilla pod, split lengthways

Gluts aside, I stick to small batches when it comes to jam and marmalade, which keeps it a reliable, small-scale operation. Peach jam, along with fig jam, tomato sauce, red peppers under oil and Carmex lip salve with sand in it, is summer jarred as far as I am concerned. Sun-ripened peaches are already sweet and need little help, just the edges brightened by lemon. It makes a lovely jam tart with chopped pistachios sprinkled on top.

If you want to peel the peaches, do so by plunging them in boiling water for 1 minute, then cooling them in cold water, at which point the skins should slip away. Cut the peaches in half, remove the stones, then cut into 5mm thick segments. Put the peaches in a large heavy-based pan, add the sugar, lemon juice and vanilla pod and leave overnight, or for at least 12 hours. If you like, you can also add a couple of crushed peach kernels.

Preheat the oven to 160°C/140°C fan/gas mark 3. Wash the jars and lids and put them into the oven for 10 minutes to sterilize. Put a couple of saucers or small plates in the fridge.

Stir the jam thoroughly, then bring it slowly to a vigorous boil for approximately 8 minutes. You'll see the jam starting to set on the handle of the spoon, and if you lift some out it will thicken. Test it by putting a spoonful on one of the chilled plates, wait 1 minute, then drag a finger through the jam: if it wrinkles and is firm, it is set. Use a jam funnel or a small ladle to transfer the jam into the warm jars, screw the lids on tightly and invert to create a seal.

Peach and almond crumble

Serves 4–6

6 ripe peaches
100g cold butter, diced,
    plus extra for greasing
75g plain flour
50–75g sugar, depending on
    the peaches and your taste
60g blanched almonds,
    roughly chopped

My dad really loves pudding, and for a while he was a member of the local Pudding Society, which met once a month to eat a bowl of soup (laying foundations, but not robbing space), followed by three puddings, which they then discussed. Innovative and exotic puddings were welcomed, but traditional puds were at the heart of it all. I think the Society would approve of this one. It's based on a favourite Jane Grigson recipe for apricot and almond crumble, and the addition of the kernels is inspired: they lend a pronounced, slightly bitter note, which is well balanced by the sweet fruit and crumble. 'Cold bowl, cold butter and cold hands, use your fingertips, and lift the flour so it can catch the air.' I can hear my granny Alice's voice when I make pastry and crumble mixtures. Don't be too thorough with the rubbing, though; you want it to be uneven, with fat bits of butter that melt as it bakes. Likewise with the almonds, you want an uneven rubble, which is why it's worth chopping your own. Wait a little before serving; this is a pudding best served warm, with cold unsweetened cream. You could also make it with apples, pears or apricots.

Preheat the oven to 200°C/180°C fan/gas mark 6 and grease an ovenproof dish with butter. Cover the peaches with boiling water, leave them for 1 minute, then cool them under cold running water, at which point the skins should peel away easily. Halve the peaches, remove the stones, then cut the halves into 1cm segments and put them in the ovenproof dish. Use a hammer to break 2 or 3 of the stones open and remove the kernel. Chop the kernel roughly and sprinkle it over the peaches.

Rub the butter into the flour with cold fingertips; you want a rough mixture with some bigger lumps of butter. Add the sugar and almonds, stir, then spread the crumble mixture evenly over the fruit. Bake for 20 minutes, then reduce the oven temperature to 180°C/160°C fan/gas mark 4 and bake for a further 20 minutes so that the top is crusty and golden.

Oranges

'*Arance, mamma, arance.*' My five-year-old, half-Roman son shakes his pinched fingers at my pronunciation of 'orange'. I can't work out what I'm doing wrong. Meanwhile, when I go into his school to do a sort-of English lesson I meet nothing but five-year-old approval from the entire class. Everything is a game! Orange is the colour they learn first because I take one from my bag and then peel it. The orange is orange. So is the Smartie, the only one that tastes as its colour promises.

Like a child making an association, I have always found lessons easier to digest when there's food involved, the fact consumed as if it really were something to eat, the information remembered like a taste. I learned Italian by reading recipes and menus, shopping and cooking. It really is a language of food, and even after twelve years I still conjugate verbs with *mangiare,* to eat. The things I learned about history in childhood were retained because they were edible. The pie shop is the reason I remember the fire of London was in 1666. It is his garden and his love of peas which reminds me that Thomas Jefferson was the third President of the United States. It's the same with school geography: the pencil line I dragged across a map to mark the spice route – the ancient trading lines that brought pepper from India, nutmeg from Calcutta across the Red Sea to Alexandria and Venice – is still etched in my head.

Years later, I find myself drawing similar maps of Sicily. Food is one way, and a most digestible one, to understand its history. You can begin, as Mary Taylor Simeti does in her masterful book on Sicilian food, *On Persephone's Island*, with Odysseus, the first foreign visitor to set foot on a Sicilian shore. He travelled the island in a state of perpetual astonishment at the abundance of grapes, pomegranates, figs, apples, wheat and legumes, cabbages and squash, cardoon and artichokes, and wild herbs. Nearly 3,000 years later the pillars of the Sicilian cooking are still there. The Greek colonizers brought cuttings of cultivated olive trees, which they grafted on to a Sicilian tree called oleaster.

The Arabs arrived in the ninth century and brought oranges and lemons, date palms and mulberry trees, rice and sugar, which would revolutionize confectionery-making across of Europe. They also invented dried pasta. The Norman occupation would displace the Arab one, but it embraced their transformation of the island. It was not until much later, the sixteenth century, that the European explorers brought tomatoes, peppers and potatoes from the New World to Europe. It would take two more centuries for the new vegetables to advance from mere curiosities to staining Sicilian food red. This is an edible timeline that suits my greedy nature. It is fitting, somehow, that Vincenzo's grandfather Orazio cultivated wheat and tomatoes, which are not only a defining Sicilian plateful, but the first and the last imports on the timeline. He also had an orange tree.

It is hard to imagine Sicily without citrus; it seems so much part of the landscape. Our ferry from Naples docks in Palermo or Catania. Either way, we have to drive through citrus groves to get to Gela, miles and miles dense with citrus trees, their deep green leaves stubbornly indifferent to the season, glinting regardless. Our first trip to Gela to open up the house was in May. On the second or third day we drove inland to a town called Caltagirone, where Vincenzo lived between the ages of six and twelve. The journey took us through acres of citrus groves where blossoming buds were erupting into thousands of tiny brilliant-white waxy flowers. Sicilians call both orange and lemon blossom *zagara*, which derives from the Arabic word *zahara*, meaning splendour, or sparkling white. That day we pulled into a lay-by so that the then-very-young Luca could pee. It had rained the day before, and when the scent hit me I fully understood what the word intoxicating means. That is what orange blossom is: it seems the very definition of perfume, something that smokes through your very being. I pulled a piece of blossom from a tree and put it on the warm dashboard. After three hours of exploring the city, the tiny sprig had scented the whole car. Six months later, in Rome, it was crisp and golden as an autumn leaf, yet it still smelled deeply of orange when you held it close. Vincenzo's mother, Carmela, had no time for my gushing: as a young woman, when she worked near those same citrus groves she would keep her car and office window firmly shut to keep out the scent, which made her feel dizzy and sick.

Vincenzo's great-grandfather Salvatore made his living from oranges. He had a small factory in Messina that extracted the essence by pressing the skins to extract the intensely aromatic and volatile essential oil from the oil glands, which was used for perfumes, soaps and creams. It was a good business until January 1908, when an earthquake struck Messina and the subsequent tidal wave engulfed the city. The factory and their home was destroyed as the town, ancient and vunerable, simply fell to the ground. Miraculously, though, his wife Angela and days-old daughter Lilla were pulled alive from the rubble. Years later, Lilla would raise two children and run her part of the family bakery

alone, much to the indignation of her late husband's family. She would also swim the narrow straight of Messina, 6 kilometres from the corner of Sicily to the tip of Italy's toe.

By the time of our late summer visit, the trees were absolutely green, the unripe fruit barely distinguishable from the leaves. When we returned in winter, oranges were blazing among the emerald boughs, and the car boots of Gela were ablaze too. There are so many oranges, too many in fact, that some are crushed by government bulldozers because they can find no market. As well as oranges and lemons, *mandarini* and *clementini* and tiny kumquats, there are also huge *cedri*, which look like giant nubbled lemons. Cut one open and you will find it is almost all spongy pith, the taste mild and sweet. *Cedro* is often candied. For my Sicilian family it was *cedro,* sliced thinly and mixed with fennel, olive oil and lemon, that was the original fruit in the orange and fennel salad we eat repeatedly throughout the winter.

Years in Italy haven't dented the fiery joy that are oranges on a tree to my northern European eyes. It is an orange that opens to bloody red when you peel one of the *tarocco* blood oranges that grow near Etna, the flesh reminiscent of raspberries. My favourites, though, are the navels that are heavy with a soft shine, each one pregnant with a tiny fruit. Vincenzo cuts a deep cross into navel oranges so they can be fanned open and dressed with salt and olive oil. I like them nude – the orange, that is – eaten over the kitchen sink.

Oranges are inherently joyful to look at, to cup in your hand and feel the weight: a self-contained universe. To stick your nail in the skin or to zest an orange, so the oil sprays on the back of your hand and the blithe scent rises up, is aromatherapy pure and simple – antidepressant, antispasmodic, antiseptic, aphrodisiac. Oranges are a tonic! Unless you are the girl I was at school with, who found even the thought of the smile of orange they used to give us during netball matches so horrendous that she hid in the toilets. For the rest of us, though, an orange a day – the whole thing, flesh, juice and zest – should be written on doctor's prescriptions: citrus against the strain of modern life, citrus therapy or some such thing. Luca, who is now five, delights in the orange trick that can be performed when a piece of peel is folded and squeezed hard in one hand, the lighter flame held close. Sometimes there is just a crackle and series of sparks, but if there is lots of oil, there's a proper roar of flame. Either way, there is a fiery scent of orange essential oils.

Oranges have three lives: the peel with pith and zest, the flesh and the juice. You could argue that the flesh and juice are one and the same, but while the segment membranes and tiny vesicles are still holding together, their form makes them very different from the juice they can be reduced to. My favourite recipes are those that use the whole orange, therefore embracing all the complex bittersweetness, like marmalade, chicken with orange, baked sardines and an orange and almond cake. I like pairs of recipes too: a lentil salad that first uses the zest, then the naked fruit, vulnerable without its orange coat, sliced for orange and fennel salad. From my Sicilian family I have learned to use orange with meat and fish as I would use a lemon, to put the empty shells on my elbows and a twist of peel on the radiator so it dries and scents the house.

Insalata di arance, finocchio e olive nere
Orange, fennel and black olive salad

Serves 4

2 large oranges
2 large fennel bulbs
100g good black olives
1 pomegranate, seeds removed
    (optional)
extra-virgin olive oil, to taste
salt

I have had many salad affairs in my life, some of which I return to from time to time in order to be reminded they are good, simply fun, or overrated. I also have three true salad loves. There is green salad, which like an evergreen is constant, month in, month out. Tomato salad, from mid-spring to mid-autumn. Then orange and fennel salad from mid-autumn to mid-spring, at which point tomatoes are ready to pick up the baton once more.

Orange and fennel is a quintessential Sicilian combination. I found the idea strange to begin with, but the combination of sweet, juicy orange and crisp fennel with its whip of aniseed quickly grew on me. Different families have different additions, such as thinly sliced red onion, pieces of red endive or *scarola*, or both. Often it is served with smoked herring, which is a wickedly

good combination. An untraditional but excellent addition is pomegranate seeds, which add their sweet but mildly acerbic nature, and also look tremendously alluring, like jewels. Back in England I have also added watercress. The ingredients are important: you need plump bulbs of Florentine fennel, sweetly sharp oranges and olives that have real flavour – look out for *taggiasche* – and good extra-virgin olive oil.

Using a sharp knife, cut both ends off the oranges so that they sit flat, then pare away the white pith. Slice them horizontally into rounds and, if you like, into halves. Trim the fingers off the fennel and discard the tough outer layers (save them for stock), but reserve the fronds. Slice the bulb in half lengthways, then each half into thin slices. Arrange the orange and fennel on a plate or put them in a bowl, dot with the olives, scatter with pomegranate seeds, if using, sprinkle with salt and the fennel fronds and zig-zag with olive oil. Toss gently and serve.

Fabrizia's orange dressing

1 large unwaxed orange
about 100ml extra-virgin olive oil
a pinch of dried oregano (optional)
red wine vinegar or lemon juice, to taste
salt

This is my friend and cookery teacher Fabrizia Lanza's dressing of olive oil, orange juice and zest, a little red wine vinegar and a pinch of oregano. Use it to dress salads of watercress or rocket, boiled vegetables, especially broccoli, lentils, grilled or poached chicken, or white fish.

Grate the zest from the orange into a bowl, then cut the orange in half and squeeze the juice into the same bowl. Add the olive oil, a pinch of oregano and another of salt and whisk. Taste and add a little red wine vinegar or lemon juice to sharpen if you think it needs it.

Reginelle
Sesame seed biscuits

Makes 50

400g plain flour, preferably
    Italian 00
1 teaspoon baking powder
a pinch of salt
grated zest of 1 unwaxed orange
170g cold lard or butter
170g sugar
2 eggs
about 50ml milk
200g sesame seeds

It is not traditional to add orange zest to these sesame-seed crusted biscotti (I have also heard them called *biscotti della regina*, or the queen's biscuits) that can be found in pretty much every every Sicilian bakery. Although I like to respect tradition, it just seemed the most obvious thing in the world to grate soft, oily flecks of orange zest into the dough. Grating and baking both bring to life the scented orange oil in the zest, so the smell in your kitchen is glorious. The baking powder means they puff up with pride, both homely and exotic. Vincenzo likes these for breakfast, his dipped in milky coffee, Luca's in warm milk. I like two or three at about 4 o'clock with tea, ideally Earl Grey, the bergamot bringing out the best in the orange. There are no two ways about it: you will get sesame seeds stuck in your teeth.

In a large bowl, mix together the flour, baking powder, salt and orange zest. Add the lard or butter, then use cold fingertips to rub the fat into the dry ingredients until the mixture resembles breadcrumbs. Lightly beat one of the eggs in a measuring jug and add enough milk to make it up to 110ml. Stir the sugar into the flour mixture, then add the egg mixture and bring everything together to form a soft ball.

Lift the dough on to a lightly floured work surface. With floured hands, roll it into a thick log about 5cm diameter, then cut this into 8 pieces. Roll each piece into a thumb-width log, then cut this into 5cm lengths, and repeat with the other pieces.

Preheat the oven to 180°C/160°C fan/gas mark 4 and line a baking tray with baking parchment. Prepare 2 bowls, one with the remaining egg, beaten, and the other with the sesame seeds. Roll the biscuits first in the egg, then in the sesame seeds, then place them on the tray. Once you have coated all the pieces, bake for about 15 minutes, or until the biscuits are golden (start checking after about 10 minutes). Transfer to a wire rack to cool.

Gelatina di mandarino
Mandarin orange jelly

*Makes 12 (or as many mandarins
as you have squeezed)*

750ml freshly squeezed
    mandarin juice
    (about 12 mandarins)
4 gelatine leaves
200g sugar

Rowntree's mandarin orange jelly, in which mandarin segments were suspended like goldfish, was a favourite growing up. If we were lucky there was also evaporated milk, which curled its way like a milky river around the craggy, softly set jelly. My dad led the way with the gargling and we would follow, three upturned faces now really looking like goldfish. I also liked the green jelly and the red jelly; any jelly, in fact, as long as it wobbled. At some point, 1985 or thereabouts, my mum started making fancy, grown-up jellies with port, Champagne and elderflower, and we liked those too – although not at the expense of Rowntree's.

Having had a happy, jelly-filled childhood, it came as a great disappointment to me that many people dislike jelly of all kinds, and that adult life does not always involve jelly. Of course I could have made them, but I didn't. A much nicer surprise was discovering that Sicilians are absolute masters of jelly (which they call *gelo*), especially watermelon, lemon and orange. It is traditionally set with cornflour, but these days also with gelatine. Particularly good is the mandarin jelly served in a mandarin shell that has been patiently emptied. Having reduced the fruit you have eased from the shell into juice, then warmed it with sugar and gelatine, you pour this warm mixture back into the shells and leave them to set in the fridge. Once set, you put the lids back on and take the fruit plate to the table. I always imagine that people will guess, but they don't. As they try to pick up a fruit the lid comes off and the orange contents, doubly scented thanks to a night in the fragrant skin, its flavour true and clear, wobbles and wobbles and wobbles.

Cut the top off each mandarin, being careful to keep the fruit intact. Use a teaspoon to help ease the fruit from the sides and scoop a couple of segments out. Now use your fingers to reach inside the fruit and carefully pull out all the segments until you have an empty shell, taking care not to damage it. Repeat with

the rest of the mandarins and put the shells on a tray that fits in the fridge.

Press the segments through a fine sieve to make juice. Measure it, making it up with a few more squeezed mandarins if there isn't 750ml.

Soak the gelatine leaves in a little cold water to soften them. Mix half the juice and all the sugar in a small pan and warm it over a low heat, stirring until the sugar has dissolved. Add the gelatine one sheet at a time, stirring to make sure it has dissolved before adding the next one. Take the pan off the heat, add the rest of the juice and stir. Pour the mixture into the empty shells and leave it to cool a little, then put them in the fridge to set for at least 6 hours.

Alternatively, you could grease a ring-shaped cake tin or mould with a little flavourless oil, then pour in the mixture and refrigerate it until set. Once set, dip the bottom of the tin in hot water to loosen the jelly, then invert it on to a serving plate.

Claudia Roden's orange and almond cake

Serves 8–10

1 large orange, about 350g
(or 2 smaller ones)
butter and flour, breadcrumbs
or matzo meal, for preparing
the tin
6 eggs
250g ground almonds
250g granulated sugar
1 heaped teaspoon baking
powder

The use of the whole orange – which means all of it: skin, zest, pith, flesh – feels nothing short of brilliant. Once boiled (for a long time, which makes the kitchen smell gorgeous) and pulped, you have an extraordinary mixture: sharp, sweet, bitter and deeply flavoured. It is then tempered by the sugar, almonds and eggs, but the opinionated flavour remains distinct, as do the flecks of bright orange, giving the cake a musky, almost spicy flavour. Claudia Roden describes it as somewhere between a cake and a pudding, which is spot on. It is good just so, or with a dollop of thick cream.

A loose-bottomed cake tin make things a whole lot easier. I use a John Lewis anodized satin tin that I pinched from my mum. The best size is 24cm diameter.

Wash the orange, put it in a pan, cover with cold water, bring to the boil, reduce to a simmer and cook for 1½ hours, or until it is extremely soft when pricked with a fork. Remove the orange, let it cool, then cut it open and remove any pips. Reduce the orange to a pulp by pressing it through a sieve, mouli or by using a blender. I use my faithful stick blender.

Preheat the oven to 190°C/170°C fan/gas mark 5. Prepare a cake tin – ideally one with a loose base – by greasing it with butter and dusting it with flour, breadcrumbs or matzo meal.

Beat the eggs in a large bowl, add the pulped orange, beat again, then add the almonds, sugar and baking powder and beat again until you have a thick, even batter. Pour the batter into the tin and bake for 40–60 minutes. Have a look after 40 minutes; it should be golden and set firm. I find testing with a strand of spaghetti helps: it should come out almost clean (almost; this is a moist cake), as opposed to sticky. If the cake does need another 10 minutes I drape some kitchen foil over the top to prevent it from getting too brown. Let it cool in the tin before turning it out on to a plate.

Bitter orange marmalade

Makes 5 standard jars

1.5kg Seville oranges or Italian
arance amare (bitter oranges)
2.3kg sugar, warmed
(I put it in a metal bowl in a
low oven for a few minutes)

My mum is a good and committed marmalade maker, principally because my dad is a good and committed marmalade eater. She eats it too, but mostly she makes it for Dad. For as long as I can remember, at some point in January she processes enough Seville oranges for my dad to have a jar of marmalade a week, plus more for us kids and guests. When I was growing up I watched and helped enough – stirring, testing, getting in the way, putting the waxy circle on each jar, sticking labels on the jars – to imagine that I would absorb the recipe by kitchen osmosis.

I didn't. It took me many years and plenty of disappointing orange syrup before I could call myself a marmalade maker. It was moving to Rome, or more specifically near the *Giardino degli aranci*, a small park that is shaded by orange trees on the Aventine hill. It is just minutes from our flat in Testaccio, but feels like another world: calm, shady and with an ideal viewpoint from which to observe this extraordinarily beautiful city, and from January to March a place to collect bitter oranges, which blaze in both the trees and well-watered papal grass. As I write this, in late October the oranges are still green, but by December they will be bright globes, and by January ready for my next batch.

I have used many recipes and collected much over the years, my favourite being Sarah Randell's from her book *Marmalade*. Her first step? Put the radio on. So you do, and the scent of orange roars. You need sugar for classic bitter orange marmalade. I have reduced the quantity over years, settling on an amount that gives a firm, clear set, without being too sweet. The best way to eat it is on hot buttered toast or stirred into a pound cake batter.

Scrub the oranges and put them in a large pan with 3.5 litres water. Simmer until the fruit is tender and the skin is easily pierced, and the water has reduced by about a third, which should take about 1½ hours. Use a slotted spoon to lift the fruit from the liquid and set aside to cool. Keep the liquid in the pan.

Once the oranges are cool enough to handle, cut them in half and scoop out the seeds and flesh. Put these into a piece of muslin or stocking, tie the end with a bit of string, and tie the package to the pan handle so that it can bob about in the marmalade as it cooks.

Cut the orange halves into strips of the thickness you like in your marmalade. Put the strips in a pan along with the warm sugar. Set the pan over a medium heat and stir until the sugar dissolves. Put a few saucers in the freezer and your scrupulously cleaned jars and lids in a warm oven (about 150°C/130°C fan/gas mark 2) to sterilize them.

Bring the pan to the boil and cook vigorously for 10 minutes, or until setting point has been reached. Drop a spoonful on a cold saucer to see if it has set: if you put a blob on a cold plate, and wait for a minute, then drag your finger though the maramlade, it should wrinkle and leave a moat, not flood back into a single blob. Once setting point is reached, take the pan off the heat and leave it for 15 minutes so that the peel can settle. Stir the marmalade, discard the pips and flesh, pour it into the warm jars and seal well.

Grapes and figs

There is a hatch between the kitchen and dining room in the house in Gela. It's about 1 metre wide and 50cm high with a sliding frosted-glass door that you don't really notice because it's never closed. It was a racy addition when the house was altered in the late 1960s, when a large, single room with a wood-burning stove at its heart was divided into three rooms: kitchen, *tinello* (dining area) and living room. Vincenzo's grandmother Sara was 5 foot 3 inches (tall for a woman in Gela), so the hole for the hatch was knocked through at just the right height for her to pass plates and dishes from the new gas stove to the table and back again. Almost 60 years and many coats of olive-green paint later, the hatch makes me feel even taller than usual – not that this reduces the pleasure of passing things back and forth.

What is it that's so enchanting about a serving hatch? I have wanted one ever since I was a Brownie, when the rock cakes we made for our baking badges felt even more important when passed through the hatch into the main hall where our parents sat, loyally washing them down with tea. Back in Gela, there is pleasure too in the hatch-shaped view you get when looking from one room to another. From the kitchen you can see the dining room table and the curtains billowing like ships in the breeze. From the table, the hatch-shaped postcard into the kitchen is of the low sink and the window from which we can see our neighbours opposite doing the cleaning, and the sideboard with its weary hinges, upon which sits a bowl of fruit.

There is always *la frutta,* and the timing of each visit is defined by what is on the plate or in the bowl, our domestic equivalent of Gela's car boots. Winter visits are orange and yellow citrus, with flashes of jewel-like ruby pomegranate seeds. Spring means cherries, sweet and sour. Summer visits begin with mulberries that stain our tongues and fingers, peaches with rich flesh the colour of a desert sunrise, then huge watermelons (which also occupy the fridge), prickly pears with their dastardly spikes, and late figs. As the air cools and August tips into

September there are grapes and more grapes, the kind that burst in your mouth and taste almost drunken. In his seventeenth-century book about the fruit and vegetables of Italy, Giacomo Castelvetro says *l'autunno per la bocca et la primavera per occhio* (autumn is for tasting, spring is for looking). It is true: having collected the summer sun, the late figs and grapes, the fruits of the more temperate days, are the most luscious and irresistible.

Along with wheat and olives, grapes and figs have been the basic food of the Mediterranean for thousands of years. Even during the hardest times, Vincenzo's grandfather Orazio felt rich because he grew them all, and with them his family could live well. Tomatoes and wheat may have been his livelihood, but grapes were his love, and with them he made wine in great vats that occupied the corner of the garage-cum-cellar. Orazio famously never drank water. He ate a lemon per day, then drank his own red wine: a litre with his second breakfast, the *calazuini* (aka *colazione*, or lunch) of bread, cheese and caponata that was eaten in the fields, and then another litre with dinner. The wine he made was for his family, as was the vinegar, and the line between them was often blurred. Occasionally, if he had more than he needed, he would hang a bunch of bay leaves above the garage door to show that he had some for sale. Even now you can still see the occasional bunch of bay leaves, sun-bleached and crisp, above a garage in one of Gela's side streets, and inside, next to the shiny new car – there is almost always a shiny car – is a vat of wine. We sometimes buy some, or sometimes we go to the next province to buy wine made by a young woman called Arianna Occhipinti, whose rebellious passion, principles and commitment to the soil, and to making natural and sustainable wine (terms that I know can be shifting sands) are to be celebrated. To walk around her vineyards in spring is to see a carpet of wild flowers, succulent grass and herbs. When we visit again in September, the vines are full of empurpled and honey-coloured grapes hanging in great droops. It is impossible not to burst them between your teeth. Taste them we do, then buy the SP68 Rosso and Bianco, which are named after the road we drive back down to Gela.

Back at the hatch, there are figs from Rosa's tree in the fruit bowl. Figs have two seasons: early ones in mid June that have ripened from last year's buds, and late figs, the true figs. Those

we find in Gela are pale green, turning almost buttery yellow when very ripe, at which point the skin cracks, gently exposing white. White too is the milky juice exuded by the stem, which was once used as rennet to make cheese. The flesh changes from a flash of pink warmth to slightly yellow; it is extraordinarily sweet, honeyed really, and so soft it seems to spill out. Left for too long on hot, still August days, they weep into the dish, turn to jam, then rot before your eyes, luring a halo of fruit flies. Grapes are more resilient, and a good job too, flung as they are into the boots of cars to be sold, inky purple, green, yellow; some the size of small plums, others like tiny pebbles. It's hard to know where to start and who is selling their own grapes: the good farmer making a bit of extra money to the upstart who jumped over the fence to pinch them. Tasting is the best way. You will be shooed away with laughter if you try to buy anything less than a kilogram, so best buy three.

Fichi, formaggio e noci
Figs, goat's cheese and walnuts

When fruit is ripe and abundant it needs nothing more than a good wash and a bowl to put it in. As in life, though, a good companion can bring out the best in it. My first choice for figs is paper-thin slices of prosciutto: sweetness with a tender, salty bite. Then there is figs with goat's cheese and walnuts – a combination rather than a recipe. For four people you need 8 or 12 ripe figs, 200g goat's cheese and 12 walnuts. You can assemble, in which case shell the walnuts and slice the cheese, then open the figs and put a slice of cheese and half walnut inside each one and press it closed. Alternatively, put figs, cheese and walnuts on a large platter, a bunch of black grapes too, then let everyone get on with it. If you can find or make walnut bread, that is lovely.

Insalata di uva e pomodoro
Grape and tomato salad

Serves 4

1 small red onion
2 tablespoons red wine vinegar
4 ripe tomatoes
5 tablespoons extra-virgin olive
    oil, plus extra for the croutons
250g red grapes
a small handful of basil
2 thick slices stale of bread
salt

There is something poetic about this September salad of two vine fruits. The last of the tomatoes, ripe with sun, with the first of the grapes, onion and vinegar sharpening edges like a heavy pencil outline. The trick of soaking the onion in a little red wine vinegar is key: it takes the eye-watering edge off the onion, while keeping all the flavour. To me, this seems a most Sicilian combination, a sort of September panzanella, although having searched through books, it isn't mentioned anywhere. Not that this matters. This is one for a warm night, to serve with grilled meat or vegetables cooked over charcoal or on a griddle pan, with the door wide open so the smoke can drift out and the warm night can drift in. Don't forget the croutons, which soak up the plentiful juices. They are the business.

Thinly slice the onion and put the slices in a small bowl with the red wine vinegar to macerate. Cut the tomatoes in half, cut away the hard core, then squeeze the juice and seeds into a sieve over a bowl.

Using the back of a spoon, press the seeds into the sieve to squeeze out all the juice, then discard the seeds. Put the tomato juice, onion and vinegar and oil in a bowl, season with salt and whisk. Chop the tomato into chunks and the grapes in half, flicking out any pips as you go. Rip the basil into little bits. Add all three to the dressing and leave to marinate for as long as you want. Cut the bread into chunks and fry them in olive oil in a heavy-based pan until golden and crisp. Add the croutons to the salad just before serving.

Salsiccia all'uva e cipolla
Sausages with grapes and red onions

Serves 4

12 slim or 8 fat pork sausages,
    or 800g Sicilian sausage
2 tablespoons extra-virgin
    olive oil
1 large red onion
2 tablespoons red wine vinegar
1 tablespoon sugar
500g white or red grapes,
    or a mixture

Meat and fruit. In a land of fragrant fruit like quinces, figs, grapes and pomegranates, with a common love of sweet and savoury and a pervasive Middle Eastern influence, I was surprised not to find more recipes for fruit with meat in Sicilian cooking. I did find, though, this recipe for sausages and grapes, which has become a great favourite, the rich, fatty sausage meat finding good companions in sweet and sharp grapes and onions.

I am told this dish was made at the grape harvest, with great whorls of Sicilian sausage cooked over charcoal. Far from fields and vines, in the domestic kitchen, it is every bit as delicious and straightforward. You can find variations of it all over Italy. For this southeastern Sicilian version you cook the sausages, then use their fat to soften the onions and grapes, add vinegar to sharpen things, then return the sausages to the pan.

In a large frying pan, fry the sausages in the oil, turning them until they are golden on all sides and have released plenty of fat. Remove the sausages from the pan and keep them warm.

If you want, you can pour away some of the fat. Thinly slice the onion, halve the grapes and flick out the seeds. Fry the onion gently in the sausage fat until soft and translucent. Add the vinegar and sugar and cook for a few minutes longer, then add the grapes. Increase the heat and cook the grapes, stirring constantly, until they are are slightly soft and opaque, which takes about 3 minutes. Taste to check the balance of sweet and sharp and add a little more vinegar and/or sugar if you want.

Add the sausages and cook, stirring, for a couple of minutes. If you can, allow them to sit for 15 minutes before reheating briskly and serving.

Dried fruit

With the leftovers from Orazio's wine making, Sara would make *mosto cotto* (grape must syrup) by boiling the must until it formed a syrup, which she then used in cakes and sweets. This summer, sitting round the table after dinner, Uncle Liborio described how the pan boiled for hours, its contents turning from liquid to an almost-black syrup, and how, when it was bottled and sitting at the top of the cellar, he would pull away the cork and take a thick sip.

Grapes, too, were dried, and the small *uva di corinto nero* (which I know as currants) were particularly valued. They are certainly sweet, but also slightly spicy, and the pip inside gives crunch. I bring bags of them back to Rome. These currants have found a way into so much Sicilian food, from the quintessential Sicilian stuffing that is stuffed into each chapter of this book, to tomatoes, rabbit, pasta. I used to be averse to sweetness in my food, but I now like it very much, as long as it is balanced with something sharp or savoury. Of course, if you don't like dried fruit, you can simply leave it out.

Figs were also dried: split and opened like a book, then left to dry in the sun, the sweetness of summer preserved to see you through the winter. Sometimes an almond or walnut was pressed into the flesh as it dried, an idea I have adopted at Christmas. Sara also made a fig syrup, a superior version of the sweet, viscous stuff I was given as a child, which, unlike the reason for taking it, I liked very much, the way the taste lingered, as the taste of dried fruits does. There are still strong Sicilian traditions of biscuits made with grape must and fig syrup, also festive sweets and breads crammed with dried fruit, a reminder that winter is a consequnce of summer, and that dried fruit are riches to celebrate. I particularly like *buccellato*, a ring-shaped pastry that is as good an ode to dried fruit as rich English fruit cake and mincemeat.

Buccellato
Sicilian fig and nut ring

Makes 12–15 slices

For the pastry
400g plain flour
a pinch of salt
grated zest of 1 unwaxed lemon
170g cold butter, diced
150g sugar
2 large eggs, lightly beaten

For the filling
500g dried figs
300g nuts, such as almonds,
    walnuts or hazelnuts
150g raisins
60g candied orange or lemon
    peel
grated zest of 1 unwaxed orange
grated zest of 1 unwaxed
    mandarin
60g honey
100ml Marsala
100g dark chocolate, chopped
a pinch of ground cloves
a pinch of ground cinnamon
1 egg
hundreds and thousands,
    to decorate (optional)
jam, honey or icing sugar mixed
    with a little water, to glaze

There are three bars opposite the Duomo in Catania: a fancy one, a working one and, in the middle, Bar Presepe, and that is where we go. Sicilian bars are inclusive – go back twice and your loyalty is repaid. Luca thinks it is his.

It is small, with high glass counters filled with patisserie, and the effect is sweetly enticing. The brioche are fat, burnished and warm, and in summer they come with a glass of granita icy enough to take your breath away. There are cakes and *cassatine* (little *cassatas*) and, at the bottom of the front counter, marzipan fruit. During our last stop before the ferry port we bought boxes of grapes, cherries and prickly pears and a *buccellato*, a pastry ring stuffed with figs, nuts and raisins. The recipe looks much more complicated and laborious than it actually is.

First make the pastry. In a bowl, mix together the flour, salt and lemon zest, then use your finger tips to rub in the butter until it resembles breadcrumbs. Add the sugar and eggs and bring the mixture together into a ball. (This can also be done in food processor, first pulsing the flour and butter, then adding the eggs and stopping as soon as it comes together.) Shape the pastry into a log, wrap it and and chill it in the fridge for 1 hour.

Meanwhile, make the filling. Soak the figs in warm water for 15 minutes, then drain them. Chop the figs, nuts and raisins very finely, then mix them with the citrus zest, honey, Marsala, chocolate and spices to make a coarse but consistent and slightly sticky mixture. Alternatively, pulse everything together in the food processor, stopping when it has just come together.

On a lightly floured work surface, roll the dough into a roughly 70 x 14cm rectangle, then lift this on to a large piece of clingfilm. Shape the fruit mixture into a salami-like log 1cm shorter than the pastry; wet hands are best for this. Put the fruit log on the middle of the pastry, then use the clingfilm to lift the sides of the pastry up until they meet and encase the filling. Seal the

pastry with your fingertips, and then roll it over gently to seal it completely, so that the seam is underneath. Bring the ends together to make a ring shape and seal the ends. The traditional pattern for *buccellato* is a series of v-shaped crimps made with a tool called a *pinza*, but the pattern can be recreated with a fork, by piercing the pastry and then dragging it slightly to expose the filling. Chill for at least 2 hours.

Preheat the oven to 180°C/160°C fan/gas mark 4 and bake for 30–40 minutes, or until golden. Once cooked, allow it to cool for 30 minutes before brushing it with the glaze and sprinkling with hundreds and thousands, if you like.

Fig compote with wine, honey and thyme

Serves 4

300ml red wine
200g runny honey
100g sugar
a few sprigs of thyme
500g dried figs

Like prunes or pears in wine, this is one for the faithful: dried figs simmered back to plumpness in honey, wine and herbs, which are, if you think about it, the flavours and scents of a Sicilian hillside. I have also added dried peaches, and I am sure pears and prunes would work well, making this both a Sicilian hillside and Blackpool boarding house with its flocked wallpaper and fruit stewed in tea, the thought of which fills me with nostalgic pleasure.

This is the sort of thing to serve after a big meal, just one or two each, before the cheese. Or with the cheese. You could also serve a couple over a simple rice pudding or beside panna cotta. The last two, eaten for breakfast with thick yoghurt, are the best.

Put 330ml water in a pan with the wine, honey, sugar and thyme over a medium-low heat and bring slowly to the boil. Reduce to a simmer, add the figs and cook until they are very tender.

Using a slotted spoon, lift the figs into a bowl. Increase the heat and boil the liquid until it has reduced to a third, then pour it over the figs and allow them to cool. Serve at room temperature, alone, or with cheese or rice pudding.

Almonds

I knew the almond sack wouldn't still be hanging on the back of the *cantina* door. That didn't stop me hoping, though, when we pulled the door open for the first time. No sack – only a rope hanging on the wall in front and some broken picture frames at the top of a concrete staircase, up which rushed the smell of a place that has been closed up for long time: musty and peculiarly sweet, like fruit that has been forgotten. Vincenzo pointed to a nail near the top of the door. This was where the sack of almonds had hung when he was a boy. We are standing where he and his cousins would have stood; from here, after checking the coast was clear, they would wriggle a nut, maybe two, out of a hole in the bottom corner of the sack, which they would hide in their mouth or pocket, then close the door and run, chewing, hoping not to be caught, but knowing they would be one day.

The *cantina* with the almond door in Gela is actually a garage that opens on to street level on the other side of the house, a storeroom for the old VW Beetle that Giuseppe (Vincenzo's second cousin) is going to revamp one day, a plough, half a dozen hoes and hoses, chairs, huge, pendulous wine carafes, the *settachai* for sieving tomatoes, a record player and countless boxes that are not ours to go through. We also find a sack, perhaps the one that contained the almonds. Vincenzo's grandfather had a couple of ancient almond trees whose generosity he would gather for the family each year, picking and then roasting the nuts in the sun. Cousin Elio promised to take us to see the land and the trees, but never got round to it, so we made do with gathering nuts from a friend's tree in early September. They were ancient trees with twisted trunks. At first it's hard to spot the difference between the leaves and the husks, especially on a ferociously bright day when looking up is difficult. Once you have seen one, though, you see hundreds. The brown husks, pitted like an alcoholic's nose, are the colour of milky coffee. Left for so long in such heat, many have split, revealing the rest of the hard, bark-like layer that needs to be cracked open to get at the nut, already toasted by the sun. The nuts, too, are the colour of coffee with a dash of milk. You bite through this dusty layer to meet pure, mild, milky-white nut.

Almond trees flower early and beautifully in February, putting on puffs of pale pink blossom like frills on the blouse of a tango dancer. The fruit can be picked when young and green, velvety pods that can be split with just a little force to reveal an immature soft white nut with a grassy taste. Green almonds can be made into a liqueur or eaten just so. Vincenzo, whose first house was a platform in an almond tree, knows all about eating them just so. Left longer, both the the green pod and nut inside turn brown and harden.

The Arabs brought to Sicily a great love of and skill in cooking with almonds, particularly in sauces and sweets, a legacy that lives on in almond milk and *pasta reale* (marzipan), which is shaped into soft almond biscuits, or coloured and then fashioned into fruits and all manner of things. Everyone in Vincenzo's family has a story about buying marzipan sweets from the nuns. I am told it is almost a lost art now, in convents anyway; perhaps the young nuns are taking on more socially committed activities. In a *pasticceria* on via Ventura in Gela, a shop that feels like a museum, we bought a luminous pink prawn, what I assumed was a mackerel and bunch of grapes. I wasn't sure how long they had been in the display cabinet. We ate them anyway, or gnawed them really, while walking back through the piazza at dusk, Vincenzo seeming more Sicilian with every step. Later, in Noto, we ate the most exquisite almond biscuits and soft marzipan delights made by the pastry chef Corrado Assenza at Caffè Sicilia. We also enjoyed gelato, granita and cassata, an elaborate triumph of sweetness: sponge cake covered with ricotta, covered with marzipan, finished with a shine of white icing and topped with crystallized fruit, the cake that is chosen for every family celebration here in Rome. Strangely, though, the memory of the bright pink prawn is the thing I can taste as I write.

For Vincenzo's grandmother Sara, the bag of almonds behind the door meant *croccante*, also called *cubbàita*: almonds or sesame seeds suspended in a brittle of sugar and honey. She would make it on the marble work surface – thwack, thwack – her hands indifferent to the hot sugar-and-honey mixture. I also make it in the kitchen in Gela with almonds bought from

the men who set up stall by the old prison wall. My hands are not indifferent. It was the other side of the family and paternal grandmother Lilla, who ran a bakery in Riesi, who made almond milk and in turn the white almond blancmange-like pudding that wobbled, the soft biscuits and fanciful cakes. It is her recipes I brought back to Rome. I hoped that someone would have a story about *pesto alla trapanese*, a Sicilian pesto made with almonds, but I might as well have have asked if they made Yorkshire puddings, so far away on the other side of the island is Trapani and its almond pesto.

When buying almonds, it really is worth buying whole ones, either already blanched, or better still, with skins that you peel off yourself. They will have a fragrant flavour and moisture from the natural oils that has usually long gone from ready-ground ones. To peel them, plunge the almonds into boiling water, let them boil for 20 seconds, then drain and squeeze one end. The skins should pop off: a pleasant faff.

Mandorle tostate
Roasted almonds

Serves 6 or more

500g blanched almonds
extra-virgin olive oil
cayenne pepper
salt (fine, or the kind you can
crush between your fingers)

A handful of roasted almonds and a glass of sparkling wine – now that is a good way to tease your appetite or, as Elizabeth David says, get the gastric juices going. This is her recipe, from her book *Spices, Salt and Aromatics in the English Kitchen*, a recipe I have made in both our Roman and Sicilian kitchens.

Blanched almonds are important. Elizabeth David is very clear about how low the oven needs to be, how you should swish the almonds in salt and wrap them in paper. She also notes that they are at their best after 6 hours – they should squeak as you bite them – and that a pound of salted almonds can be devoured in about 15 minutes. She is right, although I can never wait quite that long.

Preheat the oven to 130°C/110°C fan/gas mark 1. Rub the almonds with a little olive oil and put them on a baking tray. Bake for 30 minutes, or until they are light golden brown.

Tip the almonds on to a large piece of baking parchment and season with plenty of good salt, and an infinitesimal amount of cayenne pepper and swish them around. Gather the ends of the paper and twist them like a big sweet, then hide it out of sight for 6 hours. Serve with sparkling wine or cocktails.

Pesto alla trapanese
Almond, basil and tomato pesto

Serves 4

a large bunch of basil
(about 70g), washed and
dried
200g cherry tomatoes, the most
flavoursome you can find
100g whole skinned almonds
2 black peppercorns
2 garlic cloves
200ml extra-virgin olive oil
500g busiate, fusilli, casarecce,
strozzapreti or cavatelli
grated salted ricotta (optional)
salt

They say it was the Genovese sailors. Docking in Trapani, on the west coast of Sicily, on their way east, they brought with them ideas and culinary habits, including pounded sauces like *pesto alla genovese*, which they adapted to local ingredients: almonds, tomatoes and basil. This one became known as *pesto alla trapanese*, a fresh, aromatic sauce that traditionally coats long ringlets of pasta called *busiate*.

Although I enjoy traditional recipes, I'm going to avoid the word 'authentic' here because it is a tricky notion, and so at odds with the joyful anarchy of home cooking of which this easy, forgiving sauce seems typical. However, a set of suggestions is useful for both method and quantities. 'Pesto' comes from the word *pestare*, to pound, traditionally in a pestle and mortar, which gives a wonderful texture. Pulsing with a food processor does a pretty good job too. Some people like a very smooth pesto, while others prefer one with real texture, in which you can still see the ingredients. It's a tiny detail, but it is astonishing how the addition of two whole peppercorns pounded in, releasing heat and throat-catching spice, makes so much difference.

The classic *busiate* pasta is made by rolling the dough into a rope and then winding it around a needle, or *buso*, until they are the perfect shape to hold the pesto. If you are English, think of a ribbon around a maypole. Fusilli, casarecce or strozzapreti also work well. Traditionally, cheese is not added at the end; we add some salted ricotta.

Pull the leaves off the basil. If using a pestle and mortar, pound the tomatoes, basil, almonds and peppercorns. After a few minutes, add 1 garlic clove and some of the oil. Once incorporated, add the other garlic clove and the rest of the oil and pound until smooth and creamy. If using a food processor, pulse all the ingredients until they are chopped fine, then blend for a few seconds at high speed until creamy. If you would like more texture, you can pulse the almonds in afterwards, and roughly chop the tomatoes and stir them in by hand.

Bring a large pan of water to a fast boil, add salt, stir and add the pasta. Cook, stirring every now and then, until al dente. Meanwhile, warm a large serving bowl and put half the pesto in the bottom. Drain the pasta, tip it into the bowl and put the rest of the pesto on top. Toss and serve immediately, with some grated salted ricotta if you like.

Biancomangiare
Almond pudding

Serves 6

200g whole almonds, peeled, or 750ml unsweetened almond milk
100g cornflour
150g sugar
250ml whole milk
2 strips unwaxed lemon zest
a few chopped pistachios and/ or a sprinkling of cinnamon

Bianco means 'white', *mangiare* 'eat', so we could translate it as 'white eat'. The history and regional variations of *biancomangiare* are a portal into so much history: that of the Arab legacy, of restorative, ambiguous medieval dishes of pounded chicken and almond milk, of dishes eaten on lean days. In *biancomangiare* we find the origins of the still-commonplace expression *mangiare in bianco* (eat in white), what you do when you are not very well. As well as history, there are thoughts and recipes. I make a Sicilian version of *biancomangiare*, a soft, creamy almond pudding that wobbles.

I say Sicilian, but as with all the recipes in this book, I feel I should include a disclaimer along the lines of: 'inspired by and, I hope, respectful to Sicilian culinary history and recipes, especially family ones, but very much my own interpretation'. I love puddings set with gelatine, but for this version I use cornflour, which makes it soft and creamy rather than set, more Angel Delight than Rowntree's. Like jelly, or indeed blancmange, *biancomangiare* is divisive: you love it or you don't. For my father-in-law it is a sweet taste of his childhood, a simple-minded comfort. I share his love. Other members of the family think it is the devil's work. The addition of cornflour means it is important to cook the mixture thoroughly, stirring, for 15 minutes. You can make your own almond milk, or simply buy a carton. If you have jasmine in the garden, a flower on top is a classic and fragrant decoration.

If you are making your own almond milk, use a pestle and mortar or food processor to pound or grind the almonds to a flour. Put this almond flour in a thin piece of muslin, seal it well and submerge it in a bowl filled with 750ml cold water. After an hour, squeeze the almonds until the water is as white as milk. Alternatively, open the carton of almond milk.

In a medium saucepan, warm the almond milk, cornflour, sugar and milk over a medium-low heat and add the lemon zest. Remove from the heat and leave to sit for 10 minutes. Put the pan back over a medium-low heat and whisk gently until the pudding is thick and creamy, which will take about 15 minutes. Remove the pudding from the heat, divide between small bowls or cups, sprinkle each one with a few chopped pistachios and leave to cool for a few hours. Serve at room temperature.

Croccante
Nut brittle

Makes a piece roughly
  20cm square

250g whole almonds, pistachios,
  pine nuts or sesame seeds
flavourless oil, for greasing
200g granulated sugar
100g honey
½ lemon

Like caponata, every Sicilian cook has a recipe for *croccante* (or *cubbàita*); it is a fixture at all celebrations, religious or otherwise. In Gela, on 2 November (All Souls Day), men set up stalls in the piazza, complete with gas stoves and cold slabs. A hot syrupy mixture of sugar, maybe honey, ensnares almonds, pine nuts, pistachio nuts or sesame seeds, and is slapped down on cold surface with great aplomb. It is teeth-cracking stuff and very delicious eaten just so, smashed over vanilla ice cream, or broken into very small pieces to put in a semifreddo. It is not traditional, but I mix my nuts, to toast them lightly and chop them.

If the almonds have skins, plunge them in boiling water for a couple of minutes, drain them, then slip the skins off. If you are toasting your nuts, preheat the oven to 150°C/130°C fan/gas mark 2 and roast them for 5 minutes, or until they are very pale gold. If you like, chop the nuts roughly

Lightly grease a heatproof work surface or line a baking tray with greaseproof paper. In a small heavy-based pan, melt the sugar and honey over a low heat, then increase the heat until it is boiling at the edges – but be careful, it must not burn. Add the nuts or seeds and stir vigorously for another minute, then tip on to the prepared work surface or baking tray. Use a wet palette knife or metal spatula to press the mixture flat, then rub it with the cut side of a lemon. Allow to cool. To serve, break into pieces. It keeps well in an airtight tin in a cool, dry place.

Semifreddo alle mandorle
Almond semifreddo

Serves 4

250g croccante (see opposite)
600ml double cream
2 eggs, separated
100g icing sugar
a little maraschino liqueur,
    if you have it

One way, a smashing way, to use your *croccante*. Don't worry about the pieces being even – in fact, some tiny powdery bits and other slightly larger jagged pieces make for a nice contrast.

Break or smash the *croccante* into pieces, then use a food processor to pulse it into very small shards (this can all be done with a bag and rolling pin, if you like). Line a 1kg bread tin or other mould with foil, making sure it hangs generously over the edges.

Whisk the cream to medium peaks. Beat the egg yolks with 50g icing sugar until pale and fluffy. In another bowl, whisk the whites to stiff peaks, add the remaining icing sugar and whisk again. Fold the yolk mixture, then the whites, then the *croccante* into the cream. Spoon into the prepared tin, then cover with the overhanging foil. Freeze for 24 hours. Let it sit for a few minutes before you turn it out on to a serving dish and pull away the foil.

Chocolate and almond cake

Serves 8–10

300g whole or ground almonds
200g dark chocolate
grated zest of 1 unwaxed orange
    (optional)
200g caster sugar
a pinch of salt
4 tablespoons whole milk
5 large eggs

There has to be a chocolate and almond cake. I have accumulated several over the years, all flourless. For years I made an Elizabeth David one, then a real *torta Caprese* from a real Capri-dweller, and now I have settled on something in between, which is inspired by an Anna del Conte recipe. This is a good cake, and straightforward, which is how cakes need to be for me: something you can make without too much fuss. Whether you use whole or ground almonds depends on whether you are using a food processor or not. I do it all by hand, so I buy good fresh ground almonds (always check the date), and chop the chocolate into relatively small but rough pieces that melt as it bakes, and which make the final cake a speckled beauty. It is a dense, moist cake with fat crumbs, not overly sweet but intensely chocolatey. Much has been written about the merits of baking with almonds and no butter, so I won't bore you. I sometimes add grated orange zest, which makes it reminiscent of a Chocolate Orange, which I like, but it competes with the almonds a little. I will leave the orange decision up to you.

You can take this cake anywhere and it will fit in. Dust it with icing sugar if the occasion is celebratory, or dark cocoa if it is fancy. Vincenzo tells me it is an ideal breakfast cake, but he is Sicilian and can eat cassata first thing in the morning. I like it at about 11 o'clock with a cup of tea, at 4 o'clock with an espresso, or for pudding with cold cream.

Preheat the oven to 180°C/160°C fan/gas mark 4. Generously butter and flour a 26cm cake tin, with a loose bottom if you like. If you want to roast the whole nuts (which is nice for the flavour, but not essential), spread them on a baking sheet and toast in the oven for 4–5 minutes, then rub them with a clean tea towel to get rid of the papery skins.

If you are using a food processor and whole almonds, pulse the nuts a few times, then add the roughly chopped chocolate

and orange zest, if using, and pulse until you have a coarse mixture. Turn it out into a large bowl.

If you are doing everything by hand, chop the chocolate finely with a sharp knife, grate over the orange zest, if using, then mix it with the ground almonds in a large bowl.

Add the sugar, salt and milk to the almonds and chocolate and mix well. Separate the eggs, setting the whites aside, then beat the egg yolks into the mixture one by one. Whisk the egg whites in another bowl until they form stiff peaks, then fold them into the mixture. Scrape the mixture into the prepared tin and bake for 40–50 minutes, or until the cake is firm and just taking on some colour at the edges. Allow to cool in the tin for a while before turning out.

MEAT, FISH AND DAIRY

Beef and pork

Chicken

White fish

Fresh anchovies and sardines

Eggs

Ricotta

Beef and pork

In summer, the old centre of Gela is a place of curtains and chairs. Curtains instead of doors, in front of windows to let in the air but keep out the sun, and chairs seemingly everywhere. A common arrangement for ground-floor flats with doors that open directly on to the pavement is to have the door curtain looped over a chair on the pavement, creating a kind of tent, an extra space, a middle place that is both private and public. It is just as common to find one or two chairs in a doorway and the curtain pulled half back, which makes it appear like a domestic stage – the scene, a woman sitting, or four women talking in the house opposite, or a couple watching a TV that glows in the dark within. Several flats near us always have two or three chairs outside their door, one sometimes occupied by a box of vegetables, from which you can take what you need, leaving coins in return.

For first-floor flats and above, the curtain arrangements are just as strategic, their positions changing during the day: open, half-mast, closed, then looped over the balcony. Balcony railings are threaded with fabric to provide both shade and privacy for those sitting on chairs. The fabric is often striped, almost-nautical, cotton, lace, net, plastic or bamboo, bringing softness to the concrete and terrible disrepair. Soft, too, are the glimpses of private lives through the curtain doors. On summer nights the warren of back streets near us is quietly busy as lives spill, one way or another, into these in-between spaces.

Sometimes shops have chairs outside too, or, in the case of Quattro Canti, our butcher in via Matteotti, a metal stool. There is almost always someone sitting on the stool: Giuliano the butcher, his ever-immaculate wife, or one of his daughters or granddaughters, who wrap themselves in the chain curtain that hangs in the doorway. A curtain of huge pieces of tripe hangs from a hook in the window, some like honeycomb, others like wet sheepskin, dripping steadily into a bucket. I am used to tripe – it is as ordinary as chops and sausages on Roman butchers' counters, and as common as steak on trattoria menus, even today. This window display, however, makes a real impression when it appears every Tuesday – a stomach is a stomach, and I want to look away. Once butchered into manageable pieces, though, tripe is familiar. Like the Romans, Sicilians know how to cook offal, thanks to their resourcefulness, the need to eat everything, and the desire to eat as well as possible. Fried tripe is particularly good, as is the tripe simmered in almost the same way as in Rome, with tomato, mint and a dusting of cheese.

The shop is as spotless as the butcher's wife, and the floor often damp, having just been mopped. Compared to my butcher in Rome, whose counter is always full, the counter at Quattro Canti seems sparse and the beef and pork is in bigger pieces, complete with trotters, heads and tails, and the lamb is much older than I have become accustomed to in Rome. The birds are older too, and there is *castrato* (castrated goat), the uncompromisingly gamey taste of which is loved by some, not so much by others. The counter sums up the traditional attitude to meat in Gela, where meat is still considered something you are lucky to have, and Giuliano prepares it carefully under your gaze. The cuts are particular: the tripe, obviously; a large slice of beef muscle called *tasca* (pocket), used for a beef roll called *falsomagro* (see page 223); slices of *castrato* to be marinated in vinegar or oregano and lemon before going on the grill; *cotiche* (pork rind) to be simmered with beans; and *stigghiole* (also known as *stigghiuola*), which are intestines to be wound around spring onions. It is a shop where you have to look the meat in the eye and stomach, and there is real ceremony about this butchery, a ceremony you take home with you. This is the one side of Gela that, despite everything, is still traditional. Giuliano is keen to tell me how things are changing, though, how the culture of eight-stop shopping is being replaced by one stop, the supermarket, with its cheap, neat vacuum packs; how one of his customers dies every day and he is not sure if the daughter will keep coming; how he sells more and more breasts, but people don't want the rest of the bird. For now, though, the shop is still busy and is one of the city's best, with a proprietor who knows where his meat comes from. I am happy to take my lead from the men and women I see shopping there – many of whom remember not having meat, and see the choice to buy it as a sign

of prosperity – and to enjoy the conscious ceremony, to pay more than I would elsewhere, to make it go further, and when we do eat it, to remember that it's an occasion. This is especially true with sausage.

Buying, cooking and eating Sicilian sausage is one of the things I look forward to most when we go to Gela. There, as in much of Sicily, sausage turns a meal into a celebration, one that often takes place in one of those middle places marked out by chairs and curtains. It is always singular, *la salsiccia* (or *sosizza* in Sicily) because it comes in a long, single length. How many are you? How much do you want? You can use your arms, spreading them as wide as you want the sausage to be long. Like many butchers, Giuliano makes *la salsiccia* to order, first choosing a piece of meat and one of fat, then chopping them both with a knife while you wait. Once chopped, the meat and fat are minced coarsely, seasoned with salt, black pepper and ground fennel seeds – you say how much – then put through the machine and forced into the tubing, the pink sausage dancing on to the metal tray. Once home, you wind the sausage into a flat coil and secure it with toothpicks or skewers, which makes it look a bit like a pink ship's wheel. We grill it up on the roof.

The extension on the roof would be illegal if it were finished, which it isn't. It was built in the late 1960s to provide the extra bedroom and bathroom that occupy half the flat roof. Like almost all buildings in Gela, the roof is also home to two 300-litre tanks which receive and store the water that arrives every two days, and is criss-crossed with washing lines. For years it was also the place where Vincenzo's grandmother Sara dried tomatoes and paste into *strattu* on wooden boards angled to follow the sun. The house next door was never finished either, so the wall that divides the two roofs consists of breeze blocks wearing a rough coat of cement. The view from the roof is startling, though. From here you can look across the sprawl of Gela, the harshness of which is mitigated by its colours of bleached pink and blue and endless washing; you can see the whole expanse of the flat plateau, and beyond it muscular hills. Stand on the wall on a clear day and we imagine we can see the faint outline of Mount Etna. We have plans for it, but until then the roof remains more Roddy Doyle than Graham Green. It is a good place to watch the sun rise while the air is still cool, to dry washing (from 11 to 5 o'clock in summer, only lizards, sheets and tomatoes can bear the harsh glare of the sun-baked expanse), and then when the sun sets, it becomes a makeshift roof kitchen. The wall provides a corner for the *brace* (grill), which is comic in its tiny proportions but one of the best places I know to cook.

We are not the only ones. Most summer evenings, and on Sundays, people position their *brace* on the doorstep, balcony or roof, moving chairs and curtains accordingly so that the movable stove occupies that middle place, both public and private. Some people have larger, more sophisticated grills, and we have friends with gardens and brick ovens and fire pits and all manners of thing with which to cook outside. But in Gela the democratic *brace* is the most common. It is a metal box measuring about 70 by 40cm, on skinny legs with a lid you lift to reveal a grill and a side drawer that allows you to remove the ashes afterwards. A sort of primal urge sets in when real flames are involved, so as much I enjoy playing with fire, I stand aside while the *carbone* is arranged, fired up and allowed to turn red, then white, at which point it is deemed ready for the sausage. The coil turns from pink to opaque to golden with a steady sizzle interrupted by fierce spits as the fat hits the coals. There is wine, water, tomato and red onion salad, caponata. The thick warm air holds the scent and drifts it across the rooftops, the city crickets rub their forewings, cousins arrive with ricotta and bread, music floats from the speakers balanced on the bathroom window ledge. A feast.

Ragù di carne
Beef and pork ragù

Serves 6–8

4 teaspoons olive oil,
   or a little lard
250g pork, in one piece
250g veal or beef, such as
   braising steak, in one piece
1 large onion
1 celery stalk
1 carrot
60g pancetta
3 teaspoons tomato purée
300ml white or red wine
400ml tomato sauce (see page
   32 or 36) or passata
2 bay leaves
salt and freshly ground
   black pepper

After years of making a bolognese-style ragù with just a spoonful of tomato purée and milk to finish, this ragù of pork and beef simmered in tomato was both a change and, in a way, a return to the much-loved English bolognese of my childhood, which I have been told more times than I care to remember is not authentic. However, unlike the minced meat sauce that we stirred through spaghetti, this recipe uses whole pieces of pork and beef, which are simmered in tomato and wine with bay leaves – this is a shining moment for bay – until the meat is very tender.

At the end of cooking, the ragù is rich red and you have choices: use the sauce for pasta and eat the meat as another course or meal, or chop the meat and return it to the sauce, which is generally what I do. The texture of chopped meat in ragù is very different from mince, more like soft rags than tiny pebbles. You can, of course, make it with mince, adding a sausage too if you like; the proportions of meat are up to you, it isn't a precious or fussy recipe. While it cooks, the sauce should maintain the sort of simmer that has you checking the flame hasn't gone out. The smell as it cooks, and the taste by the end, are heavenly.

Whether you add the meat back into the sauce or not, many shapes of pasta work with ragù, including spaghetti, fettucine, penne, farfalle and potato gnocchi. In Palermo, a similar ragù is mixed with ricotta, which is then stirred through pasta. It can also be used in a baked pasta dish that my family calls *'ncasciata* (see below), which means mess, a hint as to the informal nature of the dish. Alternatively, this ragù is glorious as part of a more formal layered baked lasagne, for which you can used bought or home-made pasta. This panful is enough for 6–8 servings, depending on how much ragù you like with your pasta – you're in charge. Add it bit by bit, though, to gauge how much you need.

In a large, heavy-based pan or casserole dish, warm the olive oil or lard over a medium heat, add the meat and carefully brown it on all sides, turning it with tongs or two spoons. Finely dice the onion, celery, carrot and pancetta. Remove the meat from the pan and set it aside, then add the onion, celery, carrot and pancetta and fry until very soft and fragrant.

Add the tomato purée and wine and stir until the purée has dissolved and the wine has slightly evaporated. Add the tomato sauce and bay leaves and stir before returning the meat to the pan. Reduce the heat so the ragù is at a very gentle simmer and cook for 2 hours, stirring every now and then. Once the meat is tender, the sauce has reduced and the oil has come to the surface, remove the meat from the pan and chop or tear it roughly over a plate to catch all the juices. Return it to the pan, taste and season with salt and pepper.

Ragù with pasta

Bring a large pan of water to the boil, add salt, stir, then add 450g pasta (such as spaghetti, fettucine, penne, cavatelli or gnocchi). Cook until al dente, then drain. Warm a serving bowl, add the pasta and 50g grated Parmesan, toss, add about half the ragù (you probably won't need it all), toss again and serve.

Ragù with pasta and ricotta

Bring a large pan of water to the boil, add salt, stir, then add 450g pasta. Cook until al dente, then drain, reserving some of the cooking water. Warm a serving bowl, add 250g fresh ricotta and stir in a ladle of cooking water to thin it a little. Add the pasta, stir, add about half the ragù (you probably won't need it all), toss again and stir.

Baked pasta with ragù and breadcrumbs ('ncasciata)

Preheat the oven to 180°C/160°C fan/gas mark 4. Grease a baking dish with olive oil and dust it with breadcrumbs. Fry some long, 1cm-wide slices of aubergine in a ridged grill pan until golden, then line the dish with them, draping them over the edges. Bring a large pan of water to the boil, add salt, stir and add 400g short pasta, such as penne, rigatoni or conchiglie. Cook for half the usual time, then drain. In a bowl, mix the pasta with half the ragù, a handful of grated Parmesan and about 250g crumbled ricotta or chopped mozzarella or provola. We also add hard-boiled eggs (four of them, cut into quarters). Put this mixture in the aubergine-lined dish and fold the draped edges over the top. Sprinkle with more breadcrumbs and a little grated cheese and bake for 15–20 minutes. Allow to cool slightly before turning it out on to a plate and slicing, remembering that *'ncasciata* means mess, so don't worry if yours is one.

Lasagne

400g 00 flour and 4 eggs, or
    400g dried lasagne sheets
olive oil, for greasing
400g ricotta
500ml whole milk, plus 3–4
    tablespoons
50g butter
50g flour
1 quantity ragù (see page 214)
100g Parmesan, grated
a handful of breadcrumbs
salt

Lasagne, for me, means a dish of baked fresh pasta in many thin layers, with just enough ragù, ricotta and béchamel to hold together, and which cuts into firm but tender slices. Made well and with love, lasagne is a magnificent thing. Fresh pasta, for most of us at least, needs time and space, which is why lasagne is not something I make very often. This makes it into a celebration, and even more loved.

The preference for fresh pasta isn't snobbism about dried pasta, which is the mainstay of our diet, merely a preference. (If I use dried pasta to make baked pasta dishes, it's usually a short variety or large shells.) All that said, dried lasagne is fine here, just follow the instructions and your own experience as to the pre-cooking and the number of layers you want. As with fresh pasta, I always pre-cook dried lasagne briefly, as I feel it never cooks properly otherwise, especially when you are using a modest amount of sauce in each layer, which I do. But this is up to you, based on your own experience, and these are, of course, only suggestions.

Lasagne, or *pasta imbottita* as it is sometimes called, can be also enriched with mozzarella, a vegetable ragù can be substituted for the meat, or you can take it to the Sicilian celebratory level and put in peas, tiny meatballs or hard-boiled eggs. You decide. However you make it, it will be magnificent, because lasagne is.

If you are embarking on home-made fresh pasta, read on. First, put the radio on. On a clean work surface, make a mountain of the flour, then swirl your fist in the centre to make a wide crater. Break the eggs into the crater, use a fork to beat them, then start mixing the flour into the eggs. Once half the flour is mixed in, use your hands to bring everything into a rough ball. Knead the dough using the ball of your hand, rotating it as you go and swinging your hips (seriously) until the dough is smooth and

soft as a baby's bum – about 8 minutes, but maybe more. Let the dough rest for 30 minutes under a bowl.

Cut the dough into 4 pieces. Set the pasta machine to its widest setting, pat the first piece of dough into a flat patty and pass it through the machine twice, then place it on a floured board, rubbing the sheet with a little flour. Do the same with the other three pieces. Reduce the setting by one and pass all four sheets through again. Repeat until you have passed all four sheets through all but the last setting. I usually cut them into roughly 25cm lengths to make them easier to manage; they are going to be trimmed to size more precisely when you assemble.

Next, pre-cook the pasta, whether you're using fresh or dried. Bring a pan of salted water to the boil, turn the heat off, get a bowl of cold water ready, and have 3 clean tea towels spread out. Dip 4 or 5 sheets in for 10 seconds (or 1 minute if you're using dried pasta). Use a sieve or tongs to lift them out and plunge them straight into the cold water for a dip, then spread them out on the tea towel. The first time you do this you will think 'What the heck?' and 'Bummer!' as a sheet slithers on to the floor. Then you will find a way, and it will be fine. You do need to create a bit of space – which I do in my small kitchen – and two pairs of hands are nice. Think of it as a lasagne dance. Once all the sheets are pre-cooked, you can assemble.

Mix the ricotta with 3–4 tablespoons milk so that it is spreadable. Make a béchamel sauce by melting the butter, stirring in the flour and cooking it to a smooth, sticky paste that comes away from the sides of the pan, then gradually adding the milk, stirring all the time, to make a smooth sauce, not too thick and not too thin. Let it simmer for 10 minutes and season it with salt and pepper.

Grease a roughly 25 x 30cm baking dish with oil and smear the base with béchamel. Make the first layer of pasta, using scissors to cut it to size if necessary. Spread a thin layer of ragù over the top, then spread over some ricotta and dust with grated Parmesan. Now make another layer of pasta (patching is fine), then another of ragù, then a layer of béchamel, which will of course mix and drag the ragù – this is fine. Now more pasta, ragù and ricotta. Continue like this (I usually go for 8 layers), ending with a thin layer of béchamel, the last of the Parmesan and a sprinkling of breadcrumbs.

Once assembled, the lasagne benefits from a night's rest in the fridge before being baked, but bring it back to room temperature before cooking. Preheat the oven to 180°C/160°C fan/gas mark 4. Bake it for 30 minutes, or until the surface is golden and edges are bubbling. Allow it to rest for 10–20 minutes so that the flavours and layers can settle before cutting it. The slices reheated the next day are always the best.

Polpette in bianco
Meatballs in white sauce

Serves 6

250g minced beef
350g minced pork
75g soft fresh breadcrumbs
75g Parmesan, grated
1 heaped tablespoon finely
    chopped flat-leaf parsley
2 eggs
fine breadcrumbs, for rolling
6 tablespoons extra-virgin
    olive oil
2 garlic cloves
200ml white wine (you may
    need a little more)
salt and freshly ground
    black pepper

A friend calls it the 'blessed curse of mamma's meatballs'. The meatballs are, to the person describing them, the best, their taste inimitable; just the thought of eating them is to be transported home. Italians take this idea to quite an extraordinary level, which I have learned to appreciate, love even, despite being English. The curse is that no meatballs will ever come close, even those made by other relatives. Vincenzo's family have proved this. Uncle Liborio, who is a chef and technically a much better cook than his mother, Sara, has made meatballs with meat from the same butcher, breadcrumbs from the same bakery, the same pan and water, and standing on the same patch of floor in front of the stove. The meatballs were good, but not Sara's, and therefore disappointing. The other part of the curse is that we all have to hear about everyone else's blessed meatballs.

This recipe is for meatballs in white (*bianco*) as opposed to red (*rosso*), i.e. tomato, sauce – but you could simmer them in tomato sauce if you wanted to. There is a moment of stove-top alchemy when the escaped breadcrumbs, meat juices, wine and olive oil come together into a thickish gravy that clings to the meatballs. Served on a wide platter with the gravy poured over the top and a handful of parsley, they make for a pleasing and, due to their pop-in-the-mouth size, irresistible dish. Potatoes and greens (see page 100) or mashed potatoes make good partners.

Knead together the meat, breadcrumbs, Parmesan, parsley (reserving a little for later), eggs, a generous pinch of salt and a few grinds of black pepper. Work the mixture, kneading and then squeezing the ingredients together into a soft, consistent mass.

Pour more breadcrumbs on to a plate. Take walnut-sized balls of the meat mixture and roll them firmly between your palms into small, neat balls. Roll the balls in breadcrumbs and sit them on a clean board or plate.

Warm the olive oil in a large, deep frying pan. Crush the garlic cloves with the back of a knife so that they split but remain whole and add them to the pan. Fry gently until golden and fragrant, which should take a minute or so. Remove the garlic and add the meatballs. Fry the meatballs, increasing the heat a little and moving them around until they are brown on all sides. This will take about 6 minutes.

Add the wine, which will sizzle vigorously, and a good pinch of salt. Continue to cook the meatballs, nudging them around. As the wine reduces into a thickish gravy, scrape it down from the sides of the pan and keep the meatballs moving so they cook evenly. You may need to add more wine. After about 5 minutes, taste a meatball to see how it is cooking. You may need to cook them a little longer; you may not. Adjust the seasoning if necessary and stir again.

Once cooked, turn the meatballs on to a warm platter, pour over the pan gravy and sprinkle over a little parsley to serve.

Braciole di Carmela
Carmela's beef rolls in tomato sauce

Serves 6

6 beef slices, such as fillet,
 topside or chuck (about
 10 x 15cm and 6mm thick)
1 red onion
1 celery stalk
1 large carrot
6 hard-boiled eggs
6 thin slices of prosciutto
 or mortadella
1 small white onion
5 tablespoons olive oil
150ml red wine
700ml smooth tomato sauce
 (see page 32 or 36) or passata

The Sicilian writer and poet Pino Correnti wrote about *falsomagro* in his book *Il Libro D'Oro Della Cucina e Dei Vini di Sicilia.* He considered it the undisputed king of Sicilian meat dishes: a large piece of beef wrapped around a filling of vegetables, chopped meat, cheese and hard-boiled egg, then simmered in tomato sauce. The name translates as 'false lean', possibly because its appearance from the outside promises something lean, but when you cut it open it is clear this is not the case: instead, you discover an almost baroque filling fit for a feast day, religious or otherwise.

Most families have their own version. Nowadays, rather than making one large *falsomagro,* my mother-in-law, Carmela, makes individual ones that are often called *braciole. Braciole* are really just *involtini*, or meat rolls, with an egg inside. They don't have quite the same *behold!* moment as a large single roll, although the yolks still shine. Carmela and I have made these together on many occasions, most recently in my kitchen, which proved itself to be wholly inadequate. No long tongs or kitchen roll, a knife that needs sharpening, no meat basher or oven glove, my salt too coarse, my pepper grinder too uptight. Realizing that my hovering was as annoying as my grinder, I sat at the table and made notes. I noted the ingredients, of course, even though many of them were in *qb – quanto basta* – which means 'however much is enough', or use your common sense.

Carmela has no idea how amusing she is, especially when she is cross and using a rolling pin instead of a meat mallet. She is very specific about how to bash out the meat and snip away any muscles or fibres that might make it curl, about the arrangement of the carrot and celery and about the tying of the roll, for which she uses cotton that she keeps in her handbag, a tardis of useful things, including packets of dry and moist tissues. Like so many stew and braises, *braciole* are better after a few hours' rest, better still overnight. Just reheat the rolls gently. In Sicily the rolls are served alone, with bread for the sauce. I love them with buttery mashed potatoes.

Prepare the beef slices, if necessary pounding (or rather gently extending or stretching) them until thin, then nick the edges of each slice to stop them curling in the pan. Prepare the red onion, celery and carrot by cutting all three into similarly sized slim batons. Peel the hard-boiled eggs.

Make sure your reel of cotton is close to hand, and ideally enlist the help of another person for the tying. Spread the beef slices out on a clean work surface. Lay the prosciutto on top of the beef, making sure you leave a margin around the edge, and place an egg in the bottom half of the slice. Arrange bundles of carrot, celery and onion around the egg, tucking them in close. Bring the bottom of the slice up and over the egg, then roll it, tucking the sides in as best you can, until you have a neat, plum-like cylinder. Secure the roll with a double piece of cotton as if you were tying a parcel, so lengthways first, then the sides. Do this twice, to make sure the ends are really well sealed.

Chop the white onion. In a large deep frying or sauté pan, warm the olive oil, then fry the onion until soft and translucent. Add the beef rolls and fry them, turning them as required, until they are brown. Add the wine and let it sizzle, then add the tomato sauce and a pinch of salt. Reduce the heat and let the rolls simmer, half covered, turning them every now and then until they are cooked through, which usually takes about 1 hour. Ideally, let them sit for a while, then reheat them gently.

Fettine alla pizzaiola
Beef slices with tomato and oregano

Serves 4

8 lean beef slices, such as fillet,
  topside or rump (about
  10 x 15cm and 3mm thick)
2 garlic cloves
450g ripe tomatoes, or 400g
  good-quality tinned tomatoes
3 tablespoons extra-virgin
  olive oil
50g black olives
a sprig of fresh or a pinch of
  dried oregano
salt and freshly ground
  black pepper

Alla pizzaiola means cooked in the style of a pizza, in other words with tomatoes, olives, oregano, and swiftly. Originating in Napoli, this style of cooking meat has now diffused all over the south, everyone having their own version and thoughts about how to make it.

Cinzia is in my mind's eye when I make this, as it is her hands I've watched most often. She asks her butcher to slice the beef very thinly, then rumples the slices so they look a bit like pulled-back curtains and fit in the pan in a single layer. The rumples mean that the meat, which cooks quickly, has pleasing traces of pink in the folds. This is a dish in which oregano works particularly well, its warm, slightly camphorish scent complementing the beef and rich tomato sauce. The whole thing, from first chop to bringing it to the table, takes about 15 minutes. Bread to mop up the juices and a large glass of red wine are all I want with this.

Pound (or, if using fillet, gently extend or stretch) the beef slices until they are thin and tenderized. Make notches along the edges of each slice to stop them curling up in the pan.

Thinly slice the garlic and roughly chop the tomatoes – if you are using tinned ones, scissors in the tin are best. In a large, heavy-based frying or sauté pan, warm the olive oil and garlic over a medium-low heat and gently fry the garlic until it is fragrant. Add the tomatoes, olives and a pinch of oregano, salt and a few grinds of black pepper and simmer gently for 10 minutes, or until the sauce is thick and rich. Add the beef slices, rumpling them slightly so they all fit in the pan in a single layer. Continue cooking the slices, turning them once or twice, until they are cooked through. Move the slices to a warm serving dish, scrape over the remaining sauce, sprinkle with more oregano and serve.

Chicken

I can measure my life in roast chickens. Those cooked by my mum and both my grandmas, the weekly birds that provided two meals, one of them usually soup; roast chickens from the glistening walls of rotisseries on foreign holidays, sophisticated and exotic versions of something I already knew; the best chicken I've ever eaten, pulled from a wood-fired oven in the south of France when I was 23; the worst chicken I've ever eaten, which was put in the oven and then forgotten (by me); the feral-tasting chicken that was actually a pheasant – my brother still reminds my mum about that; the chicken I roasted for myself every other week at the tiny Mornington Crescent flat I lived in when I was at drama school, the trains that cut though Camden rattling the oven every couple of minutes; the roast chicken from the *tavola calda* Volpetti in Rome, where I would be asked *sei per petto o coscia?* (are you for breast or thigh?), which never failed to make me burn (I am both); the chicken I roasted last night, before writing this.

I know I am not alone in thinking that roast chicken with crispy skin, tender flesh and gravy made from the sticky juices, potatoes of some kind, a green salad, a blob of mustard and a glass of wine is a good meal. While it never seems to lose its ability to feel celebratory, it is not a bit fussy. Roasting a chicken is simple; roasting one well, not quite so simple, which is why we all have our own methods based on years of experience and chickens enjoyed, or not enjoyed, the bad teaching us as much as the good.

One of the worst meals I ever have eaten involved chicken. It was a sunny Sunday and we were eight. The dish was a sort of *coq au vin*, in that it was chicken and onions boiled in red wine, only not for very long, so that the wine wasn't much thicker than when it left the bottle. As the hostess served the first portion, the wine flooded the plate, fleeing, it seemed, from the chicken and onions as if wanting nothing to do with them. The chicken itself was very pale violet. It was clear that something had gone terribly wrong; the chicken wasn't even close to being cooked, but we all tried anyway, hopefully, desperately. Those with breasts fared slightly better, but those of us with thighs met uncooked flesh almost immediately, a pink alarm letting us know that all was not well. Refill my wine glass and I am pretty good at eating my way though even the most terrible plateful, but raw chicken? No chance. To start there was almost silence, then compensating conversation flowed over the flooded plates. After a very long 40 minutes, someone offered to clear the table, at which point, seizing the opportunity, several people jumped up with their own plates. 'Wait,' said the hostess, and then confirmed my suspicion that she was on some sort of drugs by asking if anyone would like seconds. What did I learn? That awful meals are sometimes wonderful in their awfulness. And never to undercook the chicken.

A good roast chicken starts with a good chicken. Having seen first hand the different ways that chickens can be raised, the worst of which was worse than anything I could possibly have imagined, I am really fussy. I only buy chicken from my butcher and pay 21 euros for a two-kilogram bird from a farm I know. We have a tight kitchen budget, which means that chicken is something we have once, maybe twice a month. Sometimes I roast it whole, at other times I joint it and use the legs and thighs for one thing and the breasts for breadcrumbs. Either way, the bones get made into stock.

In Gela, chicken also means cutlets, or *cotoletta*, one of few things for which Vincenzo breaks his non-meat-eating habit. The recipe, and most importantly the method, is *nonna* Sara's. Until the late 1960s she kept her own chickens, streetwise chooks who roamed and pecked the land that would later become via Vespa. In the 1970s and 80s, as life in Gela changed, she bought a chicken once a week from the man who drove into town with a van full of crates. She did the work, though, strangling and plucking the bird in the garage. As the years passed, Sara happily bought chicken from the market and chicken breasts from the supermarket, which she saw as progress, as her bright, light reward for years of relentless hard work. She embraced rolls of long-life cheese, cartons of iced tea and clean-cut breasts. She would never have called this a recipe, simply *pollo impanato* (breaded chicken), its siren scent luring the kids in from the street.

Pollo al forno
Roast chicken

Serves 4

1 plump free-range chicken,
    about 1.8kg, at room
    temperature
80g butter, at room
    temperature
1 unwaxed lemon
a sprig of rosemary or thyme
salt and freshly ground
    black pepper

This much I know about plain roast chicken. The bird should be dry and at room temperature. The butter should also be at room temperature so that it can be rubbed easily into all the nooks and crannies of the bird, the lemon too, as it will be easier to squeeze. I use a roasting tin only slightly larger than the bird and put the bird in the oven with its legs facing towards the back. 220°C for the first 15 minutes, then baste, then 190°C for 40 minutes, without basting. Then – as taught by Simon Hopkinson in his aptly named book *Roast Chicken and Other Stories* – I turn the oven off, leave the door ajar and let the chicken sit in the cooling oven for another 15 minutes. These minutes are vital: it is during this time, the cooking equivalent of a perfect vinyl fadeout, that the cooking finishes, the skin dries and the flesh relaxes but clings to the juices, making for a roast with properly crisp skin, succulent, tender flesh and easy carving.

Actually, carve is not the right word: cut and pull is more appropriate. Using a knife, poultry shears and my hands, I pull chicken to pieces. I do this in the roasting tin and then roll the pieces in the best sort of gravy: the buttery, lemony, nut-brown juices that have collected at the bottom of the tin. Serve it with green salad or watercress, potatoes and greens or warm caponata.

Preheat the oven to 220°C/200°C fan/gas mark 7. Pat the chicken dry with kitchen paper. Using your hands, rub the chicken with the soft butter and season generously with salt and pepper inside and out. Put the chicken in a roasting tin. Wash and then soften the lemon by rolling it back and forth across the kitchen counter while applying pressure with your palm, then cut it in half and squeeze the juice over the chicken.

Tuck the squeezed-out lemon in the chicken cavity along with the herbs, then close the opening with cocktail sticks. Don't make an expert job of this, or the chicken might puff up and burst. Put the chicken in the top third of the oven with its legs facing towards the back and roast for 15 minutes. Baste well. Turn the oven down to 190°C/170°C fan/gas mark 5 and roast for another 40 minutes. Turn the oven off, leave the door ajar and let the chicken rest in the cooling oven for another 15 minutes.

Before carving, tilt the chicken slightly so that all the juices run into the tin. Stir the buttery, lemony, nut-brown juices – scraping up the thick dark bits from the bottom of the tin – with a wooden spoon. Carve, rip, tear or pull the chicken apart in the roasting tin, letting the pieces and joints roll in the juices.

Pollo con le patate, acciughe e rosmarino
Chicken with potatoes, anchovies and rosemary

Serves 4

4 tablespoons olive oil
1 free-range chicken, about
    1.5kg, jointed into 8 pieces
1kg potatoes
2 garlic cloves, peeled and
    crushed
6 anchovy fillets
a sprig of rosemary or a good
    pinch of dried or fresh
    oregano
a pinch of dried red chillies
    (optional)
250ml dry white wine or water
salt and freshly ground
    black pepper

Apart from my pasta pan, the pans I find most useful in the kitchen are two large aluminium sauté pans, the sort you see in trattoria kitchens and throughout this book. One has a long handle, and the other two round ones. If for my first book I wished we could have included a free food mill, for this one I wished we could give away one of these pans. Mostly I use them for pasta sauces and braised vegetables – they are heavy enough to allow even cooking, but light enough to lift and flip. The one with two handles can also go in the oven, so I use it for fish, and for something I call a braise-bake, which makes it sound like a political scandal. A braise-bake is just that: a braise (an oily, steamy simmer on the stove) to start with, then the rest of the cooking done in the oven. If there are more juices than you want, you can always put the pan back on the stove again to reduce them, making it a braise-bake-braise.

This recipe is a variation of Roman hunters'-style chicken (*pollo alla cacciatora*), so the joints simmer in white wine with chopped garlic, chilli and rosemary. This version, though, includes anchovies, which season deeply, and potatoes, which soak up the plentiful juices. Because you begin on the stove top,

the meat will have a deep crust, which deepens in the oven. The potatoes get golden tops too, but underneath they will be tender and sticky. We sometimes use oregano, but rosemary is mighty here, wild and aromatic: there really is nothing like it, even if you do get a needle stuck between your teeth. Add bread, salad, wine and cheese and you have a good meal.

Preheat the oven to 200°C/180°C fan/gas mark 6. In a large, deep, ovenproof frying pan or casserole that can accommodate the chicken and potatoes in a single layer, warm the olive oil over a medium heat. Adding them skin-side down, brown the chicken pieces on all sides. Lift the chicken on to a plate. Meanwhile, cut the potatoes into 1.5cm wedges.

In the remaining oil and chicken fat (if you feel there is too much, pour some away) and over a low heat, fry the garlic and anchovies, nudging the anchovies with a wooden spoon so they disintegrate and dissolve into the oil. Add herbs and chilli if you are using it, then the potatoes, and stir until each wedge glistens.

Return the chicken to the pan, fitting the pieces between the potatoes – it doesn't matter if it is all a bit squashed, as the meat will shrink. Pour over the wine, season cautiously and cook over a medium-low heat for 10 minutes, during which time the wine will bubble. Transfer it to the oven for 40 minutes, basting the potatoes every 15 minutes. There will be lots of oily gravy.

Cotoletta di pollo
Breadcrumbed chicken

Serves 4

4 chicken breasts, halved
    horizontally
plain flour, for dusting
2 eggs, lightly beaten
80g dried breadcrumbs
20g grated pecorino or
    caciocavallo (optional)
a pinch of dried oregano
    (optional)
extra-virgin olive oil and/or
    butter for frying
lemon wedges, to serve
freshly ground black pepper

There is a reason why the classics are classics. They are smart and delicious and, once made, they quickly become steadfast in our recipe lives, their goodness and familiarity as lovable as a favourite song dancing out of the radio. *Cotoletta di pollo* is one of our classics, usually made on a Wednesday.

I am not such a fan of the inevitable smoke that follows as wayward breadcrumbs burn. This can be lessened by a good coating of egg, by shaking off excess crumbs, keeping the heat low and steady. The cheese is optional, but I think it is important for the seasoning and crispness it gives. The oregano too is optional; I like it but many don't, so I make my *cotoletta* last and add a pinch to the breadcrumbs. A tomato and red onion salad, or peeled chunks of tomato mixed with warm green beans, make good partners. Make one extra, and then you can make a sandwich the next day.

Using a meat mallet or rolling pin, flatten the chicken breasts to a thickness of 5mm. Prepare 3 plates: one with flour, one with the eggs and the third with a mixture of the breadcrumbs, cheese, oregano (if using) and some black pepper – the cheese means you don't need any salt. Working one breast at a time, dip them in the flour, shake off any excess, then dip them in the egg, then the breadcrumbs, making sure they are well coated.

Heat 6 tablespoons olive oil or butter in a large, heavy frying pan over a medium-high heat. Place 2 cutlets in the pan and fry until a crisp golden-brown crust has formed and the meat has cooked through, which will take about 4 minutes per side. Lift the cutlets on to a plate lined with kitchen paper. Add more olive oil or butter and repeat with the remaining cutlets. Serve with lemon wedges.

Polpette di pollo e ricotta e limone
Chicken balls with ricotta and lemon

Serves 4

For the meatballs

300g minced chicken breast

200g ricotta

grated zest of 1 large unwaxed
    lemon

60g soft white breadcrumbs,
    ideally from day-old bread

50g Parmesan, grated

a pinch of dried oregano

1 egg, lightly beaten

salt and freshly ground
    black pepper

To cook and serve

6 tablespoons olive oil

1 garlic clove, crushed

a sprig of rosemary

200ml white wine, or 500ml
    tomato sauce, or 1 litre broth

Chicken, ricotta and lemon make the tenderest meatballs. Hands really are best, to mix and pummel everything, and shape the balls, which should be bite-sized. You can fry them, a little wine providing a steamy braise; or simmer them in tomato sauce, which makes them even more tender and plump; or simmer them in broth.

In a bowl, mix together the chicken, ricotta, lemon zest, breadcrumbs, Parmesan, oregano and egg using your hands, and season with salt and pepper. With wet hands, shape the mixture into walnut-sized balls, and place them on a tray lined with baking parchment.

In large frying pan over a medium-low heat, warm the olive oil and fry the garlic and whole sprig of rosemary until fragrant, then remove them from the pan. Add the chicken balls and fry gently, turning them until they are brown on all sides.

If you are using white wine, add it to the pan, where it will sizzle, then let the meatballs simmer for 10 minutes, shaking the pan from time to time so they don't stick. By the end of cooking they should be tender but cooked through, in a slightly thickened sauce.

If you are using tomato sauce or broth, warm the sauce in a pan large enough to accommodate both it and the meatballs. Once the sauce or broth is almost boiling, drop the balls into it, making sure they are submerged. Turn the heat to low, cover the pan and poach for 15 minutes, by which time the meatballs should be cooked through but still tender.

Pollo con arance e olive
Chicken with citrus and olives

Serves 4

2 unwaxed oranges

1 unwaxed lemon

6 tablespoons extra-virgin olive
oil, plus extra for brushing

1 clove garlic

1 free-range chicken, jointed,
or 8 thighs

100g green olives

a sprig of fresh oregano or
marjoram

salt and freshly ground
black pepper

Every time I make this it crosses my mind that I would rather like to spend the afternoon in a silky, fragrant bath of olive oil and citrus. Preparing the marinade is more or less all the work involved. After an afternoon, all you need to do is pour everything into a baking dish, push some slices of orange and green olives in the gaps, rip over some oregano and put the tray in the oven. Chicken and citrus have a great affinity, the lemon giving edge and sharpness, the orange sweetness.

Submerged in the marinade, the lower halves of the thighs poach, while the upper parts roast until golden, and the orange slices crisp and curl at the edges. You can, if you like, thicken the cooking juices by pouring them off into a saucepan to reduce before pouring the now-thickened juices back over the chicken. Although this is a dish full of Sicilian flavours, I cannot help but be reminded of the 1970s colour supplement recipes collected by my mother, of things cooked *à l'orange* for dinner parties, and Demis Roussos.

In a bowl, whisk together the zest and juice of 1 orange and the juice of the lemon with the oil, and season with salt and pepper. Crush the garlic gently with the back of a knife so that it remains whole and add to the marinade, along with the chicken, making sure each piece is covered. Cover with clingfilm and leave it for 4 hours, or overnight, in the fridge.

Preheat the oven to 200°C/180°C fan/gas mark 6. Brush with oil an ovenproof dish or roasting tin that will hold the chicken in a single layer, add the chicken and pour over the marinade, which will come about halfway up the chicken. Add the olives and oregano, then slice the remaining orange and tuck the slices in between the chicken. Roast for 45 minutes. If the tops look as if they are browning too fast, cover the dish loosely with foil.

Once the chicken is cooked, assess the amount of liquid that remains. If there is a lot, lift out the chicken pieces and reduce

the liquid to a thicker sauce in the roasting tin, or tip it into a pan and boil it hard until it is as thick as you would like, then pour it back over the chicken. I sometimes return the chicken to the oven while the sauce reduces to give colour to the undersides.

White fish

It takes about 25 minutes to drive from Gela to the fishing port of Scoglitti – or 35 if you are in a tin-can Fiat Panda that's just clocked 200,000 miles. We make the journey often in summer, so it is familiar: flying down via Verga, past the lorries full of watermelons and peaches, and the section of ancient wall that the city spilled beyond in the 1960s. Once out of the city, the car flies even faster along the newly resurfaced Strada Statale 115, which skirts Gela's immense, monstrous and now shamefully almost-silent oil refinery; on the other side of the road there are superstores, mechanics and a lonely bar that serves decent coffee and granita.

As suddenly as a power cut, everything changes. There is space. Great expanses marked by low stone walls are covered with post-harvest stubble, some blistered and bleached by the sun. In the distance, a phantom section of motorway on stilts goes nowhere, and behind it a cemetery appears to float, mirage-like. From the back of the car, Luca keeps up a running commentary: 'Monsters! Sheep! Is that where your dead grandpa is?' He is, and Uncle Salvatore too, in the family tomb, a miniature house in a long terrace with other miniature houses, each one a well-tended shrine decorated with pictures, toys and flowers. Later that second summer, on one of the hottest days of the year, we will all go to the cemetery to reunite Vincenzo's grandmother Sara with her husband and eldest son.

Near another section of ghost motorway we turn into a lane flanked by bamboo so tall it feels like a tunnel. When we emerge, everything opens up again, hills dotted with olive trees whose silvery-green leaves glint in the fierce June sun. There are vivid green vines – the only things tenacious enough to hold on to their colour – and along the side of the road, swathes of dusty-green *fichi d'India* plants, whose clusters of cactus-like fleshy leaves have spikes that fly at you. Neither a fig nor from India, *fichi d'India* are plum-shaped fruits that are also covered in spikes. In June, the fruit that grows like fingers from the sides of each leaf is still green; by August it will be bright pink, and the seed-riddled flesh will be coral. Vincenzo has inherited his grandfather's nerve for picking the fruit, though he does curse the fact that he is still pulling spikes from his clothes days later. The small green figs from a nearby clambering tree are easier picking; the tree seems almost part of an abandoned house, the back section of which is a mountain of rubbish so well established that it has its own weeds reaching for the sky. Behind the house hills rise, their great contours seeming almost muscular, dusty yellow with rich green stripes of vines. The great contours make me catch my breath, but it is the land as a whole, with its staggering contrasts, that makes my heart feel full. It is here, more or less, that Vincenzo's grandfather Orazio farmed for 70 years.

You don't need a sign to see that you are passing from one province to the next. Ragusa feels completely different from our province of Caltanisetta: there is order and production, and soon the space is filled with hundreds of green houses. Every few minutes a young man passes on a bicycle, pedalling through almost impossible heat, no doubt on his way to pick fruit. Gela is agricultural too, but this part of Ragusa is the profitable agricultural heart of Sicily, much of it under a plastic roof, even in August. The plastic flashes past, the reflective surfaces playing tricks with my eyes. They seem endless, until they do end and it is green again, the smell of salt indicating we are near the sea. This journey always strikes me as a sort of summing up of our part of Sicily, of the riches, the marks and scars left by everyone who has visited, from the Greeks to the petroleum giant. It is a songline for Vincenzo's family, the agriculture and the industry that helped a daughter but betrayed a son, the life and the death. The car seems to breathe with relief as we shoot down the home straight to the sweeping coast and the sea.

Scoglitti is a small town on the coast, pretty but not a bit twee, and a popular place for Sicilians to have a summer home. We go there to buy fish or eat fish. If we are buying, the boats come in at around half past four. A waiting crowd will have gathered on the dock in a low building at the end of the port for the auction. The crowd is keen and experienced, so we stick to the fringes. It is always good to be reminded that fresh fish doesn't smell anything like fish, but like wet stones and sea water, like iron and flesh. Crates are unloaded and some, especially those that

appear to contain the coveted *gamberi rossi*, or blood-red prawns (which really are the colour of a pin-prick tear of blood, thick red) are put directly into vans, and then fly away. Other boxes, filled with more prawns, large fish and crustaceans – the best of the catch – are also carried off to local trattorias. The rest of the crates are brought through to the covered area, where they are stacked on low metal trolleys. Through cracks in the crowd we watch as another box of prawns seems to go for an extraordinary price. By the time we get a look-in there are sardines and anchovies, pale-pink prawns and mullet mottled with coral, great flat skate like waterlogged kites with dragon tails, the long silver *spatola*, which look remarkably like a belt a glam rocker might have worn in 1972, and small mackerel with blue-green iridescent tiger striping along their backs, some still flapping desperately, others taking their last gasping breaths. The first time I made a bid I asked for a kilogram of mackerel. Somebody laughed – here, everything is by the crate. In my bid

to look slightly less foolish, perhaps, I took a crate that must have been 6 kilograms, which was then tipped, or rather poured, into a blue plastic bag. That night the roof smelled of blackened and blistered flesh as we feasted on mackerel. I then spent much of the night boiling and boning fish and putting it in jars, something I am in no hurry to do again.

If we are there to eat fish, we go to Sakalleo, a restaurant in the middle of town. The small interconnecting rooms make it seem smaller than it actually is, which is nice. It is functional and comfortable. Like most of the fish restaurants in Scoglitti, the menu consists of tasting menus, the only real choice being at which point you stop: after the antipasti, pasta or secondi. The owner's daughter is half French and fabulous, with red lips and denim hotpants. There is not much room for manoeuvre; she tells us in a deep voice that rolls from her lips: 'I know what you want.' And you don't doubt it. The antipasti start arriving, little dish after little dish: an oyster each; peeled, blood-red prawns that are some of the most plump and pure I have ever eaten; slices of raw sea bass cooked with lemon; cubes of octopus and butterflies of anchovy; enormous yellow mussels stretching like acrobats across their shells; tiny clams called *telline* that taste like a liquor made from sea water; sardines rolled up so they look like little fat birds; and *spatola* with almonds and breadcrumbs, served with sweet onions. If we are particularly hungry we might have a plate of spaghetti with a sauce made from mullet broth, with clams and bottarga. If we are feeling flush we have whole roasted fish. You are simply brought dessert, which isn't so much a dessert as a finishing point: a bowl of lemon sorbet, a cold, clean, sweet-and-sour full stop. Then, as if to get you going again, there is a pistachio biscuit, the outside crisp and the inside soft and green, which in turn leads to coffee. After dinner we always walk along the seafront, joining locals and tourists, mostly French, on the nightly *passeggiata*, or stroll. You always know the Sicilians: they are the elegant ones, the heels higher, the clothes crisper, the hair sleeker, *la bella figura* in movement; my shoes always feel flat, my hair frizzy. I enjoy the way the sultry, salty night clamps itself to our skin and the sea that has provided our supper has become a huge black expanse, sometimes still, other times rising and falling in huge swells, on the far side of which is Tunisia and Africa. Vincenzo might have another espresso, as he is driving. I don't, as Luca and I are going to sleep all the way home, our sandals and toes filled with sand, our faces and lips covered in the finest layer of salt.

I used to be intimidated by cooking fish, staying safe with neat fillets safe behind plastic. You just hadn't met the right fishmonger, my fishmonger told me, and he was right, to a point. I now get enormous pleasure from cooking fish, and simple preparations are what it demands. The most important thing is freshness, so peer in close and ask questions. Look for bright eyes, firm skin, bright red gills and a smell of wet stones and sea water, like iron and flesh.

Pesce in padella con finocchio e limone
Sautéed fish with fennel and lemon

Serves 4

2 fennel bulbs
6 tablespoons extra-virgin
    olive oil
4 sea bream fillets, about 100g
    each, skin on
½ unwaxed lemon
salt

Fish and fennel make a good pair – if you like fish and fennel, that is. It is a combination you meet again and again in Sicily, from robust dishes of pasta with sardines and powerfully flavoured fronds of wild fennel, to elegant plates of paper-thin raw fish and sweet bulb fennel marinated with lemon juice, to fish dishes spicy with fennel seeds or fragrant, feathery fronds.

For this recipe you want bulbs of sweet Florentine fennel, the rounder and plumper the better. The recipe begins in much the same way as braised fennel: the slices are cooked in a little water and their own fragrant juices until they are tender and the juices are sparse and sticky, which is important. You then push the fennel to the sides of the pan and add the fish, which is covered at first so that it steams, then uncovered to finish it off.

Trim the base and fingers off the fennel and pull away the outer layer if it seems very tough or damaged. Cut the fennel into 1cm slices lengthways and soak them in cold water for 10 minutes, then drain.

In a frying or sauté pan with a lid, and large enough to hold the fish in a single layer, warm the olive oil, adding the fennel almost immediately, turning it so that each slice glistens. Add 120ml water and cook over a low heat until the fennel is tender and most of the water has evaporated, which usually takes about 12 minutes.

Push the fennel to the sides of the pan and turn down the heat. Add the fish to the pan skin-side down, sprinkle it with salt, squeeze over the lemon, cover the pan and cook for 5 minutes. Turn it over and cook, uncovered, for 3 more minutes, by which time it should be cooked through.

Pesce con crosta di pane e mandorle
Fish with an almond and breadcrumb crust

Serves 4

60g whole blanched almonds
150g dried breadcrumbs
grated zest of 1 unwaxed lemon
a pinch of dried oregano
(optional)
4–8 fish fillets, such as mackerel,
bream or sea bass
extra-virgin olive oil
salt and freshly ground
black pepper

In much the same way that they find their way into the cracks and corners of your kitchen, breadcrumbs have found their way into every chapter too, despite having one of their own. Here they are in one of their most reliable roles: as a topping, which crisps in the oven, providing a contrast to the soft fish below. Maybe that is damning them with faint praise, which is where the almonds, lemon, salt and pepper come in, bringing some texture and edge. You may, of course, decide that reliable is what you're after.

It was at Sakalleo, the fish restaurant in Scoglitti, that we first ate this, made with belt-like *spatola*. At first we didn't notice the almonds, just a lovely flavour, so we sat chewing with can't-put-my-finger-on-it faces. Vincenzo was the first to get it: almonds, toasted to give the breadcrumbs a rich, nutty texture and crunch, with a hint of lemon too and plenty of seasoning. I took the idea home, where it bounced around the kitchen like a ball: on pasta, as a stuffing, on fish. On all sorts of fish. Our favourite is cod – essentially fish fingers – but mackerel also works well, its thick, milky flesh a sturdy match for the coarse, nutty crust. Fish and breadcrumbs need a foil, something sweet, sour, salty, pungent to offer contrast. A salad of tomatoes, red onion and capers is a brilliant and typically Sicilian combination.

Preheat the oven to 200°C/180°C fan/gas mark 6 and line a baking tray with kitchen foil or greaseproof paper. Roughly chop the almonds and mix them with the breadcrumbs and lemon zest, salt and pepper and a pinch of oregano, if using.

Brush the fish fillets with olive oil, then dip the fillet side of the fish in the breadcrumbs, pressing so it is well coated. Place the fillets skin-side down on the baking tray. Once all the fillets are on the tray, zig-zag them with olive oil. Bake until the fish is cooked through and the crumbs are golden, which will take 10–15 minutes, depending on the thickness of the fillets – you need to keep an eye out, and taste.

Pesce al forno con le patate
Baked fish with potatoes

Serves 4

1 large bream, about 800g,
  or two smaller fish,
  about 350g each
1kg potatoes
extra-virgin olive oil
lemon slices and flat-leaf
  parsley (optional)
salt

A whole fish cooked on a bed of sliced potatoes was the first dish my friend, the superb cook and teacher Carla Tomasi, cooked for us. It came after *pasta e fagioli*, and before a green salad and *zuccotto*, all eaten on her long table overlooking her beloved garden.

Having spent many years protecting fish with layers of potatoes or salt – what a palaver – or protective packages of foil or parchment, I found the idea of roasting a whole fish naked, but for a little salt, unnerving, but I trusted Carla. If you use a smaller fish, the potatoes may need a head start, but with a large fish, say 700g, thinly sliced potatoes will cook in the same amount of time, the potatoes under the fish having the benefit of a slight steaming, those at the edges crisping. Far from being dry, the fish skin toughens with the heat, under which the flesh can bake and steam. Rip off the skin and you are met with a puff, and soft flakes. Be generous with the oil and salt on the potatoes. This is an absolute favourite Friday supper for us three; all you need is lemon wedges and a green salad. Bream or bass, or flat fish like halibut or turbot all work well here.

If your fishmonger hasn't done it already, scale the fish by wetting it and then using the blunt edge of a knife to scrape the scales away, then rinse again. Gut the fish carefully by piercing the belly with a small, sharp knife near the small hole in the middle of the belly, then slitting it open to just below the gills. Use your fingers to pull out the internal organs, scooping right up towards the head. Use a fingernail or the point of the knife to scrape away any blood or dark innards clinging near the spine and in the neck – this is important, as they are very bitter. Dry the fish carefully inside and and out with kitchen paper.

Preheat the oven to 200°C/180°C fan/gas mark 6. Peel the potatoes and slice them thinly. Don't worry too much if you have the odd uneven slice that is thick at one end and thin at the

other; they will all be welcome. Rub a roasting tin with olive oil, put the potatoes in, zig-zag with more oil, season with salt and toss everything well. Rub the fish with salt, filling its belly with lemon slices and some parsley if you wish, then place it in the middle of the potatoes. Bake for 30 minutes, or until the flesh is opaque, not glassy, which you can check by pulling back a little skin near the spine where the flesh is thickest. Waiting for 5 minutes before you eat, to let the juices settle, is a good idea.

Pesce alla ghiotta
Fish in spicy tomato sauce with capers and olives

Serves 4

1 onion
2 celery stalks
100ml extra-virgin olive oil
500g fresh tomatoes, or peeled
    plum tomatoes without juice
a pinch of red chilli flakes
50g salted capers, rinsed
60g green or black olives
4 fish fillets, about 120g each
1 heaped tablespoon chopped
    flat-leaf parsley
salt and freshly ground
    black pepper

In short, you make a rich tomato sauce, bolstered with caper and olives, then poach fish in it. This dish is from Messina, and traditionally would have been made with swordfish, but I have used salt cod, cod, bream and hake, all of which worked well. *Ghiotta* means gluttonous, which is perhaps how this *saporitissimo* (well flavoured), warm and deeply spiced sauce might make you feel. Rather like the Neapolitan pasta sauce *puttanesca*, which includes the same intensely flavoured ingredients, the exact proportions can only be personal. Use the quantities here as a guide rather than definitive instructions. I love capers, so I have been heavy handed, but I only want warmth, not fire, from the chilli. In summer I make this with fresh tomatoes, peeled and roughly chopped, which makes for a softer, sweeter sauce. In winter I make it with tinned tomatoes, which sometimes need a teaspoon of sugar to balance the acidity. You can serve it alone, with bread for juices, or with rice, couscous or plain boiled potatoes.

Finely dice the onion, then pull the strings off the celery and dice that too. In a large, deep frying or sauté pan, which will eventually accommodate the fillets in a single layer, gently fry the onion in the oil over a medium-low heat until soft and translucent. Add the celery, stir and cook for a couple of minutes, then add the tomatoes and chilli and simmer gently for 10 minutes. Add the capers and olives and simmer for a couple of minutes more.

Take the pan off the heat and arrange the fillets, skin-side down, in the pan in a single layer, then ladle some of the sauce over the fish. Put the pan back over a low heat and simmer very gently, spooning more sauce over the top every now and then, until the fish is cooked through. Sprinkle with parsley and serve.

Fresh anchovies and sardines

Insistence was needed to convince my *pescivendolo* (fishmonger) here in Rome to get me some sardines. Did I know how bony they were, how difficult to digest, especially at night? 'Are you sure you don't want anchovies?' he said, pointing to the polystyrene box where they lay, small and slender, their blue bodies streaked with silver, eyes bright. I was sure – the plan was *pasta con le sarde* (pasta with sardines). At this point he agreed to get me some for the next morning, but I had to promise I would come and collect them, as he wouldn't be able to sell them to anyone else.

In Gela it is the other way round: crates and crates of sardines outweigh the anchovies by some measure. Sardines have always been plentiful in the bay of Gela, and other fish too, which is why, since the city was founded in around 688 BCE, it was a town of fishermen who lived off the unpredictable but generous sea. This sea would also shape the life and work of an ancient Greek called Archestratus, who was born in Gela, a gourmet of such rare talent that he could taste the difference beween a mullet caught when the moon was waxing and one caught when it was waning. In her book on Sicilian food, Mary Taylor Simeti describes him as a fourth-century Michelin inspector who toured the island and reported back, in poetry, on what he ate. No fragment of poetry survives that suggests he ate sardines from the bay of Gela, but I like to imagine he did, sprinkled with just a little salt and vinegar. The importance of Gela itself waxed and waned: it was founded, destroyed and rebuilt several times under the Greeks, a tiny settlement under the Romans, an almost non-existent one under the Arabs, rechristened as Terranova in AD 1233 by the Holy Roman Emperor Frederick II, then ruled by the Spanish as part of the Kingdom of Sicily. Through all this, the wealth of the sea has played a fundamental role in its wealth. All this changed, as did the physical appearance of the bay, when the oil company Eni built the refinery, which inflated the population in an almost grotesque way on a promise that was never kept, polluted the water and ruined livelihoods. Fifty years on, the almost-closure of the plant means the sea is good once more, and filled with tiny silver darts flashing through the water, captured by great nets and brought up the hill in baskets and boxes by men in caps and Adidas tracksuits, old world and new cheek to cheek. Buying fish at the *pescivendolo* near the Duomo is a joy, a skill and a competitive sport, not least establishing and maintaining a place in the queue. Sardines, mackerel, octopuses, prawns and mullet are overlooked by Jesus on the cross and at least five men who, apart from the one who cuts the swordfish with a cleaver as long as his arm, have ambiguous roles. I take my lead from the locals and use my elbows and eyes, glad that I can almost recite from memory Jenny Baker's wise, almost poetic advice from her book *Simply Fish*. Eyes should be full and bright (not dull and sunken). Body should be firm and springy (not limp and spongy). Skin should be glistening (not dull and dry). Gills should be bright red (not dull or grey). The smell should be of the sea (not fishy). I wish I was as full, bright and firm as a fresh anchovy.

Unlike Scoglitti market, where you have to buy three, in Gela you can buy just one kilogram, but no less. Unless you're a really early riser, the sun always catches up with you in summer; oily fish deteriorate more quickly than a pale Englishwoman in August's searing heat. Anchovies and sardines do not demand fussy preparation and fanciful cooking as I once thought, but they do require some speed. Get home, clean them and cook them by the end of the day. Sardines and anchovies are cleaned in more or less the same way, which is called the *linguetta* (little tongue) style in Sicily. For sardines you need to scrape away the scales, which you can do with your finger under running water. Pull off the head and the fins, but not the tail, then use your finger to slit open the belly and remove the guts, if they haven't already come away with the head. Holding the fish belly upwards, use your fingers to open out the body like a butterfly, then use a fingernail to ease out the spine. Rinse away any extraneous bits and bones, then pat it dry and lay it open, skin-side down, like a fleshy butterfly until you are ready to use it.

We should eat more oily fish! It was a campaign in the early 1980s, at least by my grandma Phyllis, although she meant the contents of tins. I have a real soft spot for a night in with a tin of sardines on toast or on pasta. Plentiful, cheap, sustainable,

fiddly but rewarding, Rome's anchovies and Gela's mackerel and sardines have made an oily-fish eater of me. Frying them deeply into curls or pan-frying them until burnished are particularly good ways to cook both; grilled over charcoal too, served with boiled potatoes, green sauce and a warm night. Both anchovies and sardines are delicious marinated. You need very fresh, scrupulously cleaned fillets, which you sprinkle with a confetti of finely chopped garlic, lemon zest, parsley and chilli, then cover with a mixture of 2:1 olive oil and lemon juice. Anchovies and sardines can also be baked, stirred into a pasta sauce or rolled up like little fat birds.

Alici impanate
Deep-fried anchovies

Serves 4–6

500g fresh anchovies
100g fine dried breadcrumbs
   or polenta
oil, for frying, such as olive,
   groundnut or sunflower
lemon wedges, to serve
salt and freshly ground
   black pepper

It is often a nice moment when you realize that something you do often has become a ritual. Children, habitual and observant, are often the ones who confirm this, reminding you that buying new school shoes should always be followed, regardless of the season, by an ice cream, that a particular walk means a particular drink at a particular bar, that Thursday is pizza night, that on Friday you fry (and hope said child conks out). I have no fear of frying, with door and beer open and hair in a shower cap. I use a small pan, which means I don't need too much oil for it to be 7–8cm deep. You want it to reach 175°C or, for those of us who can't find the thermometer, the point when a cube of bread dances around and takes 30 seconds to turn golden.

There are various ways to prepare anchovies for frying. You can leave them naked, or dip them in seasoned flour or a light batter, or you can dip them in fine breadcrumbs, which means they darken to deep gold and put on a crisp coat, a pleasing contrast to the tender fish within. If the oil is hot enough, the fillets will take a less than a minute to crisp and curl, at which point you need to scoop them out with a slotted spoon, drain them on kitchen paper, spritz them with lemon and eat them as quickly as possible. While you have hot oil, why not make some *panelle* (see page 316) too?

Clean the anchovies as described on page 256, making sure you wash and pat them dry carefully. Put the breadcrumbs on a plate and season them with salt and pepper, then drag the fish through the breadcrumbs. Bring the oil to frying point and fry in small batches, lifting them out as soon as they are deep gold. Drain on kitchen paper, sprinkle with salt and serve with wedges of lemon.

Pasta con sugo e alici fresche
Pasta with fresh anchovy and tomato sauce

Serves 4

500g fresh anchovies

400g large or cherry tomatoes, roughly chopped, or 24 small ones

1 garlic clove

6 tablespoons extra-virgin olive oil, plus extra to serve

100ml dry white wine

a handful of flat-leaf parsley, finely chopped

500g spaghetti, farfalle, penne or paccheri

salt and freshly ground black pepper

There are two ways to make this, which you could argue is actually two recipes, in which case you have two for one! The first way starts with the anchovies, then there is wine and a simmer before adding the tomatoes for the last few minutes so they are just cooked through. The anchovies collapse completely and benefit from the boozy simmer, and the tomatoes, despite adding flavour, feel more like a garnish. The other way (my favourite), is tomatoes first and then, once they have become a rich red sauce, you add the anchovies to poach in it. Of course, the fillets break up when you stir them in, but you still find nice pieces ensnared by the pasta. I peel the tomatoes, because although I have no problem with skins on most occasions, here I think it is nice to have a more unbothered sauce, and peeling is no trouble if you have the pan of water for the pasta.

Both methods make excellent use of the tomatoes' acidic companionship for the almost-milky, well-flavoured flesh of the anchovies. Be bold but wise with the salt and pepper – it brings out the flavours. This could also be made with sardines, but don't tell my fishmonger in Rome.

Clean the anchovies as described on page 256. Bring a large pan of water to the boil for the pasta, which you can also use to peel the tomatoes, if you like. Plunge them into the boiling water for 20 seconds, then into cold water, at which point the skins should slip away.

To follow the first method, gently crush the garlic, but keep it in one piece, if you want a milder flavour, or finely chop it if you want a stronger garlic flavour. In a large frying or sauté pan, warm the olive oil, then add the garlic and fry it very gently until it is lightly golden and fragrant, but make sure it doesn't brown.

Add the anchovies to the oil in the pan and fry them for 2 minutes, or until the flesh is white, then add the wine and simmer for 5 minutes. Add the tomatoes and parsley and season with salt and pepper, then cook for 5 minutes, squashing the tomatoes with a spoon, until the anchovies are barely cooked.

To follow the second method, add the tomatoes to the pan, and cook, stirring, for 10 minutes, or until they are very soft and collapsed. Add the wine and let the pan bubble, sprinkle over the parsley and place the anchovies over the top. Let them poach gently until the flesh is white. If it is ready before the pasta, you can pull the pan off the heat and then reheat it gently.

Meanwhile, add salt to the boiling water, stir it and add the pasta. Cook it until al dente. Drain the pasta and add it to the saucepan, stir and divide it between bowls, making sure everyone gets enough sauce.

Pasta con le sarde
Pasta with sardines and wild fennel

Serves 4

500g fresh sardines
a large bunch of wild fennel
    greens
1 large onion
50g currants
6 tablespoons extra-virgin olive
    oil, plus extra for frying
8 anchovy fillets
150ml tomato sauce (see page
    32 or 36; optional)
50g pine nuts
500g bucatini, spaghetti or
    casarecce
200g dried or soft breadcrumbs
salt and freshly ground
    black pepper

After early spring rain, wild fennel can be found on the steep banks of the Tevere river near Ponte Testaccio. We know because one day while out for a walk, we saw a figure crouching in the distance. As he straightened, we could see he was wearing a cap and holding a bunch of green. Vincenzo knew immediately: he was a Sicilian collecting wild fennel. You have to hunt for it, pulling apart the undergrowth like closed curtains to find the young plant reaching hopefully for the light. The wayward cousin of bulb fennel, wild fennel has a slightly swollen white stem from which shoot tufts of feathery fronds. Pick a piece and stroke your cheek – it feels almost silky, its young colour an optimistic green that darkens as it grows older. The scent is grassy and fragrant, the flavour a very pronounced version of the wispy fronds you find on fennel bulbs: pure aniseed and a touch of bitterness.

Rome is one thing, Sicily another. Around the feast of San Giuseppe on 19 March, the island is covered in edible weeds, including soft tufts of wild fennel that people still collect to eat and store for the winter. Left unpicked, the fennel grows into wiry bushes that eventually shoot up into giant plants with lacy, umbrella-like heads filled with seeds, which are also collected. Many other plants masquerade as fennel, so you need to know what you are looking for and and where to look. Salvatore, one of the caretakers at my friend Fabrizia Lanza's cooking school, is a sort of wild fennel diviner who knows where and when. Fabrizia herself, like her wild-herb-loving mother Anna, is a protector of traditional recipes and the use of defining Sicilian flavours, most notably Palermo's iconic *pasta con le sarde*, a dish that brings the economic wealth of the sea and land together, binds it with tomato and stirs it though pasta. There is a legend that says that, having landed on the beach at Mazara del Vallo in southwest Sicily, Euphemis of Messina ordered his cooks to look around for what they could find to eat. The hillside provided them with wild fennel, raisins and pine nuts, the sea with fish, and using these things the cooks created this dish. It is a pleasing legend, which, whether true or not, ties the dish to a place and time and reminds us of the riches that once thrived – and still thrive – in Sicily.

In traditional recipes, the wild fennel is boiled to eliminate some of the bitterness, then cooked with tomato and currants, which lend sweetness. Even so, wild fennel is a uncompromising flavour, combined with the tender flesh of the sardines. Traditionally, long pasta is used and the dish is finished with toasted breadcrumbs. It's one of the things I look forward to most when I visit Fabrizia's school, and the first thing I order when we go for lunch at Piccola Napoli or the perennially rowdy Ferro di Cavallo trattoria in Palermo.

I am usually reluctant to give recipes that require difficult-to-find ingredients such as this one, but I include it here as an important and, I hope, inspiring recipe that might spur improvisation. You can make a good variation with ordinary bulb fennel: just slice it thinly and then blanch it, then simmer it in the sauce. I also make a storecupboard version, otherwise known as a night in with tin of sardines, again with very finely sliced bulb fennel and anchovy breadcrumbs. Or perhaps you will choose to make a mental note for when you go to Palermo and order a plateful for yourself.

Clean the sardines as described on page 256. Trim away any particularly tough, dry or damaged parts of the fennel and wash it thoroughly. Bring a large pan of salted water to the boil, add the fennel and cook it for 5 minutes, then lift it out with tongs and set it aside, reserving the water for cooking the pasta. Roughly chop the blanched fennel.

Thinly slice the onion and soak the currants in a little warm water to plump them. Warm the olive oil in a deep frying or sauté pan over a medium-low heat and gently fry the onion until soft. Add the anchovies and stir until they have disintegrated into the onion. Set 4 sardines aside for a garnish if you want to, then add the rest to the pan, along with the tomato sauce, if you are using it, and the blanched fennel. Cook for 10 minutes, stirring every now and then; the sardines will break up. Drain and squeeze the currants and add them to the pan along with the pine nuts, then cook for a few minutes more.

Bring the pan of water back to the boil, add the pasta and stir. Cook it until al dente. While the pasta is cooking, toast the breadcrumbs in a small pan with a little olive oil and season with a little salt and pepper, then tip them into a bowl. Now, if you have reserved any sardines, use the same pan and fry them in a little olive oil, turning them carefully so as not to break them.

Drain the pasta, then either add it to the saucepan, stir it and serve from there, putting a fried sardine on top of each bowl and handing round the breadcrumbs separately. Alternatively, put half the sauce in a large, warmed shallow serving bowl, tip the pasta on top, cover with the rest of the sauce and toss gently. Place the fried sardines on top, scatter over the breadcrumbs and serve.

Sarde a beccafico
Sardines stuffed like little birds

Serves 4

16 fresh sardines (about 800g)
6 tablespoons extra-virgin
   olive oil
2–4 preserved anchovy fillets
150g dried breadcrumbs
25g currants, plumped in hot
   water then squeezed dry
25g pine nuts
2 tablespoons finely chopped
   flat-leaf parsley
grated zest and juice of ½ lemon
1 clove garlic, very finely
   chopped (optional)
16 bay leaves
½ orange
salt

Beccare means to peck, and *fico* fig, and a *beccafico* is a small Italian songbird that grows plump and sweet on a diet of sun-ripened figs. The idea is that sardines, when rolled around a breadcrumb stuffing with the tips of their tails mimicking a beak, look rather like the plump, fig-eating bird.

These are real nostalgia food for Sicilians, the combination of ingredients – fish, breadcrumbs, bay, citrus – providing a heady, scented reminder of another home, an idealized one perhaps, all tucked up in a dish. It does look charming with the tails and tips of leaves peeking out. Some people also add a piece of orange along with the bay leaf. Like the baked anchovies, the dish steams below and bakes above, getting a slightly crisp top. There are many ways to make them, but this is the way that works for me. Sardines are a faff to fillet, but worth it.

Preheat the oven to 180°C/160°C fan/gas mark 4 and grease a small baking dish with oil. Clean the sardines as described on page 256.

Prepare the filling by warming 2 tablespoons of the oil over a low heat in a frying pan. Add the anchovies and stir until they disintegrate, then add the breadcrumbs and toast them for a minute or two, stirring constantly. Remove the pan from the heat and add the currants, pine nuts, parsley, a little lemon zest, the garlic if you are using it and 2 more tablespoons oil. Mix thoroughly.

Open a sardine and place it skin-side down, then put a heaped teaspoonful of the filling on it and roll it up towards the tail. Place it in the baking dish so that the tail is pointing upwards. Repeat the process with the rest of the sardines, alternating them with bay leaves, making sure they are tucked in neatly so they can't unroll. Squeeze over the orange and lemon juice, zig-zag over the remaining oil, season with a pinch of salt and bake for 10 minutes. Serve hot, warm or at room temperature.

Timballo di alici
Baked anchovies with breadcrumbs

Serves 4

extra-virgin olive oil
500g fresh anchovies, cleaned
100g soft breadcrumbs from
   day-old bread
2 tablespoons chopped
   flat-leaf parsley
grated zest of 1 unwaxed lemon
salt and freshly ground
   black pepper

This one of my mother-in-law's specialities, although (unlike many Sicilian home cooks I know, who possess an inherent confidence, almost arrogance, about their home cooking) Carmela never believes us when we tell her how delicious her *timballo* is. The anchovies are arranged in a tin like the spokes of a bike wheel, topped with a mixture of breadcrumbs, lemon zest and parsley and zig-zagged with olive oil. Simple. The topping crisps and protects the fish, which bake and steam gently underneath. I use a shallow metal tart tin, which gets hot quickly and means that the timballo needs a matter of minutes in the oven. Serve it with bread and a green salad, or an orange and fennel salad (see page 166).

Preheat the oven to 180°C/160°C fan/gas mark 4. Grease a metal tin (I use an old cake tin around 30cm in diameter) lightly with olive oil, then arrange the anchovies as if they were the overlapping spokes of a wheel, making two layers if necessary. In a bowl, mix the breadcrumbs, parsley and lemon zest and season them with salt and pepper. Sprinkle the mixture evenly over the fillets, then zig-zag with more olive oil. Bake in the middle of the oven for 12–15 minutes.

Eggs

Ideally there are always two half-dozen cartons of eggs in the kitchen. I don't mind if one carton is already open – I feel reassured by the sight of one in progress and one in reserve, and the knowledge that if all else fails, at least we have eggs, and therefore a meal.

'Eggs are in deep trouble. Take care when buying them,' wrote Jane Grigson in 1974. They are in just as deep now, with production ever more intensive and labels often misleading, so we have to take even more care, especially those of us who live in cities and aren't lucky enough to know the hens our eggs come from. Take care, ask questions, be fussy and read boxes: there are bad and good eggs out there. We usually get eggs from our butcher, who gets them from the farm that supplies him with chickens. Occasionally, my friend Cinzia gives us eggs from her friend's chickens in her home town of Velletri, about 45 minutes north of Rome. She messages on her way back, *ho uova per te*, I have eggs for you. So I walk up the road to collect them, safely wrapped in a neat packet made from a series of clever folds. Back home, it is usually Luca who unwraps them: *careful, careful,* he whispers. I am never absolutely sure I believe him.

A smooth, perfect oval; all eggs are beautiful, even those born in circumstances that don't bear thinking about. Fresh eggs, though, from chickens that have run, flapped and pecked at grains, worms and kitchen scraps, have textures, colours and speckles that are a joy to behold. You really have to crack Cinzia's eggs to break them. A decisive tap with a knife blade is best for the shell that cracks rather than collapses. Because the eggs are so fresh, the plump white clings protectively to the yolk, which is more reddy-orange than yellow, a colour that explains why in Italian the yolk is called *il rosso*, the red. Whip these with sugar over the heat and your *zabaione* will be the colour of a desert sunrise. At my parents' house in Dorset too, where the kids collect eggs from the coop, the deeply coloured yolks are a thing of beauty. During his recent trip to Dorset,

Vincenzo pricked a just-collected egg, made a pin hole in the top of it, threw back his head and drank the egg through the hole, something he used to do in Sicily as a boy. The expression about teaching your grandmother to suck eggs finally made sense. I was not tempted.

Eggs are accomplished things, multi-talented in fact. They can be the star, possibly taking you by surprise; Sicilians love to hide eggs in baked pasta or at the heart of a meat roll called *braciole* (see page 223). They are just as happy to co-star, share a plate or be the supporting player without whom the whole thing might fall apart. Eggs emulsify, enrich, bind and even whip themselves into peaks. Quite simply, eggs are marvellous.

They are also the ultimate fast food, an exercise in simplicity and pure flavour. Boil, crack, beat: a four-minute boiled egg with bread, butter, salt and lots of black pepper could well be my perfect meal. Nothing else feels so complete. A three-minute fried egg, possibly with a slice of prosciutto draped over at the last moment so that the fat melts into the yolk. A 45-second omelette, maybe with herbs, rolled or folded and eaten with a glass of wine. And then there is the faithful answer to the Sunday night question: what are we going to eat?

Uova con pomodori
Red eggs

Serves 4

4 ripe tomatoes
4 tablespoons olive oil
4 large eggs
a pinch of dried oregano
   or some ripped basil
salt and freshly ground
   black pepper

Red eggs is the answer for my nearly-5-year-old. For me too, when tomatoes are in season with a good balance of sweet and acidic. It is a set of moves I know well: grab your pan by the handle. Peel your tomatoes if you like, then chop them, or if they are really soft, crush them with your hands, then fry them in olive oil with a pinch of salt, which hastens the water away. Add lightly beaten eggs and fry neatly or messily, seasoning with more salt and pepper and some herbs if you wish. Bring the pan to the table with bread and tell everyone to tuck in. It goes without saying that some salted ricotta on top is nice.

If you can be bothered, peel the tomatoes by plunging them into boiling water for 30 seconds, then into cold water, at which point the skins should pull away easily. Chop the tomatoes roughly. In a large frying pan, warm the olive oil, then add the tomatoes and cook for a few minutes, stirring every now and then, until the water has evaporated and the tomatoes are saucy.

Beat the eggs with the herbs and season them with salt and pepper. Now you have two options. Either scrape the tomatoes from the pan into the eggs, wipe the pan clean, warm some more oil and pour in the tomatoes and eggs, then cook them into a firm frittata. Turn it by inverting it on to a plate, then returning it to the pan. Alternatively, pour the eggs over the tomatoes in the pan, stir with a fork and cook, with no worries about turning it, until you have something that looks like scrambled eggs.

Mozzarella in carrozza
Mozzarella in a carriage

Serves 2

4 slices of white bread,
    crusts removed
100g mozzarella, at room
    temperature, sliced
2 large eggs
olive oil and butter, for frying
salt and freshly ground
    black pepper

This is often the answer. It is somewhere between eggy bread, fried bread and a grilled cheese sandwich. I make it for a late supper when I'm alone, or for the three of us for a early meal, possibly with a tea-towel apron in front of the TV. As is the case with most simple things, a little bit of care goes a long way: cut the crusts off the bread, beat the eggs properly with a fork, then season them boldly. I fry in a mixture of olive oil and butter, which I heat until hot but not smoking before carefully lowering in the sandwich to fry first on one side, then the other. The carriage is ready when it has a burnished golden crust and the mozzarella has melted obligingly to the edges. It is not only more delicious with good, milky *mozzarella di bufala*, but also neater too, as the moisture in the cheese helps everything stay together. If your mozzarella isn't as milky as you'd like, try Anna del Conte's trick of dipping the sandwich first (quickly) in milk, then in flour before the egg coating. A couple of anchovies make a very delicious addition.

Make sandwiches from the bread and mozzarella, making sure the cheese is evenly distributed but just short of the edges. Press the sandwiches together gently and cut each one in half. In a soup dish, beat the eggs with a fork and season them with salt and pepper. In a frying pan, warm 1 tablespoon olive oil and small knob of butter over a medium heat. Working one sandwich at a time, dip one side, then the other, purposefully in the egg, then fry on each side until crisp and golden. Remove and drain on kitchen paper. Eat before frying the second sandwich.

Uova trippate
Eggs cooked like tripe

Serves 4

8 eggs
1 heaped tablespoon finely
    grated Parmesan
1 heaped tablespoon finely
    chopped flat-leaf parsley
butter or olive oil, for frying
500ml tomato sauce
    (see page 32 or 36)
salt and freshly ground
    black pepper

A variation on the egg and tomato theme. This time, the eggs are made into thin omelettes first, which are then sliced into fat ribbons and stirred into the sauce. For those familiar with the Roman dish of honeycomb tripe cooked in tomato sauce with mint, you will recognize the similarity both in method and appearance – hence the name. This is a bit more work than red eggs, and easily dismissed, perhaps, as nursery food, but it is really good.

In a large bowl, beat the eggs lightly with a fork, add the Parmesan, parsley, a little salt and a few grinds of black pepper.

Make 3 omelettes. Warm a little butter or olive oil in a small frying pan over a medium heat, then add a third of the egg

mixture and swirl it round, using a wooden spoon to ease it away from the edges, until it has set. Flip it over and cook the other side, then slide it on to a plate. Repeat to make two more. Once the omelettes are cool, roll them loosely, then cut them into 1cm-thick strips. Warm the tomato sauce, add the strips, stir gently, and serve with bread and a crisp salad to follow.

La stracciatella
Egg drop soup

Serves 4

1.2 litres good-quality
   chicken stock or broth
3 large eggs
3 tablespoons semolina
3 tablespoons grated Parmesan
1 tablespoon finely chopped
   flat-leaf parsley
a little grated nutmeg

A Roman classic. This is a curious soup, the semolina, eggs and cheese curdling into a tangle of *stracci* (little rags), which are suspended in the soup. It is, though, straightforward to make and absolutely delicious and soothing, nourishing too. Whenever I have chicken broth I try to save a little so I can make myself a bowl of this.

Set aside about 250ml of the chicken stock and pour the rest into a large pan. Bring it to a gentle boil. In a bowl, whisk together the eggs, semolina, Parmesan, parsley, a grating of nutmeg and the reserved cold stock. Pour the egg mixture into the gently simmering stock and whisk vigorously for 30 seconds, then reduce the heat to low and continue cooking, whisking every now and then, for another 4 minutes or so. Serve immediately, either from a large soup tureen or directly from the pan.

Eggs baked in greens

Serves 4–6

600g chard or spinach
50g flour
500ml milk
1 bay leaf
50g butter, plus extra for
    greasing
1 onion studded with 3 cloves
50g Parmesan, grated
a small handful of breadcrumbs
6 large eggs
salt and freshly ground
    black pepper

You can make this with bright, deep-green chard with great fleshy stems, or spinach. The greens are steamed and mixed with a well-seasoned béchamel, which makes it rather like creamed spinach, in which you make holes and then bake eggs.

Wash the chard and cut the stems off the leaves, trimming off any tough ends and pulling away any stringy bits. Cut the stems into short lengths, then roll the leaves into cigars and chop them roughly. Bring a large pan of water to the boil and add some salt. Add the stems first and boil for a few minutes, add the leaves and boil for a few minutes more, or until tender, then drain.

Put the milk in a pan along with the bay leaf and onion, warm it a little and then leave it to sit for 30 minutes. Melt the butter in a heavy pan, stir in the flour and cook for 2 minutes, until it is a sticky paste that comes away from the sides of the pan, without allowing it to brown. Remove the bay leaf and onion and then, over a very low heat, pour the milk gradually into the paste, whisking constantly. Increase the heat a little and bring the sauce to simmering point, whisking, until the sauce thickens to the consistency of thick double cream. Turn down the heat and let the sauce simmer gently for 20 minutes. Stir in all but a small handful of the grated Parmesan, taste and season with salt and pepper.

Preheat the oven to 180°C/160°C fan/gas mark 4. Grease an ovenproof dish with butter and dust it with breadcrumbs. Mix the chard with the béchamel, pour it into the dish and use a spoon to make 6 holes in the mixture. Carefully break an egg into each hole. Bake for 30 minutes, then let it sit for 10 minutes and eat it warm.

Summer salad of farro, eggs, tuna and capers

Serves 4

250g farro
50g capers in salt
4 eggs
1 small red onion or 2 shallots
3 ripe tomatoes or 12 cherry
 tomatoes
a handful of basil
200g tuna in olive oil, drained
100g black olives
extra-virgin olive oil
salt and freshly ground
 black pepper

I considered giving farro its own chapter, so useful and good is this sturdy grain. A early form of wheat, farro (sometimes called emmer wheat) was a staple grain in early Roman times, thanks to its high protein content, vitamins and slow release of energy. It is often confused with spelt, which is also wheat but a different variety, although the two are often interchangeable. Roman soldiers marched on farro, I tell my chip-, ketchup- and legionnaire-loving son, which works, miraculously. Farro is a stalwart grain, and looks a bit like plump brown rice, and it has a truly pleasant taste: mild, nutty and chewy. If you buy it polished and cracked (often labelled as quick-cook), it needs no soaking and cooks in about 20 minutes.

In winter I use farro in bean soups in much the same way I would use pasta, adding it towards the end of cooking so that it swells and absorbs the flavours. Farro pairs especially well with borlotti beans and lentils, and you could add a handful to the Sicilian lentil soup (see page 326). It is summer now, though, with its long, slow days and indecisive appetites, and farro comes into its own in the form of a salad that can be eaten either now or later, and could stand alone or sit alongside a lamb chop, and be made to go a bit further with extra ingredients if more guests turn up. With farro as your base, anything goes. Eggs and tuna are favourites, along with capers, tomatoes, olives perhaps, some chopped red onion, which makes it a sort of farro Niçoise, I suppose.

Rinse and drain the farro, then put it in a pan, cover it with about 7cm water, add a pinch of salt and bring to the boil. Reduce the heat to a simmer and cook for 15–20 minutes, or until the farro is tender but still has some bite. Drain and set aside.

Meanwhile, soak the capers in cold water for 10 minutes, then drain and chop them. Hard-boil the eggs, then drain and peel them when cool enough. Finely dice the onion and roughly chop the tomatoes. Tear the basil into little pieces.

Put the farro in a large bowl, add all the other ingredients except the egg, season with salt, pour over some olive oil and toss very well. Halve or quarter the eggs and put them on top. Serve, ideally while the farro is still slightly warm.

Mayonnaise

Makes 8 generous servings

2 egg yolks, at room temperature
300ml extra-virgin olive oil
(or half olive and half
sunflower or groundnut oil)
juice of ½ lemon or dab of
Dijon mustard
salt

I use extra-virgin olive oil for everything, including mayonnaise, which makes it green tinted and strongly flavoured, the very thought of which brings some people out in hives. You can use half olive and half a neutral oil, it's up to you. I also make it by hand, because I enjoy it. This is a task made easier by an olive oil jug with a very thin spout, a patient pourer (Vincenzo), and a small bowl that is heavy enough to stay still without holding it. I adore mayonnaise with lemony chicken and plainly roasted fish. I am heavy-handed with the lemon.

In a heavy bowl, start whisking the egg yolks with a generous pinch of salt. After a few minutes, when the yolks are thick and sticky, start adding the oil very gradually – by very gradually I mean drop by drop at first, and then a very thin stream. Do not rush, and keep whisking as you add the oil.

Keep adding the oil until the mayonnaise seizes into a very thick ointment; at this point you can relax and add the oil in a slightly thicker stream. Keep whisking until you have a smooth, silky and firm mayonnaise. You may not need to add all the oil. Add a few drops of lemon juice or a dab of mustard, whisk, taste and then, if necessary a few drops more. Add salt as you wish.

Zabaione
Zabaglione

Serves 4

6 egg yolks
80g sugar
grated zest of ½ unwaxed
    lemon (optional)
100–200ml dry Marsala
    or strong coffee,
    according to taste

Recipes, like people, are easily put into categories. I had filed *zabaione* in the fussy dinner party category, along with puff pastry starters and anything with a glazed sauce or served *à l'orange*; it was a pudding that would most likely be whipped up by a rather capable woman who had spent time in Italy, then done a cooking course at Leith's School of Food and Wine. I knew it was a light custard, and therefore might split, and somewhere along the line I had picked up the idea that you need a copper bowl.

It was Vincenzo one Saturday morning, whisking up egg yolks and sugar in the milk pan like his grandmother used to do it in Sicily, who changed my perception. Suddenly the glamorous hostess has a vest on and is listening to Pino Daniele. We ate it for breakfast with shots of espresso and sponge fingers.

You don't need a copper bowl or a bain marie, just a heatproof bowl balanced over some hot water. Whisking steadily, you will see the air being incorporated and the *zabaione* expanding like a marvellous hole filler. It is indeed a great pudding for a dinner party, made performance-style in front of your guests. I also sometimes make it the day before and serve it cold, by which time it has settled and thickened. It is also nice for breakfast, in which case take the coffee option, or maybe not. The addition of lemon with coffee may seem odd, but it works, the zest lending its clean, incomparable scent to the rich, aerated pudding – in the same way, perhaps, as a curl of lemon zest in an espresso is said to cure a headache and lift the spirits. I have seen recipes for *zabaione* with 200g sugar for 6 eggs, but 80g is more than enough for me. Of course, sugar is a personal thing, as is the amount of Marsala or coffee.

Put the egg yolks, sugar and lemon zest, if using, in a heatproof bowl that will fit neatly over a pan, then whisk vigorously until the mixture is pale, frothy and has almost doubled in volume.

Put a little water in a pan, bring it to the boil, then reduce the

heat so that it is barely simmering. Set the bowl over the top – it must not touch the water – and start whisking.

Once the egg and sugar mixture has thickened into a custard, begin adding the Marsala or coffee gradually, whisking as you do so, until the mixture is richly yellow, thick and creamy. Remove from the heat and allow to cool. To serve, pour it into glasses or little bowls.

Brutti ma buoni
Ugly-but-good biscuits

Makes 50-60

250g hazelnuts

150g egg whites (usually about 4 large eggs, but don't worry if you are slightly over or under)

200g caster sugar

There is always a great trayful of these on the bottom shelf behind the glass counter in our local bakery in Rome. Ugliness, like beauty, is in the eye of the beholder, and I have never thought these biscuits *brutti*. I find their bumps and knobbles charming and I am a great lover of hazelnuts, dense and buttery, sweet and abiding, especially when ground into flour for crumbles and biscuits – these being the very best biscuits, a bit crisp and a bit chewy. If you grind the hazelnuts finely you get a more compact biscuit, and if you chop them coarsely they are more like nut clusters. There are various ways to make these Roman favourites; this version involves cooking the mixture twice, first in a pan, which thickens the mixture, then in a low oven, like meringues, which gives them a crisp, dry outside and tender centre.

Preheat the oven to 130°C/110°C fan/gas mark 1. If you are using whole hazelnuts, toast them briefly in the oven, then grind them to a flour in a food processor, or chop them by hand.

Using a balloon whisk or electric beaters, beat the egg whites until they are pure white and stand in stiff peaks. Using a metal spoon, fold in the sugar, then the cooled hazelnuts.

Transfer the mixture to a heavy-based pan over a low heat. You want the mixture to thicken, so cook gently, stirring and scraping the mixture from the sides, for about 10 minutes.

Use 2 teaspoons to make small walnut-sized mounds of mixture on a baking tray lined with baking parchment. Bake for 40 minutes, or until pale and crisp on the outside and chewy in the centre.

Ricotta

The moon may not be made of cheese, but cheese can look like the moon. The round, rippled mass of curds, with its pool-like craters filled with whey, creates a lunar landscape when sheep's milk is turned into cheese. We arrived at just the right moment: cheese tourists gathering around a vat the size of a tractor wheel, to look at the moon. I have stood in that white-tiled room, in a square modern building in the middle of a sheep farm in central Sicily, many times, and each time I am surprised by the way the air, thick with steam and sweetly lactic, clings to your skin and fills your nostrils, how the room feels like a warm and milky surgery. Having waited for us to arrive, Filippo, the sheep farmer, lifts a spoonful of curds on to a plastic plate, which sags at the weight, and sets it aside. Then, using a metal pole, he breaks our gathered silence as he cuts the curds with a slashing movement and lets the whey drain away with a sucking gurgle, leaving pure white, almost-dry curds. The amount Filippo can cup in his hands is impressive: 15cm piles of curds lifted and pressed by hand into perforated white plastic baskets. Once full, each basket is pressed again before being flipped and inverted into another basket, revealing deep imprints. This new-born cheese is *tuma*. When lightly salted, which sharpens its flavour, it becomes *primo sale* (first salt). Both are mild in flavour but unmistakably sheepish. With further salting and time, the *primo sale* becomes pecorino, which will be aged for three, six or twelve months, or possibly more, depending on demand.

Now for the ricotta. The vat of cloudy, faintly yellow leftover whey is enriched with a little more whole sheep's milk, which is *ri-cotta* (re-cooked) until it curdles again. This takes time, and Filippo stirs rhythmically as he has done for nearly 50 years, his intuitive movements based on a lifetime of experience. He continues uninterrupted, even when his phone rings, and he wedges it under his chin to talk to his wife. Eventually, curds appear, loose like scattered clouds scudding across a pale milky sky. Once the ricotta is ready, he moves quickly, this time using a slotted spoon to lift it into smaller baskets, setting aside another plateful for us to taste.

The first plateful of curds that Filippo set aside contains *cagliata*, which comes from the word *caglio* (rennet), so you could translate *cagliata* as 'coagulated', which always make me think of grammar lessons and verbs. Sitting on the plate, the *cagliata* is smooth and silky, its texture like softly set blancmange and its taste delicate and sweet. The second plateful is what Vincenzo's family call *ricuttedda*, or *ricotta con sieru,* an almost soupy curd of ricotta in even thinner whey. Both are the very definition of ephemeral, food that couldn't travel much further than plate to mouth. You need a spoon. Tasting helped me to understand what Vincenzo had been talking about for all these years, the reason he would stand on the steps of his grandmother's house waiting for the ricotta man to pass on his bike, which was slung with horn-like wicker cones, called *cavagna,* filled with fresh, piping-hot ricotta. The kids would have a bowl into which the man would pour the ricotta and they would drink it there and then, throwing their heads back, or pour it over bread.

Very few shepherds still work the way Filippo Privitera does. He is a shepherd, worker, craftsman and alchemist, transforming milk and rennet into cheese. With only two Ukrainian helpers, he looks after 300 sheep, milking them by hand twice a day, for 365 days a year, in order to make his cheese and ricotta this way, as it has been made for centuries. Filippo is supported fiercely by my friend, the food writer Fabrizia Lanza, who sees protecting him and the techniques passed down through generations as an imperative. His cheese is bought by Fabrizia's family and used at her cooking school and winery, but it is not valued in the same way by many locals – another example of the complicated relationship Sicilians have with their culinary heritage. Filippo points to a *Wall Street Journal* article about him in a plastic folder pinned to the wall, as proud of it as he is about his cheese. He is also proud of his son, who comes into the room at one point to say hello. He has no interest in carrying on his father's work. We drive back to Fabrizia's, the ricotta in a white tray balanced on my knees and keeping them warm.

Until the 1970s there were dozens of Filippos in Gela. Vincenzo terrifies and delights Luca with his stories of being sent down the steps at the end of via Mazzini to see the

toothless local shepherd and collect cheese and milk. The house in front, or rather the remains of the house in front, was formerly home to a family of eight, who also kept sheep on the ground floor of their house. Occasionally they too would give Vincenzo's grandmother cheese in exchange for wheat and tomatoes. She would salt the cheese in the cellar, which would see them through the winter. Times and habits were changing anyway in Sicily in the 1960s, but the construction of the oil refinery in Gela accelerated change, and ricotta production was industrialized, then complicated by suffocating regulations. Today these factory farms produce decent sheep's milk ricotta, but it is not the same.

Once again, I found the answer in a car boot. I was visiting Rosa's, and a man was sitting on a chair just outside her shop, his face turned up to the sun. Suddenly I was part of what felt like a clandestine cheese deal and followed him across the road to his Fiat Punto. He opened the boot and there it was, that familiar smell, thick and sweetly lactic and ovine. He pulled back several towels to reveal a polystyrene box in which were baskets of ricotta made by his brother, sitting in a sloshing bath of whey. I bought two, and a round of young pecorino studded with black peppercorns. On our way home, we picked up bread from the baker, and Elio from his work in the garage, and then sat at the table eating thick slices of bread with warm ricotta, dried oregano, olives, olive oil and salt (see page 122).

Warm ricotta from a shepherd or a car boot is all very well, but only if you live near the shepherd or the boot, which we don't most of the time. In Rome, though, we can find fine sheep's and cow's milk ricotta. Romans are rightly proud of their ricotta, but it isn't the same as that found further south – it is denser and has always spent longer away from the vat, according to the Sicilian. I enjoy both. I also have no problem with the stuff in tubs. Certainly it is a very different sort of ricotta, usually made from cow's milk and so without that distinctive sheepishness; it is also pasteurized, which imparts a different flavour and a fine, smooth texture. But the tubs will keep, and they are endlessly useful. They will work for all these recipes if they are the only type you can find.

Ricotta is one of the most hard-working and essential ingredients in our kitchen. It is as useful as an egg, going on bread, on top of vegetables, caponata, greens and potatoes, where it turns them from a side dish into a meal. A slice of ricotta is a good companion for honey, crushed nuts, ripe or poached fruit, all of which are as happy to be pudding as they are breakfast. For a trusty quick supper, while cooking some pasta I mix 250g ricotta with 50g Parmesan and lots of black pepper in a bowl, thinning it with a little starchy pasta-cooking water, then add the cooked pasta. A spoonful of ricotta makes a good addition to pesto, frittata or gnocchi, and is an essential addition to our beloved Sunday lasagne. And the cake, a trusted and beloved one for the baking inhibited, which is made more or less every week: 400g flour, 180g sugar and 2 teaspoons baking powder, mixed with 200ml olive oil, 4 eggs, a 250g tub of ricotta and the zest of 2 lemons, then baked for 50 minutes. It is in my first book, and now here too.

Anelletti con pomodoro, basilico e ricotta
Anelletti with tomato sauce, basil and ricotta

Serves 4

a few sprigs of basil
500ml simple tomato sauce
 (see page 32 or 36)
50g salted ricotta
200g fresh ricotta
500g dried pasta, preferably
 anelletti
freshly ground black pepper

Anelletti means 'little rings', and is the name for a shape of dried pasta much loved in Sicily; it is also the distant cousin – and I won't hear a word said against them – of Heinz' spaghetti hoops. Despite their finger-tip size, anelletti are dense and take a deceptively long time to cook, which is why they are often used for baked pasta, especially moulded *timballi* and stuffed vegetables. They can also be cooked and served with sauce. When I stay with Fabrizia, on the day we visit Filippo, when one of us has travelled back with a plastic tray of warm ricotta on our lap, we have anelletti with tomato, basil and a spoonful of fresh ricotta. It is a patriotic plateful, which you swirl until the creamy pink sauce clings to every ring. We also eat rings and ricotta 500 miles away in Rome, with bags of anelletti brought back from Sicily. You can use other shapes, both long and short; penne and spaghetti work particularly well, I think.

If you have time, put a sprig of basil in the tomato sauce and let it sit for a while. Grate the salted ricotta and mix it with the fresh ricotta, along with a few grinds of black pepper.

Bring a large pan of water to the boil, add salt, stir, then add the pasta. Stir again and cook until al dente. Meanwhile, warm the tomato sauce gently.

Once the pasta is cooked, drain it and add it to the tomato sauce, stir and divide between warm bowls, top with a spoonful of the seasoned ricotta, a thin line of olive oil and a sprig of basil.

Ricotta al forno alle herbe
Baked ricotta with herbs

Serves 4

500g fresh ricotta, drained
a handful of breadcrumbs
100g fresh herbs, such as basil,
    parsley or mint
2 large eggs
50g salted ricotta, Parmesan
    or pecorino, grated
salt and freshly ground
    black pepper

Ricotta is often baked in Sicily – really baked, until the outside has blackened, and inside its dark protective coat the cheese is smoky and firm. This dish is reminiscent of Sicilian baked ricotta, the surface puffing up so that the soft inside pulls away. A few more eggs and it would be considered a frittata, but the ricotta is the star here, along with masses of green herbs – whatever you have, such as parsley, mint, basil, dill or wild fennel. The sweet acidity of a tomato salad would make it a good partner.

You will need an ovenproof dish or cake tin about 23cm in diameter and 4cm deep. Grease it with butter, dust it with breadcrumbs and preheat the oven to 190°C/170°C fan/gas mark 5. Make sure the ricotta is well drained – this is particularly important with the fresh sheep's milk variety – I sit mine in a sieve over the sink for at least an hour, or until it no longer emits a milky residue.

Chop the herbs very finely, then mix them with the ricotta, eggs, grated cheese, salt (you won't need much) and black pepper. Alternatively, you could blend the herbs with 100g ricotta in a food processor, which will give you a smooth, vivid green, then mix in the rest of the ingredients by hand. Scrape the mixture into the prepared tin and bake for 30–40 minutes, or until it has puffed up, seems set and is coming away from the sides of the tin.

Salted ricotta

Fresh ricotta is an ephemeral, perishable thing, especially in Sicily during the summer, when even taking it home to Gela seems detrimental. A way to preserve it is to salt it heavily in order to make *ricotta salata* (salted ricotta). If we bring one thing back to Rome from Sicily, it is this: the symbol of the two kitchens, and for me this was the ingredient that was missing in Italian food: a soft, crumbly sheep's milk cheese that could be put on everything, a gap feta had previously filled.

I wish I had known Vincenzo's grandmother Sara when she was a younger woman; she sounds like a force of nature, a farmer's wife (not that this is all she thought she was) who knew how to preserve everything her husband grew in order to feed her family. By the time I met her, although she still had an infamous appetite and brief moments of absolute lucidity, especially with her grandchildren, a series of strokes had stolen her. His mother, Carmela, has complicated feelings about Gela. Not that she isn't proud of where she came from, but she is sometimes reluctant to talk about it. Her brother Liborio is the keeper of everything, probably because he took much of what he learned from his mother and translated it into his work as a chef. He is not a bit precious, though, howling with laughter at the memory of the boiled aubergines that looked like insoles – he ate enough of them as a boy to last him a lifetime.

It is Liborio, sitting at the kitchen table in Gela, who describes how *nonna* Sara made bread, preserved the tomatoes, reduced the dregs of the wine to must and salted the cheese. He paints a picture of her putting ricotta in box filled with salt, how the liquid drained away and the ricotta, with its ridged edges, hardened first into a texture like damp chalk and then, once the salt and time had done their work, into a hard grating cheese that lasted them well.

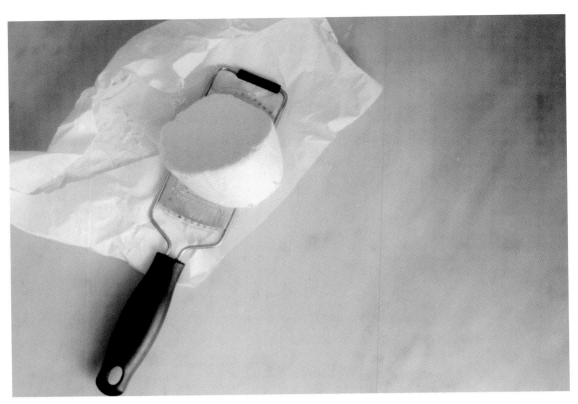

Insalata di pomodoro, cipolla e ricotta salata

Tomato, onion and salted ricotta salad

Serves 4

500g sweet cherry tomatoes
1 large mild, white or red onion
   or several spring onions
a splash of good-quality red
   wine vinegar (optional)
extra-virgin olive oil
100g salted ricotta, grated
salt

I asked for a tomato salad; I was brought what I thought was a plate of cheese. Then I looked closer and saw there were tomatoes and sliced spring onions with a moat of olive oil, hidden under a thick blanket of cheese. The combined taste of sweet cherry tomatoes, mild onions and the salty, creamy cheese, which I first ate in an average trattoria in Catania, was so wonderful I wanted to shout. I still feel much the same, and despite repeated eatings I show no signs of tiring of its charm. It goes well with lamb and the baked ricotta above, but really I just want it on its own.

Cut the tomatoes in half and arrange them in a single layer on a large plate. Thinly slice the onion. If it is strongly flavoured, soak the slices in a mixture of two thirds water and one third vinegar for 10 minutes, then drain. Arrange the onion on top of the tomatoes, sprinkle over a little salt, zig-zag with oil, then cover with a generous layer of salted ricotta.

Ciliegie sciroppate con alloro
Cherries in syrup with bay leaves

'There is always a chance it will explode,' said Gabriella, her almost-smile suggesting that the possibility of cherries, wine and sugar seeping between the terracotta tiles and dripping through her roof was a risk she was prepared to take. We were in Abruzzo, sitting at her table after a very long, very good dinner at their *agriturismo* (farmhouse inn) in the hills near Loreto Aprutino. Before us was a small glass of inky-purple liquid: Gabriella's sour cherry liqueur, made by steeping sour cherries in Montepulciano d'Abruzzo and sugar in a large, teardrop-shaped glass bottle on the roof for 40 days and 40 nights during high summer. As we tried not to slide under the table, I wondered how Gabriella managed to put the bottles on the roof, how she got the steeped cherries out and what she did with them, could I have another glass? One answer came the following morning, when we were served the steeped cherries, wrinkled, dark and boozy, on ricotta.

Nine months later, in Rome, the first of the cherries, some crimson, others deep purple, have splattered the market with colour and we have been eating them greedily by the kilogram, spitting stones into our fists and grabbing another handful in a sort of cherry race. Then, at the small farmers' market in the old slaughterhouse, I found the first of the sour cherries, paler than usual, sweet as much as sour, reminiscent of almonds and almost the wrong side of perfect ripeness.

Back home, I remembered Gabriella's roof and followed my instincts. I put them in a pan, along with a few sweet cherries, bay leaves, red wine and some sugar, then let it all bubble into a fragrant, syrupy, shirt-staining stew. The precise quantities are not important, but as a guideline, for four people I would say 400g pitted cherries, ideally a mixture of sweet and sour, 300ml red wine, 130g sugar and 3 bay leaves. Everything goes in the pan at the same time, is brought slowly to the boil, then reduced to a simmer for about 12 minutes, until the cherries are completely tender. If the sauce is not thick enough, lift the cherries out

and set them aside, reduce the syrup by boiling it until it is the
thickness you like, then return the cherries to the pan. They need
a partner, such as a slice of fresh ricotta; the combination with
soft, creamy cheese, the dark red and the white, is stunning.
Eat them also with mascarpone, Greek yogurt or next to a plain
cake. They will keep for a week in a sealed jar in the fridge.

Ricotta, miele e pistacchi
Ricotta, honey and pistachios

This could be breakfast, in which case bread or toast, on to which you can squash the ricotta, honey and nuts, is essential. Alternatively it is a lovely pudding, possibly with fruit; pears and figs go particularly well. Whip the ricotta with a little milk to make it softer and more spoonable. Honey is as magical as the plants and bees it comes from – always look out for a good local one. Sheep's milk ricotta is ideal, but cow works well too.

Cassata

Sicilian layered sponge, ricotta and marzipan cake

*Serves 10 Sicilians
or 15 non-Sicilians*

For the marzipan
150g blanched almonds
    or ground almonds
150g icing sugar, plus extra
    for rolling
a squeeze of lemon juice
green food colouring

For the sponge cake
5 eggs
200g sugar
150g plain flour
2 teaspoons baking powder
a splash of Marsala or orange
    flower water

For the ricotta filling
400g ricotta, ideally
    sheep's milk
150g caster sugar

For the icing
250g icing sugar
a squeeze of lemon juice
candied fruit, such as orange,
    lemon or pumpkin, to
    decorate

Our lives changed for the better when Sicilia e Duce appeared on via Marmorata. We had been clocking its progress ever since the sign went up on the whitewashed window. Work took a longer than expected, but eventually a proper Sicilian *pasticceria* (pastry shop), run by a Sicilian family, opened 200 metres from our flat in Rome. There was no grand launch; one day the door was simply open, and we were some of the first in, greeted by a warm wave of yeast from the brioche buns on the counter, and next to them, crisp, blistered tubes of fried pastry to be filled with ricotta. The long glass counter was a shrine to Sicilian sweetness, with a dozen or so types of soft almond biscuits, fluted lozenges of quince paste, marzipan fruits, glistening *mini di Agata* (St Agata's breasts with cherry nipples), various deep-fried crescents of pastry filled with ricotta. Then the triumph of the fridge, and sweetness: the cassata.

The word *cassata* comes from the Arabic *qas-ah*, the name for the large terracotta dish with slanting sides which is used to make this, Sicily's most famous cake. It was the Arabs who transformed Sicilian – and European – cooking by introducing Sicilians to the cultivation of sugar cane, and this cake along with it. It is quite something: layers of sponge soaked in alcohol and filled with heavily sweetened ricotta, covered in green marzipan, topped with a sugar glaze and decorated with candied fruit and squash.

For Vincenzo's family, cassata is the preferred cake for every celebration: birthdays, name days, Sundays, family gatherings, births, christenings are all toasted with a sweet slice. It wasn't made at home, though – cassata was bought from the local *pasticceria* and then brought home in a domed paper box, which sat on the sideboard until it was time. I was taught to make cassata by Fabrizia. The most complicated things can be made to feel entirely possible by watching someone, and Fabrizia has it down to an absolute art. Sometimes I know she would rather teach us to make bread or cheese, but we always want the cassata. She rolls the strips of marzipan for the sides with swift and confident movements using a nifty wooden wallpaper border roller, dampens the layer of sponge with bergamot, then cuts the candied fruit with a mandolin. It is bejewelled, arabesque beauty, a Liberace of a cake that laughs in the face of plain cakes being the best – although I do like a nice plain cake. Cassata is a project; ideally you want to to make the sponge and marzipan the day before. Two pairs of hands are nice, as is a glass of Marsala as you cook. It is a spectacular cake.

To assemble the cassata you need a cake or pie tin with sloping sides, about 23cm in diameter and 4cm deep. First, make the marzipan. Grind the almonds in a food processor if you are using whole ones, then mix them with the icing sugar and about 70ml water and a little lemon juice to bring everything together to a soft paste. Knead for 1 minute, then add a few drops of food colouring and knead again until the paste is pale green. Wrap it in clingfilm and set aside.

Next, make the sponge cake. Preheat the oven to 180°C/160°C fan/gas mark 4 and grease and dust with flour a 23cm loose-bottomed cake tin (an ordinary cake tin; not the one with sloping sides). Separate the eggs and beat the yolks in a bowl with the sugar until light and fluffy. Sift the flour and baking powder over the egg and sugar mixture and fold them in. Whisk the egg whites to soft peaks and fold them in too. Pour the mixture into the prepared tin and bake for 20–30 minutes, or until it is golden and a skewer comes out clean. Allow to cool before turning out.

For the filling, the ricotta should be well drained. I put mine in a sieve for at least 1 hour, pressing it gently from time to time, until it is firm and leaves no watery residue when it sits on a plate. Press the drained ricotta through the sieve into a clean bowl so that it is creamy, and beat in the sugar.

Line the cassata tin with clingfilm and dust the worktop with icing sugar. Roll out a long, 5mm-wide strip of marzipan and use it to line the sides of the tin, cutting it to size with a knife and then sealing the join and pressing it into the clingfilm on the sides of the tin. A little patchwork is never a problem as long as you press it carefully.

Using a serrated knife, slice the cake into long 5cm-wide slices and then, trimming them as necessary, make a single, patchwork layer of sponge to cover the bottom of the tin. Sprinkle over a few drops of Marsala or orange flower water. Next, put a thick layer of the ricotta cream over the sponge, using the back of the spoon to even it out. You should use it all. Now arrange another patchwork layer of sponge cake slices on top of the cream and press down gently. Sprinkle over a little more Marsala or orange flower water. Cover with clingfilm and leave to chill for 1 hour.

Make the icing by mixing the icing sugar with a few drops of lemon juice, and water if you need it – it should be dense but still run slowly from the spoon.

Turn the cassata out on to a plate, so that the bottom becomes the top, then carefully pull away the clingfilm. Press the sponge top down gently so that the marzipan provides a tiny lip or edge around a sponge crater; pour in the icing to completely cover the top up to this edge. Allow the icing to set for 30 minutes, then decorate with candied fruit as you wish.

STORECUPBOARD

Chickpeas

Lentils

Preserved anchovies

Flour

Bread

Chickpeas

Every Wednesday morning, Enzo puts several kilograms of dried chickpeas in a large plastic tub that once contained olives, then covers them with cold water. They sit. By Friday morning, the chickpeas are plump, almost double the volume of two days before, and the water is tinted ever-so-slightly yellow. On good days the light floods into that corner of Testaccio market, illuminating the domed glass counter and filtering through the tinted water, making the whole tub radiate sunshine, a Roman tradition alive and glowing. Enzo drains the chickpeas, then puts 250g portions into clear plastic bags, which he spins, knots and piles on top of the counter of the stall he runs with his wife, Lina. Other stalls on the market do the same, many advertising the fact with a *ceci bagnati* (soaked chickpeas) sign sellotaped to their counter. It's the same all over Italy on Fridays, the day on which chickpeas are traditionally eaten, many people still observing the practice of eating a lean, meatless meal.

More often than not, the pre-soaked chickpeas are simmered into almost buttery softness for a soup, which is thickened with pasta. This, *pasta e ceci*, is a dish that sums up the Italian genius for taking the simplest, sustenance-level ingredients and letting time and heat work their everyday alchemy, transforming them into something much greater than the sum of their parts. As in life, with advice and experience we all find our own way: there are as many ways to make *pasta e ceci* as there are cooks. Some are simple survival recipes, literally chickpeas, their broth and pasta; others more complex, with a foundation of carrot, celery and onion, maybe some pork fat, anchovy or rosemary, and may or may not blush with tomato. However it is made, *pasta e ceci* is particularly reassuring and satisfying. Ask a Roman, or a Sicilian for that matter, about their favourite dishes and they might well mention *pasta e ceci*. You can use tinned chickpeas, but soaking and cooking dried chickpeas has benefits: the starchy cooking liquid, rich with nutrients, is the not-so-secret key to giving flavour and body to the final dish.

The first time I saw fresh chickpeas was in a field in the middle of Sicily with my friend, the cookery teacher Fabrizia Lanza. The plant is small with round, slightly feathery leaves. After the flowers come the chickpeas, which develop in small green pods which pop when you press them – really pop, possibly shooting the one or two chickpeas some distance. We burst our pod, which is slightly velvety on the outside, smooth outside and tough – then pulled out the chickpea, small and pale green like a plump hazelnut that ends in a nifty point. Fresh chickpeas taste like creamy, grassy peas with a hint of chestnut. There is an evocative description by Giacomo Castelvetro in his early-seventeenth-century book about the fruit and vegetables of Italy of ladies sitting on doorsteps, waiting for the countrywomen returning from the fields with baskets full of tender, young chickpeas, which the ladies then buy to nibble, just for fun. 'Nibble' is a good word. On another visit to Fabrizia, Mario, a chef at her cooking school, made up a soup of fresh chickpeas and white and sweet Sicilian onion, extra-virgin olive oil and salt. I can still remember the taste.

After a few weeks in the sun, the pods are pale yellow and crisp as a crisp, and you can roll them open in your fingers. The chickpea inside is familiar, yellow and hard. Very recently dried chickpeas don't need that much of a soak back into softness; the older they get, though, the harder they become, which is why you should always look at the date on the packet. Very old, hard nuts, like human hard nuts, will never change their ways, however long you soften and simmer.

For the dried chickpeas that most of us can find, soaking is fundamental. Advice varies as to how long to soak for; Enzo suggests 48 hours, never changing the water. When my eyes went wide, he just laughed and reminded me that once covered, you do nothing, just wait. Enzo's 48-hour chickpeas cook in less than 30 minutes and are always tender as can be. I find 24 is enough, though, and despite being disorganized, I have now got in the habit: a packetful skittled into a bowl last thing at night and left in full view to be cooked the following evening, in time for dinner. Once soaked, the chickpeas need to be covered with fresh water, brought to the boil and then simmered until tender enough to squash easily between your fingers. They can also be baked in the oven: cover the drained chickpeas with two fingers

of water, add a clove of garlic, some sage and olive oil, bring to the boil and bake for 1¼ hours. Freshly cooked chickpeas are rather like creamy chestnuts and will keep for up to 5 days in the fridge, if protected by their cooking water. And when you don't want to soak, chickpeas are the legume that best survives being tinned – in fact, tinned chickpeas are brilliant and I am almost as devoted to them as I am to frozen peas, a tin turned into soup, blended into a sort of houmous or simmered with some simple tomato sauce being particular faithfuls.

Pasta chi ciciri
Pasta with chickpeas

Serves 4

300g dried chickpeas
200g pork, in one piece
1 small onion, halved
1 celery stalk, cut into chunks
a sprig of sage or rosemary
250g small dried pasta, such as
    ditalini or pastella, or 300g
    fresh maltagliati
6 tablespoons extra-virgin
    olive oil

There has to be a recipe for *pasta e ceci* (pasta and chickpeas). I learned to make it in Rome, where it is traditionally eaten on Fridays. However, there are versions of it from all over Italy, all of which are merely guidelines until you make the dish your own. This set of guidelines is from Sicily, where it is called *pasta chi ciciri,* for which you do need to soak the chickpeas and to make a pork broth, which was new to me. Having given up its best for the stock, the pork, now mildly flavoured, is removed, but could be eaten in a well-seasoned sandwich. The best pasta to use, I think, is fresh *maltagliati*, which means badly cut pieces. I either make my own or cut up fresh lasagne sheets. It's a straightforward one-pot dish in five steps, which means that ideally you should listen to Dave Brubeck's 'Take Five'. One: make a broth with the pork; two: add soaked chickpeas and seasoning, onions, herbs, celery. When the chickpeas are tender and the broth tasty, three: add the pasta and stir, otherwise it sticks. Right at the end, four: add the soul of the dish, the extra-virgin olive oil. Five: eat.

The day before, cover the chickpeas with cold water and leave them to soak for 24 hours.

In a large, heavy-based pan, cover the pork with 1.5 litres water and a pinch of salt, bring to the boil, then simmer, skimming off any foam. After a good hour, remove the pork and add the chickpeas, onion, celery and herbs and continue to simmer. Once the chickpeas are soft and nearly cooked, check the amount of liquid and add a cup of boiling water if it seems low. Remove the vegetables, add the pasta and a pinch of salt, increase the heat a little and continue cooking until the pasta is al dente. Keep stirring so that the pasta doesn't stick. In the final minutes add the olive oil, then serve.

Zuppa di patate, ceci, zucchine e rosmarino

Potato, chickpea, courgette and rosemary soup

Serves 4

1 large white onion
6 tablespoons extra-virgin olive oil
1 large sprig of rosemary
1 large potato
2 medium courgettes
1 small piece dried red chilli, chopped, or a pinch of red chilli flakes
800g tinned chickpeas, drained
grated pecorino, to serve
salt and freshly ground black pepper

At the time of writing, we have been eating this repeatedly. Not only because it is simple, the sort of soup that takes a little more than 30 minutes – I get it going as soon as I get in the door while I still have my coat on – but also because it is pure, simple and good. The potatoes collapse slightly, giving the soup texture, the courgette is tender, the rosemary is appropriately camphorous and noisy and the chickpeas are chickpeas, therefore good. You could blend it, but I like it brothy, and with croutons fried in olive oil or butter. You could, of course, soak and cook your own chickpeas, in which case use the broth too.

Chop the onion. Warm the olive oil and onion in a heavy-based pan over a medium-low heat and cook until the onion is soft, then add the rosemary and cook for a minute or so more. Dice the potato and courgettes, then add them to the pan along with the chilli, stirring until each piece is glistening with oil. Add the chickpeas and 1 litre water. Bring the soup to a gentle boil, then reduce the heat to a simmer and cook for about 30 minutes, or until the potatoes are starting to collapse. Season with salt and pepper, bearing in mind that you're going to serve it with grated cheese.

Ceci al rosmarino
Chickpeas with rosemary

Serves 4

250g dried chickpeas,
    soaked for 24 hours,
    or 2 x 400g tins
1 large white onion,
    or 6 shallots or spring onions
5 tablespoons extra-virgin
    olive oil
a large sprig of rosemary
salt and freshly ground
    black pepper

In his collection of Italian folktales, Italo Calvino includes one called *Cecino* (small chickpea). It is the story of a poor couple who long for children, but can't have them, and even if they could, they are so poor they wouldn't be able to feed them. One day, while the wife is soaking chickpeas, another, older woman passes by the window and asks for something to eat, at which the childless woman shoos her away. Angry, the old woman curses the pan, saying all the chickpeas will turn to children. The next morning the pan is full of children, a dream and nightmare come true, since they barely have enough to feed themselves. Distraught, the wife kills the children by stamping on them and then, even more distraught, sits and weeps. Suddenly she hears a tiny voice, for one has survived; he is Cecino, and he will be their son. Luca loves this story of wishes and stamping, of an only son, and (for now) demands it when we have chickpeas.

The strident, sap-green flavour of rosemary works beautifully with chickpeas, which is why it is included in so many recipes. For this Roman side dish, you soften an onion in extra-virgin olive oil, then add the cooked chickpeas and stir long enough for the flavours to *fare amicizia*, or make friends. If you like, you can mash or purée some of the chickpeas for a creamier texture. I often make this as an accompaniment for roast leg or braised neck of lamb, both of which love rosemary too. For this recipe, the chickpeas must be really tender. If you are doubtful about cooking your own, used tinned.

Drain the chickpeas, put them in a large pan and cover them with well-salted water. Cook over a very low heat until they are quite tender, then drain. Chop the onion. In a large frying pan, warm the oil, add the onion and fry it gently with the rosemary needles over a low heat until the onion is very soft. Add the drained chickpeas and cook for a few minutes longer. Season with salt and black pepper and serve.

Chickpea flour

Vincenzo has a plan. To begin, we drive up to Tuscany to stay with his uncle near Livorno and eat *cecina*. The next day we continue up the coast to Genoa, where we eat *farinata*. At the port of Genova we put the Panda on the night boat to Sassari in Sardinia, where we eat *la fainé*. After two days in Sardinia we catch another night boat to Palermo, where we eat *panelle*. To finish, we will cut down the heart of Sicily to our house in Gela, where we eat our final *panelle*. A journey in search of *cecina*, *farinata*, *fainé* and *panelle*, all variations on the same theme: chickpea flour mixed with water into a batter, then baked or fried with olive oil until it forms a firm pancake the colour of sunshine.

Chickpea flour is made from ground chickpeas, so it has the same, sweet, creamy, nutty flavour with a touch of bitterness about it. Its consistency reminds me of cocoa or talcum, so fine it seems almost weightless; stick your finger in it and it sinks into a silky nothingness. Chickpea flour is as ancient as chickpeas themselves, and I am sure there must be chickpea flour ley lines to discovered, showing how these dishes migrated, with whom and how they evolved.

To make *panelle,* no doubt a legacy from the Arabs, chickpea flour is cooked with water in much the same way as oats are for porridge or maize flour is for polenta: slowly, over a steady heat and with a steady beating hand until it forms a thick paste. It is then spread on a cold surface, where it sets enough to be cut into squares and fried until crisp on the outside but still soft inside, with a texture somewhere between a pancake and a set savoury custard. The resulting squares are sandwiched in soft roll to make *pane e panelle*, bread and chickpea fritters, which remind me of a chip butty: cushiony and likely to stick to the roof of your mouth, but with crisp edges. Vincenzo's love of *panelle* is second to no man's. As a very small boy a man would come on a Vespa with a bottled gas and frying pan combination ingeniously attached. When he was older he would head to the *friggitoria* on corso Vittorio Emanuele after school, where he would order a bread roll called *mafalda*, which was made with a zig-zag of dough that would be split and filled with just-fried *panelle*. Or it can be eaten alone, perhaps with a generous spritz of lemon. For me, it all began with Fabrizia's *panelle*, which are classic and prove that form informs flavour: the same mixture, shaped and sliced in a different way, can seem like another thing entirely. She fries in extra-virgin olive oil. 'Why people have a fear of frying I will never understand,' she says as she lifts yet another slotted spoon full of crisp *panelle*. *Panelle* and a beer, or a glass of something with bubbles, has the power to transport me. *Panelle* are a simple stroke of cooking genius, the perfect balance between frugality and liberality, and are absolutely bloody delicious.

Panelle di Fabrizia
Fabrizia's chickpea fritters

Serves 6–8 as an antipasti

300g chickpea flour
olive oil, for frying
lemon wedges, to serve
salt

For the twenty-fifth anniversary of Fabrizia's cooking school, hot plates warming great bowls of olive oil were set up in the courtyard, and Giovanni and Enza stood frying batch after batch of *panelle* to be passed around. Fabrizia is happy to share the secrets of her *panelle*, perhaps because she knows that hers will always be the most delicious. She has a particular whisk, which has just a few straight prongs, each with balls on the end. (A balloon whisk works well too.) She also has a dozen or so plastic plates with ridged edges, and it is these that give her *panelle*, which are cut into triangles rather than squares, their distinctive form, with thin, fluted edges that rupture into crispness: the best bit. The procedure may sound bizarre or difficult, but it is neither. You smear the thick mixture on to several of your plates (this way, you can see which one works best), imagining that you are plastering something circular. You wait for it to set a bit, then peel it off; it looks like a curious Japanese face mask. This soft,

floppy disc can then be cut into slim wedges and fried in hot oil until it is crisp. Now you need to move fast: sprinkle them with salt and cut wedges of lemon while someone opens the wine or the beer, and eat. Ideally the first one should be so hot that it sizzles in you mouth.

In a large pan, whisk together 1 litre cold water and the chickpea flour until it forms a smooth batter with no lumps. Tip the batter into a large, heavy-based pan over a medium-low heat and whisk steadily. After 10 minutes or so, the batter will start thickening, and now you really need to whisk to make sure it doesn't stick to the bottom. Once the mixture is coming away cleanly from the sides of the pan, it is ready.

Now, moving swiftly, use a spatula to smear the batter on to a clean marble surface, a large flat tin, or plates. The layer should be 3–5mm thick. Let the mixture cool completely. If you have spread it on to a work surface or tin, it can be cut into squares where it is. If you have smeared it on to plates, peel off the layer of batter carefully and cut each one into slim wedges.

In a pan or deep frying pan, heat the oil to frying temperature, which is 180°C, or when a cube of bread dances on the surface of the oil and turns golden after 20 seconds. Fry the panelle in small batches until they are crisp and golden. Lift from the oil with a slotted spoon on to kitchen paper to drain briefly, then transfer to a serving plate. Sprinkle with salt and serve straight away, with lemon wedges.

Farinata
Chickpea pancake

Serves 4-6

150g chickpea flour
100ml extra-virgin olive oil
salt and freshly ground
    black pepper

Then there is *farinata*, which, like its cousins *cecina* and *fainé*, is the same batter as *panelle*, but baked. I came to *farinata* after *panelle* and had the same sinking suspicion that I do with any oven-baked version of a fried thing, like chips, fish or fritters. I was wrong: chickpea batter is every bit as good baked as it is fried, and it is simpler, which is why it has become a bit of a staple in our house.

After whisking the three ingredients together you let them rest, which is important. The batter is suspiciously thin and you may well think that nothing good will come of it. The quantity of oil, too, is surprising, as is the way it floats on the surface in psychedelic, lava-lamp-like bubbles. Have faith and bake the sunshine-yellow batter in a shallow tin until it's firm, golden

and slightly flaky on top. Once you've scored it and eased it out of the tin, it looks like a piece of fat, flaking pancake, and tastes softy nutty and toasty.

As is so often the case with Italian recipes, the baking time is *qb* or *quanto basta*: however much it needs. In my oven, in a shallow enamel baking tin, my *farinata* takes 30 minutes. You can use a non-stick pan, and real aficionados have special copper-edged tins. I don't find the easing and scraping with a wooden spatula, and the crispy, dark-gold bits that stick to the edges of the tin waiting to be chiselled away by the cook, to be a chore, though. *Farinata* is ideal as an antipasti, cut into small squares and finished with salt and black pepper, and maybe some lemon. It is also a versatile accompaniment, with anything really: fish, meat, and I particularly like it with with greens cooked in olive oil, stewed red peppers or, as they do in Liguria, scattered with chopped rosemary and onions cooked in olive oil.

Using a balloon whisk, mix together the chickpea flour with 450ml water and a good pinch of salt until you have a smooth batter. Allow the batter to rest at room temperature for 2 hours.

Preheat the oven to 180°C/160°C fan/gas mark 4. Use a slotted spoon to skim off any froth that has risen to the surface, then whisk the batter again.

Pour the olive oil into a baking tray or ovenproof dish. Tilt the dish so that the base and sides are well coated with oil. Pour in the batter and then use a fork to distribute the oil into the batter. It will not incorporate entirely, but will look bubbly and a little like mottled paper.

Bake for 20–30 minutes, or until it is set firm and golden on top. Allow to cool for about 5 minutes before using a knife and spatula to ease it from the tin in squares or triangles. Grind over plenty of black pepper and eat while it is still warm, ideally with beer.

SAPORI DI **PARCO** SERENO

LENTICCHIA
DI CASTELLUCCIO
DI NORCIA

Presidio Slow Food

PRODOTTO TIPICO
AZIENDA AGRICOLA ROSA CIARROCCA
LENTICCHIE
santo stefano di sessanio
A AGRICOLTURA BIOLOGICA

Lentils

I remember as much about the earth as the lentils. It had rained what turned out to be the last rain for months the night before we walked around Francesco di Gesu's land near Villalba, in central Sicily, to learn about ancient varieties of wheat and the cultivation of chickpeas and lentils. The late-morning June sun, high and glaring, meant everything seemed dry, but underneath the earth was still damp. We had been told to wear sensible shoes. I was wearing clogs, which are in their own way sensible, just not here. The clay-like earth stuck to my wooden feet in huge tenacious clumps, from which sprouted great tufts of wheat and grass. I tried to stamp as I walked, but succeeded only in collecting more earth and wheat with each step until I could barely lift my feet, such was the weight. Eventually I left one behind and hopped back to pick it up. Then, balancing like a stalk, I found a stick to scrape away the mud. I turned the clog over to discover that the great clump of mud – enough to make a wonderful pot – was studded with crisp brown pods and small green lentils.

Today, mechanical methods are generally used to harvest lentils, but here the *lenticchie di Villalba* are still harvested by hand. A few days before we visited, the plants, which are annual and grow to almost 50 centimetres high, had been cut back, then forked into piles. Testament to the power of the Sicilian sun, which I could feel burrowing into my shoulders, the recently bright-green plants were now piles of stalks and leaves so crisp and dry they almost seemed burned and blistered. On closer examination we found pale bronze finger-tip sized pods with the texture of tissue paper, which only needed to be rubbed ever so slightly to reveal one or two green lentils. Francesco explained the traditional process. The piles are shifted on to huge mats, then beaten with a stick to separate the lentils from the pods. The dry plants are then hurled high in the air with a blunt-tipped pitchfork so that the lentils drop to the ground. The hope, too, is that during the process some slight breeze will whisk away some of the pieces of stalk and pod. Further sorting of hand-harvested lentils takes places in enormous sieves, which are swirled to separate the wanted from the unwanted, the dust and chaff from the lentils. It sounded extraordinary and poetic to the woman in clogs, although I know it is extremely hard, costly work in every sense.

Back in Rome, Andrea, the owner of our local trattoria here in Testaccio, tells me similar stories about lentils in Abruzzo called *rascino*, tiny slate-grey ones from the dry uplands of Castelluccio in Umbria. These are the most prized variety, and like the Villalba lentils are protected by DOP and Slow Food status, since larger, more robust varieties that can be harvested mechanically appeal more to farmers. Lentils are the most ancient pulse, part of the human diet since Neolithic times and one of the first crops to be domesticated. Both the Greeks and the Romans prized lentils for their taste and nutritional value: lentils have the highest protein content of any vegetable, and a decent amount of phosphorus and iron to boot. Both the Italian *lenticchia* and our word lentil come from the Latin *lens culinaris*, the little lens-shaped seed you can cook. Luca takes that to mean they will make him see well. I hope so, but the generations of myopics in our family don't bode well. Even more than sight, *lenticchie* are associated with good fortune, especially when eaten at New Year with a fat, rich sausage called *cotechino*. The more you eat, the more money will come to you during the following year.

It was Andrea who cooked the most memorable lentil dish. As is so often the case, circumstances play a role in the memory. It was my first day out after three days in bed and, feeling tender but hungry, as though escaping from my house prison, I ventured to the trattoria that feels like home. Andrea had boiled the tiny, very dark-red lentils with whole garlic *in camicia* (in its shirt or papery skin) and *alloro*, the bay that grows so vigorously here in Rome. He brought the bowl to our table by the wall next to the window, and in it were boiled lentils in a little of their own broth, with croutons and extra-virgin olive oil. Simple, but in that moment they seemed the Platonic ideal of lentils with their individual, earthy flavour, just soft and floury enough to absorb the flavour of the garlic and the bay.

I am devoted to lentils, and we eat them in one form or another most weeks. It is no coincidence that I keep my lentils near the bay leaves, as the two love each other. As with all legumes, the first thing to do when choosing lentils is to look at the date on the packet: ideally you want those that have been harvested within the last year or two. With time, lentils become harder, drier and more tasteless, and will not soften into anything, however hard you try. Unlike Indian lentils (and remember the word there has a much broader context, spilling over into split peas), Italian lentils generally keep their shape and lentil integrity, unless of course you purée them, which we will come to later. Most Italian and Sicilian lentils do not need soaking, making them extremely useful for someone as disorganized as me. I always look over lentils to make sure there are no tiny stones or pieces of grit in them, then wash them, but you might not find that necessary. They generally cook in about 25–40 minutes, the exact time depending on how old they are. I start tasting after 20 minutes, looking for the moment the lentils are tender and soft but not squidgy; still distinct and holding their shape.

Zuppa di lenticchie
Sicilian lentil soup

Serves 4

1 onion

1 carrot

1 celery stalk, with leaves

6 tablespoons extra-virgin
  olive oil

1 small potato

a pinch of dried chilli flakes

a pinch of dried oregano or
  a bay leaf (optional)

250g small brown or green
  lentils

a squeeze of lemon (optional)

salt

With just a little extra water and a blast in a blender, braised lentils turn into purée, and with a little more water and another blast, soup. I have been given numerous variations on this soup, some blushing with tomato, others scented with fennel, bay, rosemary or marjoram. This version has the joy of the mountains: Sicilian oregano. The soup can be made more substantial with the addition of cooked pasta, rice or some toasted bread at the bottom of the bowl. You can of course put some guanciale or pancetta in the soffritto if you wish, which lends flavoursome and fatty notes. The potato is my addition; it disintegrates during cooking but gives an almost silky body to the final soup. The lemon may sound like an odd addition but it sharpens the edges nicely, and is optional.

Finely dice the onion, carrot and celery. Warm the olive oil in a heavy-based pan or casserole dish and fry the onion, carrot and celery until they are soft and fragrant. Peel and roughly chop the potato and add it to the pan along with the chilli and oregano. Stir, add the lentils, stir again and then add 1.5 litres water. Bring the soup to a gentle boil, then reduce the heat to a simmer for 20–40 minutes, or until the lentils are tender. Season with salt.

The soup can be served just so, or some (or all) of it can be passed through a food mill or blended with a stick blender to a purée (I pass half through the food mill). Serve it alone or ladled over some toasted bread, with a little more olive oil on top and a squeeze of lemon, if you like.

Zuppa di lenticchie e castagne
Lentil and chestnut soup

Serves 4

350g chestnuts, cooked and
    shelled, or vacuum-packed
    cooked chestnuts
4 tablespoons extra-virgin olive
    oil, plus extra to serve
100ml white wine
1 tablespoon tomato purée
    (optional)
1 onion
1 carrot
1 celery stalk
250g small brown lentils
1 bay leaf
a few stalks of flat-leaf parsley

Chestnuts are a bother to peel. Many Italian recipes suggest that you score them with a knife, then boil them, then peel. I find this the most exasperatingly painful task, as scored, boiled chestnut skin is sharp. I score the nuts across the curved side, then roast them for 15 minutes or so, wrap them in a clean tea towel for 5 minutes to steam away, and peel them while still warm. Lentils and chestnuts make a good pair, earthy and warm, and this is a most beautiful and soothing soup, a variation on a recipe from Lazio for chickpea and chestnut soup. The Christmassy air of chestnuts means there something rather celebratory about it.

Break the chestnuts into small pieces. Warm the olive oil in a frying pan, add the chestnuts, stir for a minute or so, then add the wine and tomato purée, if using, and let everything bubble for a couple of minutes.

Chop the onion, carrot and celery. Rinse the lentils, then put them in a pan, cover with 2 litres water and bring to the boil. Skim off any froth, then add the onion, carrot, celery, bay leaf and parsley, turn down the heat and simmer for 30 minutes, or until the lentils are tender.

Remove the bay leaf and parsley, use a slotted spoon to lift out half the lentils and purée them with a stick blender, then return them to the pan. Add the chestnut mixture and cook for a minute or two longer (for a creamier soup, purée it after you have added the chestnuts). Serve with a swoosh of olive oil.

Braised lentils

Serves 4

1 onion
1 celery stalk
1 carrot (optional)
6 tablespoons extra-virgin
    olive oil
250g small brown or green
    lentils
1 bay leaf
salt and freshly ground
    black pepper

This is one of my essential recipes. There is a similar one in my first book, but it seems important here too since it is both useful and delicious, and easily doubled up, in which case it will provide two or three meals. You have two choices: you can cook the lentils with the vegetables and water until the lentils are tender and most of the liquid has been absorbed. Quite how much liquid is left is up to you: some people like their lentils quite brothy, others prefer them drier. The other method is to boil the lentils until tender first, drain them, then add them to a soffritto of onion, celery and carrot that you have already prepared. It very much depends on your taste, what suits you and how you are going to serve them. I generally opt for the one-pan method, for one-pan reasons, although I think I prefer the flavour of method two, which is clearer somehow. Either way, serve the lentils with rice, sausages, game, pork belly, oily fish or with a poached or fried egg on top.

For the first method, finely dice the onion, celery and carrot (if using). Warm 5 tablespoons olive oil in a heavy-based pan or casserole dish and fry the vegetables with a pinch of salt until soft and fragrant. Add the lentils, stir again and cook for a few minutes so they toast ever so slightly, then add 1 litre water. Bring to a gentle boil, then reduce to a simmer for 20–40 minutes, or until the lentils are tender but not mushy. Season with salt, and pepper if you wish, then stir through the rest of the olive oil.

For the second method, bring a pan of well-salted water to the boil, add the lentils and the bay leaf and cook until they are tender. Meanwhile, finely dice the onion, celery and carrot, if using. Warm 5 tablespoons olive oil in a heavy-based pan or casserole dish and fry the vegetables with a pinch of salt until soft and fragrant. Once the lentils are tender, drain them, add them to the vegetables and cook for a few minutes longer over a low heat. Season with salt, and pepper if you wish, and stir through the rest of the olive oil.

Insalata di lenticchie, arance e erbe
Lentil salad with orange zest and herbs

Serves 4

250g small brown or
    green lentils
1 clove garlic, whole and
    unpeeled
2 bay leaves
1 celery stalk
2 large unwaxed oranges
a large handful of mint
5 tablespoons extra-virgin
    olive oil
juice of ½ lemon
a large handful of flat-leaf
    parsley
salt

Cooking for others is usually a mixture of sensations, of pleasure and love with duty or necessity. Cooking is also full of private moments, dead ordinary things that are extraordinarily good and should enjoyed selfishly: tasting as something cooks, the feel of something ripe, an orange maybe, then the hot scent as you grate the zest from the fruit, each push across the rough metal ridges unleasing another wave. Chopping mint and parsley is another pleasure. You can be bold with the amount of fresh herbs here, making it as much a salad of parsley and mint as it is lentils, rather like a lentil version of tabbouleh. Of course, you will get herbs stuck in your teeth. The orange dressing, sweetly sharp from the juice and essential oils from the zest, works well with the lentils. If I am making this there's a very good chance I will use the flesh of the orange to make a fennel and orange salad, the sweet orange flesh and crisp fennel contrasting and complementing in equal measure. Good too, is a fillet of grilled or pan-fried fish, the heat of which reawakens the essential oils in the orange zest when you put it on top.

Put the lentils in a medium pan with the garlic, bay and celery and cover with 1 litre cold water. Bring the lentils to the boil, then reduce the heat to a simmer and cook for 20–25 minutes, or until the lentils are tender. Drain, discarding the garlic, bay and celery.

Meanwhile, make the dressing in a serving bowl or lipped dish. Grate the zest from the oranges, tear the mint into little pieces, chop the parsley and mix them with the olive oil, lemon juice and a good pinch of salt. Tip the lentils into the bowl and toss with the dressing. Leave to sit for 5 minutes, toss again and pour over a little more olive oil for shine.

Lenticchie in umido con alloro
Lentils with garlic and bay

Serves 4–6

500g small brown lentils,
    such as Castelluccio,
    Rascino or Villalba
5 fresh bay leaves
4 garlic cloves
1 slice of bread per person
extra-virgin olive oil
salt and freshly ground
    black pepper

This is Andrea's way with lentils, the simplest one, naked really, which, if the lentils are good, is an excellent way to appreciate their unique, fragrant flavour. It is also a recipe in which I am reminded how indispensable bay is, with its sweet, balsamic flavour and hint of nutmeg. Be bold with salt and pepper: the lentils will suddenly taste like lentils. The bread and olive oil need to be good too. I have also served lentils cooked this way with sausages. Grill four, then nestle them in the lentils 10 minutes before serving, and spoon over some of the sticky sausage juices from the pan. They are also nice stirred into rice, with a hard-boiled egg, a squeeze of lemon and some more olive oil.

Put the lentils in a heavy-based pan, earthenware pot or casserole dish with a lid, cover with 1 litre water and add the bay and the (unpeeled) garlic cloves. Bring the lentils slowly to the boil, then reduce the heat, cover the pan and simmer until the lentils are tender but not mushy and there is just a little liquid left. Depending on the age of the lentils, this will take anything from 20–40 minutes from when the water boils.

Meanwhile, cut the slices of bread into chunks and fry them in olive oil until golden and crusty. Ladle some of the cooked beans and a little of the cooking liquid into each serving bowl, top with some croutons and pour over some olive oil.

Preserved anchovies

The anchovy lady is at Testaccio market on Saturdays. Always dressed in a pale blue housecoat, she parks her small metal trolley near the pet stall at a busy intersection in the market building, visible from four entrances. In the old market, which was the bosky, clamorous heart of Testaccio, she was one of several women, along with the egg lady, the honey lady and the greens and herbs lady, who sold only one thing, but she was the only one of them to move to the new, bright-white market on the other side of Testaccio. Here, she seems both at home and out of time. Her trolley is just large enough to accommodate a large tin of anchovies preserved in coarse salt, a wad of waxed paper and a roll of clear plastic bags. Tongs and cloths hang from the sides of the trolley like tassels that swing as the market gets busy and vociferous shoppers push past. She usually has a portion in her hand: half a dozen headless fish encrusted in salt on a piece of paper. If she doesn't have one ready she uses tongs to lift the fish from the damp crystals. Either way, she is swift. At a *sì* or a nod, the paper is rolled into a salami and put in a bag, which is knotted and in your hand before you can open your purse.

If you had to tell the history of Roman food in objects, a tin (or perhaps a wooden tub) of salted anchovies would be a good one to choose. Salt was vital to the ancient Romans, which is why their cities were built close to the sea, and therefore to saltworks, the great wide white pans on to which the sun beat down. The sea also provided fish – tuna, mackerel, sardines as well as anchovies – that was salted in a vast industry at the heart of Roman commerce. The contents of a barrel of anchovies in ancient Rome was probably much the same as what you'd find in a tin now. They are decapitated, but not gutted or boned, then simply packed tightly in layers with salt. It is the action of the salt on the enzymes in the guts that creates the distinctive, powerful colour and rich, searing flavour. The ancient Romans also used the fish scraps and innards to make various sorts of sun-fermented fish, long-lasting concoctions that were used liberally in cooking rather like Asian fish sauce or Worcestershire sauce are now. Salted anchovies are still used in much the same way, as the deep seasoning at the bottom of various soups and stews.

It is worth seeking out anchovies preserved in salt. Their smell is pungent, even for an anchovy lover, and I don't imagine many haters would put themselves nearby. The anchovies need to be prepared, the salt brushed away, the belly nicked with a fingernail and then the fish opened like a butterfly so you can pull away the backbone, which almost unzips. This is more satisfying than fussy. Once rinsed again and blotted dry on kitchen paper, the fillets are ready for use, or to be stored in olive oil.

Then there are anchovies preserved in olive oil. These are the ones I remember from my childhood, in small, slim tins with curved edges and a round key you pulled up and back with a sort of suck, or very small jars, in which case the anchovies might be rolled around an olive or bit of red pepper. I was a pantry-climber and fridge-raider from a young age, and I tasted everything I could; my fingers got into jars of jam and chutney, plastic tubs of glacé cherries, Rowntree's jellies and pots of gherkins and anchovies. Even before anchovies came my dad's pot of Gentleman's Relish, a paste of anchovies, butter, herbs and spices also known as Patum Peperium, and which comes in a distinctive squat round pot, formerly ceramic but nowadays made of plastic. The paste is a dull greyish-brown and the taste is loud, salty and fishy. Alone it is too much, but spread thinly on hot buttered toast it paved the way for anchovies, which I would eat from the tin. These are prepared differently from the salted ones: they're brined, then preserved in oil. There are various grades, and it's not food snobbism to say that really cheap ones taste terrible – acrid, spiteful and ruinous to food. They give anchovies a bad name. Decent-quality anchovies in olive oil, however, are fat, pink and delicious. There are also the very best anchovies from Spain, but they are out of my budget. I always have both salted and oil-preserved anchovies in the fridge and use them interchangeably, the in-oil ones probably more often as they involve less faff.

For me, anchovies are indispensable as ingredients and seasoning, star or chorus. In the chorus they are hard-working team players, savoury and salty, seasoning deeply and discreetly.

That said, I once told my sister (an anchovy hater) that, when used carefully, the fishiness of anchovies disappears, but she could still sniff them out at several paces. You, the cook, are in charge of using them judiciously or generously, keeping in mind they can be a bully. In Rome, anchovies are melted into soffritto (the softened onion, carrot and celery that forms the base of so many dishes), where they deepen flavour; they can even be tucked deep inside lamb or stuffings, where they season from the inside out, making the meat seem somehow meatier. Pounded into the base of sauces, they can share the stage, as when stirred into wilted onions, or be soaked up greedily by breadcrumbs, melted or mashed into butter. Anchovies just on their own with bread and butter is hard to beat. In Rome, this is called *pane, burro e alici* and is eaten as an antipasto – something *saporito* to excite the appetite in anticipation of a meal. There is something about sinking my teeth into a layer of cold butter that I find irresistible. They are just as nice spread on toast, which is excellent cut into soldiers and dipped into a soft-boiled egg, or tossed with vegetables, especially sprouting broccoli, or spring greens. As the star, they can be draped on pizza, over salads, or noughts-and-crosses style across roasted red peppers. I see the fact that my second name is Alice, after my maternal grandmother, as a highly significant reason for my love of the small, salty fishes: in Italian, the word for anchovy is *acciuga* or *alice*.

Anchovy butter

10 anchovy fillets
150g butter, at room
temperature

On bread or toast, or stirred into vegetables. Mash the anchovies hard against the side of a bowl – a fork is best. You can use salted ones you have cleaned or oil-preserved ones you have drained.

In a shallow dish, use a fork to mash the anchovies into a rough paste, then mash the butter into the anchovies and mix until the anchovies are distributed throughout the mixture. Scrape the anchovy butter on to a piece of greaseproof paper, then roll it up so that the butter forms a log, twist the ends like a sweet and put it in the fridge to chill. Cut off slices as you need them.

Broccoli ripassati in padella con alici
Broccoli with anchovy

Serves 4

1 fat garlic clove
6 tablespoons extra-virgin
    olive oil
6 anchovy fillets
a pinch of chilli flakes
800g broccoli

I often get the pan, olive oil and garlic ready beforehand, then just leave the pan sitting by the stove, the garlic, peeled, crushed but still whole, starting to give its sunny perfume to the oil and the room. Once you put the pan on the heat, go slow, over a low heat: you want bring out the sweet, subtle scent; if you burn it, it turns into a bitter bully. You could melt the anchovies over the heat (again, go slow), or balance the pan over the broccoli water to form a makeshift bain marie – the steamy heat is enough to help the anchovies dissolve.

Sweet, cauliflower-like Romanesco, familiar, fleshy Sicilian broccoli and slender, sweetly bitter purple sprouting broccoli: all pair well with the rich savouriness of anchovy melted in olive oil. We often have this piled on toast, or topped with an olive-oil fried egg. You could also serve it with pasta, a classic southern Italian combination. Remember to keep the broccoli-cooking water – so lift the florets out with a slotted spoon – then use this faintly green and nutrient-rich water to cook the pasta.

Bring a large pan of salted water to the boil. Finely chop the garlic if you want a strong flavour; crush it gently with the back of a knife if you want a milder flavour. In a large frying pan, warm the olive oil over a low heat, add the garlic and fry gently until it is fragrant. Now place the frying pan over the pan of boiling water, add the anchovies and stir until they disintegrate. Add the chilli flakes and stir again. Keep the pan warm.

Cut the broccoli into florets, put them in the boiling water and cook until tender – it should be easily pierced with the point of a knife at the thickest part of the stem. In the last moments of cooking, warm the anchovy mixture again, then add the drained broccoli to the pan and nudge it around until each floret is glistening. Serve immediately.

Pasta, alici e cipolle
Pasta with anchovies and onions

Serves 4

2 large white onions
    (about 300g)
50ml extra-virgin olive oil
50g butter
150g salt-packed anchovies
    or 12 anchovies in oil,
    drained
500g dried pasta, such as
    spaghetti, bucatini or
    linguine, or fresh egg
    tagliatelle or fettucine
freshly ground black pepper

A favourite lunch. You know the way onions soften and collapse into a sweetly savoury mess when you cook them down in olive oil? Well, to that add butter, which mellows everything even further. Then, like the life and soul arriving at a party and turning the music up, jolt everything by adding anchovies. The collision of soft and mellow with the rich, searing saltiness is nothing short of lip-smacking.

Ideally you want mild white or red onions. Don't rush the onions: let them cook slowly and gently, and do the same when you add the anchovies: they should dissolve, not sizzle into the onion.

Bring a large pan of water to the boil for the pasta. Very thinly slice the onions. In a large frying pan, warm the oil and butter over a low heat, then add the onions, stir, and cover. Leave to cook gently, lifting the lid and stirring from time to time, until they are incredibly soft – this will take about 15 minutes and the onions should not colour.

Add the cleaned anchovies to the pan and continue cooking over a low heat until they have disintegrated and vanished into the onion, which will take another 5 minutes.

Meanwhile, add salt to the pasta water, stir, then add the pasta and cook until al dente. Drain the pasta, reserving some of the cooking water, add to the onions and anchovy and stir, adding a little of the cooking water if you think it needs it. Alternatively, tip the drained pasta into a warm bowl, add the sauce, stir and serve.

Peperoni al forno con alici e olivi
Roasted red peppers with anchovies and olives

Serves 6–8

5 large red or yellow peppers
a handful of small black olives
12 best-quality anchovy fillets
    in oil
extra-virgin olive oil
salt

Isn't a pile of red peppers one of the most brilliant sights, wherever you find them, at a market or corner shop? Even a plastic packet can't come between us and the bright joy that is postbox-red peppers. I enjoy them raw. The American writer Molly O' Neill sums up their 'sweet, sometimes herbaceous, always sunny crunch'. But when cooked they become another thing completely, transforming from crisp to soft and silken enough to wrap around your fingers like fabric, their flavour sweetly intense and ever-so-slightly smoky. I'm a sucker for roasted peppers.

The best way of roasting them is over charcoal. It can also be done over a gas hob, though (use a long fork, be patient and turn them steadily), or in the oven. Once the peppers are collapsed and charred, put them in a plastic bag, or in a bowl covered with clingfilm, and leave them for a steamy rest, during which time their skins will come away from the flesh. Pull off the skins, then tear the peppers into thick strips and dress them with olive oil and a little red wine vinegar or, better still, with anchovies and olives, which I am sure is some sort of umami perfection. We have these with bread and salty cheese, as a starter or a meal in itself. They are also good with roast chicken, in a sandwich, or torn and stirred into pasta.

Preheat the oven to 220°C/200°C fan/gas mark 7. Put the peppers on a baking tray and roast for about 30–40 minutes, turning them every now and then, until they are soft, blistered and charred.

Tip the peppers into a bowl and cover tightly with clingfilm. Leave the hot peppers to steam for 10 minutes; they will collapse further and the skins will steam away from the flesh. You could also put them in a plastic bag to steam them.

Once the peppers are cool enough to handle, pull away and discard the seeds, stalk and any membranes. Cut or tear each pepper into thick strips and arrange them in a shallow dish.

Strain (to remove the seeds) some of the pepper juices from their bowl or bag over the strips. Criss-cross the peppers with the anchovy fillets, dot with olives and pour over a little olive oil. Allow the peppers to sit for at least an hour at room temperature before serving.

Roast shoulder of lamb with anchovies, garlic and rosemary

Serves 4

1 garlic clove
4–12 anchovy fillets in oil, drained
1.5kg lamb shoulder
2 sprigs of rosemary (choose softer, younger needles if possible)
250ml dry white wine
salt and freshly ground black pepper

My mum: 'What would you like when you get home to England?' Me: 'Roast lamb, potato gratin, watercress salad and lots of red wine.' Anchovies as deep seasoning is well illustrated with roast lamb, where a few fillets stuffed into incisions in the meat melt and season it deeply and beautifully. Alongside the anchovy, stuff in a sliver of garlic and a tuft of rosemary. A shoulder on the bone, which is almost impossible to find in Rome because the lambs sold are so small, is best for this, so it is something I enjoy when I am back in England. It is important to stuff the trio of flavourings deep inside, and also to rub the joint with olive oil (some would say butter) and a little salt.

The last time I wrote about this dish a reader commented that my suggestion of 4 anchovy fillets was timid, and that they would use at least 12 fillets for a shoulder; this seemed brazenly bold to me, but is a good reminder of how our tastes vary. I think lamb cooked this way needs a nice soft accompaniment, then a green salad with some peppery leaves for afterwards.

Preheat the oven to 220°C/200°C fan/gas mark 7. Slice the garlic and cut the anchovies in half. Use a small, sharp knife to trim away any excess fat from the lamb shoulder and make 10 or so deep incisions in it. Widen the incisions just enough to stuff half an anchovy, a slice of garlic and a small sprig of rosemary inside each one. Sprinkle with salt and plenty of pepper.

Put the meat in a smallish roasting tin and roast for 30 minutes. Turn the oven down to 160°C/140°C fan/gas mark 3, pour the wine into the bottom of the tin and roast for a further hour. Once cooked, cover with foil and leave to rest for 20 minutes. Lift the meat on to a board to carve it. Use a wooden spoon to scrape any sticky bits off the bottom of the roasting tin into the liquid, then pour it into a small pan and set it over a high heat to reduce a little. Pour some over each serving of lamb.

Flour

A bag of flour is just a bag of flour. It is stout and commonplace, a kitchen basic sealed by thick folds, the contents of which are neither tempting – this is no place in which to dip a finger – nor does it promise gratification any time soon.

But a bag of flour is also a bag of flour, and therefore full of promise! Bread, pizza, tarts, pastry, pies, scones, crumbles, cobblers, cakes, buns, biscuits, crackers, playdough and pasta all begin with this stout and wondrous bag. Come to think of it, you *should* open the bag and stick your finger in to feel the weightlessness of fine flour, or the silkiness of coarser flour. To open a bag of flour makes me feel like Roald Dahl's George holding his marvellous medicine, touching 'with the very tips of his fingers the edge of a magic world'.

Magic and work. Our garage basement in Gela is a sort of museum to wheat and flour. In the corner under the stairs is the once-horse-drawn plough that Vincenzo's grandfather Orazio used to turn the land. Against the wall are the sickles, pitchforks and hula hoop-sized wooden sieves that were used for the harvest before he invested, along with other farmers, in a *mietitrebbia* (combine harvester). Across the road in the middle of the cousin's garage is the lid that covers *la fossa*, the underground silo that once contained *frumento* (wheat grains). Like most local farmers, Orazio grew *grano duro* (hard wheat, *Triticum durum*), which is particularly suited to Sicily's soil and climate. It is still cultivated all over the island, although not in anything like the quantities it once was. Sicilian *grano duro* is gold in colour and nature, its story as long and Daedalian as the story of the island itself.

My mother-in-law, Carmela, is wary of reminiscing, especially if she senses me erring towards romanticism; she shrugs off my questions and says she can't remember. Then she does remember, and, like George removing the cork from his medicine, the memories come spilling out and she can't stop talking. After our conversations she will often call Vincenzo back five or six times, shouting a new detail, correction or word down the phone as if it was a pipe, instructing him to write it down for me in Sicilian and Italian: *u frumentu, il frumento,* wheat grains. She can remember her father taking her to his still-lush wheat field around Easter, picking a stem of wheat, flaming it for a second to singe away the green husk so that she could taste the infantile berry, like grass and milk. She describes the rattling train journey to Falconera during the June harvest to take food to her father and uncle, how the reapers would wade through the rippling sea of gold with their sickles in a long line, behind them the gatherers, and how they would all sing. In the 1950s, Sicilian farming was still overwhelmingly traditional. It was her older brother who followed his father into farming, but Carmela, precise and observant, remembers details, the taste of the air, the reaping and stacking into stooks, the threshing and grading. She can describe the cane silo that was used to store the grain for daily use, and the deep *fossa* that contained the grain to be sold. An oxygen-less layer hovered over this grain as it aged and fermented, occasionally causing a worker to faint. Carmela was often the one who went with her father to take the family grain to the mill at the end of the road, where it was stone-ground under his watchful eye.

Durum berries are brittle, which means they shatter when ground into coarse *farina di grano duro* (or *semola*), then on a second milling they become a finer, silky flour called *farina di semola remacinata*. This butter-yellow flour was turned into dough for pasta and for bread, kneaded in a wooden box called a *madia*, then shaped into large loaves that were covered in sesame seeds and baked in the wood-fired oven in the old kitchen, later in the communal bakery. Even Carmela allows herself to indulge in memories of this bread, with its firm bottom and real crust covered in tiny seeds and a substantial, chewy crumb. It was the staff of life, never taken for granted and never wasted. Vincenzo's grandmother Sara kept making her own bread until the early 1960s, much later than most, and she was very proud of that fact, although she was just as proud of giving up making it, for, like having more meat, and plastic bowls, buying bread was a sign of prosperity. She continued making pizza, though, and filled bread pies called *impanata* with flour made from the wheat her husband grew. Thirty miles inland in

Riesi, Vincenzo's paternal grandmother Lilla also turned flour into bread, *impanata* and trays of pizza for the family bakery. She would use soft wheat flour, again a sign of prosperity, for bread rolls, soft olive oil rolls and cakes. But her bread was always made from durum wheat.

These days, I can find Sicilian flour and pasta made from it more easily in Rome than in Gela, where the local wheat is whisked away, and the flour for sale is shipped in from the other side of the world. Not that I am fanatical or snobbish about the sort of flour I buy, just aware that flour made from well-cultivated wheat is a very different substance from the highly industralized stuff. A bag of flour may just be a bag of flour, but bags vary. In Italy I look for Italian or Sicilian-grown wheat from a specific place, a farm, or mill which may or may not be organic. *Farina di grano duro* (*Triticum durum*), also called *farina di semola*, is made from hard durum wheat and is a more finely ground version of the semolina we British use for pudding. *Farina di grano tenero* is made from soft durum wheat. I keep an eye out for flour that is *macinata a pietra* (stoneground), which doesn't damage the grain as much as modern milling with its massive steel rollers, therefore preserving more nutrients and more flavour. The numbers refer to how finely the flour is ground, oo being the finest grade, then o, 1 and 2 being progressively coarser; in Italy they can refer to hard or soft wheat flour. I use soft o and oo flour for cakes, fresh egg pasta and half the focaccia dough. I use hard wheat *farina di semola* for things that benefit from more substance, such as pasta made with water and my sturdy *impanata*, although soft flour works too. In the UK, hard durum wheat flour is usually labelled oo flour for pasta; check on the back to see if it is made from hard durum wheat. Plain flour is made from a softer wheat.

My friend and teacher Carla Tomasi, whose skill and love of working with flour is second to none, laughs at my insistence on tipping the flour into a mountain. She thinks a bowl or container is much neater. The mountain, though, feels liberating. I pour the contents of the bag straight on to the work surface, then use a fist to enlarge and swirl it into a volcano, into which I crack eggs or pour water, put diced butter or olive oil, then put my fingers into a magic, marvellous, glutenous world.

Impanata
Stuffed bread pie

Serves 8

For the impanata
10 dried yeast or 20g fresh yeast
1 tablespoon sugar
500g strong flour, ideally 00
    hard durum wheat or strong
    white bread flour (plain flour
    will also work)
10g salt
2 tablespoons extra-virgin
    olive oil
1 egg, lightly beaten

For the chard, potato
    and anchovy filling
600g chard, blanched,
    drained and chopped
600g cooked potato, chopped
8 anchovies, finely chopped
1 egg
salt and freshly ground
    black pepper

For the cheese and
    anchovy filling
500g mozzarella, well drained,
    or tuma or primo sale,
    chopped
8–16 anchovy fillets or
    8 slices of ham, chopped
salt and freshly ground
    black pepper

If a pie has a top and a bottom, then *impanata* is a pie. The name translates as *in bread,* the filling being encased in bread. There are lots of names and variations of this, and every town has a different version with its own set of folds or pinches, and a particular filling. My father-in-law, Bartolomeo, who spent his childhood living over the family bakery, fondly remembers an *impanata* with wilted greens, potatoes and anchovies. In Catania, we enjoy something similar called *scacciata*, which is filled with *tuma* cheese and anchovies, flying deliciously in the face of any suggestion that two don't go together. My version borrows from both *impanata* and *scacciata*.

The twist and pinch to seal the top and the bottom is important, as is the thickness of the dough and a good ratio of filling to dough: you want a decent bread border, which provides a handle but is not too thick. Cheese and anchovy *impanata* is best eaten straight out of the oven, so the cheese pulls into great long strings; the others benefit from a rest, so that they are warm rather than hot. They are also good at room temperature, but are easily reheated. Cooled, *impanata* is just the sort of sturdy thing you want for a picnic.

Dissolve the yeast and sugar in about 200ml tepid water. In a large bowl, mix the flour, salt and olive oil, then add the dissolved yeast and enough extra water to bring everything together into a soft dough (this is usually another 100ml for me, so about 300ml water in all, but it can vary a lot). Knead the dough until it is smooth. Put the dough in a lightly oiled bowl, cover with a clean tea towel or cling film and leave in a warm, draughtless spot for 2 hours, or until it has doubled in size.

Make your choice of filling by mixing all the ingredients and seasoning well with salt and pepper.

Preheat the oven to 200°C/180°C fan/gas mark 6 and brush a roughly 30cm-diameter metal cake tin or pie dish with olive oil.

Turn the dough on to a lightly floured work surface and knead it for about 30 seconds. Pull away two thirds of it and flatten it with your fists, then roll it into a circle 2cm larger than the tin. Lift this circle into the tin – it will hang over the edges. Rub the dough with olive oil and add the filling, making sure it is evenly distributed. Roll the remaining dough into a circle the size of the tin, lift it on to the filling, then bring the overhang up and pinch and twist it to seal it. Prick with a fork, then brush with egg and poke a few holes in the top with a fork. Bake for 35–45 minutes, or until golden and puffed up.

La torta salata di Carla
Carla's savoury tart

Makes 6–8 slices

200g plain flour, or soft wheat
    00 flour
200g strong white bread flour or
    hard durum wheat 00 flour
10g salt
2 tablespoons extra-virgin
    olive oil

For the filling
400g boiled potatoes
500g cooked greens, such
    as courgettes or broccoli
100g goat's cheese
a handful of roasted peppers
    (optional)
2 eggs, lightly beaten,
    plus another for glazing
50g Parmesan, grated
grated nutmeg (optional)
salt and freshly ground
    black pepper

Unlike the previous recipe for *impanata*, the dough for this recipe doesn't contain yeast. There was a *torta salata* such as this on the counter the first time I walked into Carla's kitchen, and we ate still-warm slices leaning up against her counter. It was the first recipe she gave me, with the instruction not to worry too much about the precise quantities, but rather the feeling of the dough – to practise and to make the recipe my own.

More than the pastry, this savoury tart begins with leftovers, such as the two boiled potatoes that I could eat while I clear up but don't, because now I have an excuse to make Carla's tart. Once the first piece is in place, things come together quickly: the end of the cheese and the red pepper stew, those last two courgettes. Once you have your filling (the ingredients given here are just a template, you can use anything), you make the dough, which is as simple as it gets: flour, warm water, a little olive oil, salt. No yeast means no rising, so the dough is ready immediately, the piece for the base slightly larger so that it come up and over the rim. Now you arrange your filling, the potatoes roughly, the courgettes cooked and chopped filling the gap, the cheese crumbled over the end of caponata shared evenly, a couple of beaten eggs poured over the top.

'Practise' is not the kind of advice we welcome in this age of fast and infallible recipes, but this is sort of recipe you need to make few times to get a feel for it, especially stretching the dough to a reasonable thinness – it is pliable, so you can tug – and twisting it closed. Once cooked, the dough is sturdy, very much a container for the filling, but if you brush it with egg it is firm *and* tasty.

In a large bowl, mix the flour with the oil and enough water – add it slowly – to form a soft, pliable dough. Knead the dough on a lightly floured surface until soft and smooth. Cover it with an upturned bowl until you are ready.

Chop the potato, greens and goat's cheese, then mix them in another bowl. Add the roasted peppers, if using, eggs, Parmesan, salt, pepper and nutmeg if you are adding it. Mix well.

Preheat the oven to 180°C/160°C fan/gas mark 4 and oil a 23cm tart tin. Cut two thirds of the dough away, then roll it into a circle large enough to fit into the bottom of the tin, come up the sides and hang over a little. You can tug the dough. Press the dough into the base. Put the filling into the case and spread it out evenly. Roll the last third of the dough into a circle, place it on top, then pinch and twist the top and the bottom together. Paint with beaten egg, prick it in the middle and bake for 1 hour, or until golden (I sometimes pull it out halfway through cooking and paint it with more egg). Serve just warm, or at room temperature.

Sfincione
Sicilian pizza

Serves 8 generously

12g fresh yeast or
    6g dried yeast
1 teaspoon sugar
500g strong white bread flour or
    hard durum wheat oo flour
2 tablespoons extra-virgin
    olive oil
salt

For the filling

1 large onion
2 tablespoons extra-virgin
    olive oil
300ml tomato sauce
    (see page 32 or 36)
8–10 anchovy fillets, chopped
150g mozzarella or caciocavallo,
    chopped
125g toasted breadcrumbs
dried oregano, to taste
salt and freshly ground
    black pepper

Sfincione means spongy, but I think soft and plump is the best way to describe this deep Sicilian pizza, which feels closer to a focaccia than the crisp or raised edges of pizza I know from Rome and Naples. Traditionally there is lots of topping: a rich sauce of tomatoes and onions into which you press or pinch anchovy, cheese and then – a quintessential Sicilian touch – toasted breadcrumbs. As you can imagine, there is no room for daintiness when you eat a slice, which feels like biting into a bread pillow.

There used to be a stall at the market in Testaccio run by a Sicilian couple, and from time to time they would make *sfincione*. Like a dog with sixth sense, Vincenzo would always be there on the right day. The stall has closed now, so to bridge the hungry gaps between our visits south I sometimes make this.

Make a sponge by mixing the yeast with 150ml warm water and the sugar and leave it for 15 minutes, or until frothy.

Meanwhile, thinly slice the onion. Warm the olive oil in a pan, add the onion and fry until soft and translucent. Add the tomato sauce and simmer for 10 minutes.

Put the flour and the frothy sponge into a big bowl, add another 350ml warm water, some salt and the olive oil and bring everything together into a soft, elastic dough (adding a little more warm water if necessary.) Knead the dough until it no longer sticks to your hands or the work surface.

Lightly oil a roughly 35 x 50cm baking tin or two 23cm cake tins (in which case divide the dough in two) and press the dough into the tin with your fingers. Press the anchovies and cheese firmly and evenly into the dough. Spread the tomato and onion sauce over the top, then sprinkle with the breadcrumbs and oregano, if using. Leave it to rise in a warm place for 2 hours.

Preheat the oven to 210°C/190°C fan/gas mark 7 and bake for 30 minutes, or until cooked through.

Focaccia

Makes 1 large or 2 smaller
focaccias

200g plain flour or soft wheat
00 flour
200g strong white bread flour or
hard durum wheat 00 flour
50g 0 flour (coarser hard wheat
flour; alternatively, just use
250g strong white bread
flour)
10g salt
1 tablespoon (8g) fast-action
dried yeast
1 tablespoon extra-virgin
olive oil
310g tepid water
a sprig of rosemary (optional)

'No one who cooks cooks alone,' wrote Laurie Colwin, and it's true – you are cooking with the person who taught you, whether a relative, friend, TV cook, writer. It was Carla who is with me when I make this focaccia, which she describes as ticking all the right boxes: a firm bottom with a soft, chewy, mouth-engaging crumb. When we give cooking classes together, there is almost always a focaccia in the oven, filling the room with its scent, ready to greet the students. Carla is very clear that if you want to add rosemary, you should chop it finely and sprinkle it on top when it comes out of the oven, so that its flavour and oily scent is still lively. The dough freezes very well in balls in lightly oiled plastic bags.

In a large bowl, mix the flours, salt and yeast. Add the olive oil and 310ml tepid water gradually, mixing with your hand from the centre outwards and incorporating the flour until you have a consistent mass of soft dough, which will be a little sticky. Cover and leave to rest for 15 minutes.

Sprinkle a work surface with flour and turn out the dough. Knead it gently, using the ball of your hand to bring the edges in and then stretching them out. Work for about 3 minutes, then cover the dough with a upturned mixing bowl for 20 minutes. Repeat the kneading for another 3 minutes, then put the dough back in a clean, lightly oiled bowl to rise for 1 hour.

Grease a 32cm round tin with oil (alternatively, you could cut the dough in half and bake it in two 18cm tins). Turn the dough back out on to the work surface and then, working gently, press the dough into the tin. Cover with a clean tea towel and leave to rest for another hour to rise.

Preheat the oven to 220°C/200°C fan/gas mark 7. Use your fingertips to dimple the surface and brush it with olive oil. Bake for 15–20 minutes, rotating the tin once, until the bread is golden and the base firm. Brush the focaccia with more oil if you think it needs it, chop the rosemary and sprinkle it on top.

Fresh cavatelli

Serves 4

300g hard durum wheat oo
    flour (sometimes labelled
    pasta flour)

Anyone can mix flour and water to a dough. It takes knowing hands, though, to get the proportions right, to knead the two into a smooth dough, then shape it, and experienced ones to do it quickly. To watch such hands make orecchiette or cavatelli, or use a rod to make busiate or fusilli, is to watch an extraordinary and dextrous set of moves that transforms a mass of dough into tiny ears, curls, ringlets, spirals.

In Sicily, flour-and-water pasta has been made for over a thousand years, dating back to the Arab domination, and before Marco Polo was born, thus exploding the myth that it was he who brought the idea from China. When scholars talk about the first pasta in Sicily they are probably talking about busiate, which is considered to be the oldest Sicilian pasta shape. Part of the large fusilli family of spiral and twisted pasta, the name *busiate* comes from the Arabic *bus*, the name of the plant whose long, smooth and slender stems were used for both knitting and shaping pasta. The women in Vincenzo's family made busiate and other shapes of flour-and-water pasta, which were eaten straight away or dried, until the late 1950s.

Like observing well-practised hands doing arpeggios on a piano, it is hard to imagine that you will ever be able to do the same when you first see someone making fresh pasta – it is a blur of twists and rolls. Then the person slows down, the blur becomes a move and it seems more possible. Of course, your hands don't do exactly what you want them to do, and it can feel exasperating. But when you persist, the shape is a delight. I have made busiate with Fabrizia Lanza and the women of the church in Gela, none of whom still make it for their families, but their hands still know how. My hands, on the other hand, do not, yet.

I am much more comfortable with a rather more basic shape called cavatelli, which is typical of Molise but is also made all over the south. The dough is the same as for busiate: flour and water. What is so satisfying about mixing flour and water? Is it that we are transported back to our childhood, to plasticine and playdough? I am back at the table in our old house with the waxed red cloth, my brother putting dough up his nose. First the mountain, then a volcano, and into that a pool of water...

I use cavatelli as I would busiate, so with Trapanese pesto made with almonds, tomatoes and basil. It is also good with ragù, or broccoli – Romanesco, sprouting or traditional green – cooked until tender and then recooked briefly in lots of olive oil scented with garlic and a little chilli.

Make a mountain with the flour on a work surface, make a well in the centre and add 100ml water. To begin with, use a fork to incorporate the flour from the sides, then once the dough is stiff use your hands. Flour varies, as does room temperature and humidity, and so in turn does the amount of water that the flour will absorb – so add it bit by bit, being led by the feel. Once you have a soft ball, neither too sticky, nor dry, but rather tacky, knead it using the heel of your hand, rotating the ball as you go. You need to be firm and energetic. Put on the radio and swing your hips. It is ready when it is soft and smooth, which takes no less than 8 minutes. Let the dough rest under an upturned bowl or clean tea towel for 30 minutes.

There are many ways to make cavatelli: you can use a little ridged board or the tip of a rounded knife, or I use my fingers for the most primitive version. Pinch off a walnut-sized piece of dough and then, on a work surface dusted with flour, use your hands to roll it into a slim rope roughly 5mm thick, then cut it into 2.5cm-long pieces. Now put the tips of your index, middle and ring fingers on the piece of dough, press, and as you do push or flick the piece, the idea being you make three indents and the flicking action curls the dough across the board so that you have a sort of indented canoe. The first one will be odd, the second worse, but then you will get the hang of the movement. Anyone can mix flour and water, and the only way to get knowing hands is to practise, which then becomes experience. Speed will come, I'm told. Cavatelli take about 4 minutes to cook in salted water.

Brioche con tuppo
Sweet yeasted buns

Makes 10–12

100ml milk
5g dried yeast or 15g fresh yeast
500g plain flour or soft wheat
    00 flour
140g sugar
5 eggs, lightly beaten
150g soft lard or butter,
    at room temperature
sugar, for glazing
salt

A *tuppo* is a bun, which, as in English, is also the word you use to describe hair when coiled up on your head. This means you could describe Sicily's *brioche con tuppo,* or sweet yeasted breakfast bread, as a bun with a bun. The buns with buns in our local bar are almost fantastically terrible, pale things, suffocating in a plastic wrapper and tasting faintly of banana, yet another reminder of how dislocated industrialization and convenience is sweeping Sicily. Gagliano, the owner, apologizes for his brioche; once there was a bakery in Gela that made them fresh, but now he buys them in from a factory. As if to make up for the buns, the almond granita he makes and serves with the brioche is some of the best I have ever tasted: a pale, icy cream with bits of whole almond served in a wide glass on a saucer. It is a ritual so fine that I am happy to forget the brioche, almost.

In our regular bar in Catania, the brioche are comely and burnished. If I lived nearby, I wouldn't think of making brioche. But I don't; instead I dream of eating them, which prompts me to make them from time to time. Brioche need an eight-hour rise, the thought of which makes my heart sink a little, but like jumping in the water or going for a brisk walk, that doubt disappears as soon as you begin, and is replaced by the smell of yeast, then the dough. I tend to make brioche in winter – so not for serving with granita, but with milky coffee and a real newspaper.

Warm the milk until tepid and dissolve the yeast in it. Sift the flour into a bowl, add the sugar and a pinch of salt and stir. Add the milk-yeast mixture and 4 of the eggs. Mix, then add the lard or butter and work it in until the mixture is consistent. Knead firmly for 5 minutes, pausing, if you like, to lift and then throw the dough on to the work surface, which apparently helps with elasticity. Put the dough in a bowl, cover it with clingfilm and leave it to rest in the fridge for 8–10 hours.

Line a baking tray with baking parchment. Split the dough into 10 equal parts. Working one part at a time, pull off a small piece and roll it into a round ball. Shape the larger piece into a round, slightly flat ball and make an indent in the middle of the top of the larger ball. Press the small ball into the indent. Place the brioche on the baking tray and repeat with the rest of the dough. Whisk the remaining egg with a little sugar, then brush the brioche with this mixture and leave them to rise in a warm, non-draughty spot for another 75 minutes, by which time they should have doubled in size.

Preheat the oven to 180°C/160°C fan/gas mark 4. Before baking, brush the brioche with more of the egg-sugar mixture. Bake for 15–20 minutes, or until the brioche are golden.

Bread

The first thing on the table, the last thing taken off, and the final chapter in the book, but no less significant for it: bread.

We smelled Rodolfo's bakery before we found it. Cutting up one of the narrow alleys that link via Garibaldi and via Buscemi to get back home to via Mazzini, the usual lingering smells of detergent on the clothes strung out to dry from every balcony and rubbish fermenting in bags were joined by the thick scent of baking bread. But from where? The half-dozen small bakeries that, until 20 years ago, had punctuated every other street in our part of town had closed, or so we had been told. We doubled back like a trio of sniffer dogs set upon a scent, but couldn't work out where it was coming from and eventually gave up. The next day I went back to have another look. Walking around the old part of Gela can feel a bit like a game of snakes and ladders – you take alleys that seem to give you an advantage only to find yourself sliding all the way back down a long, curved road. I was ready to give up when I caught the smell again, and saw a trestle in the middle of the road. Panificio Rodolfo Placenti is easy to miss because there is nothing to see: its plain front and metal door covered with a metal curtain are no different from other houses, and the small sign is difficult to read. The scent, though, is unmistakable, with an intensity and deliciousness that pulls you through the door into a room about seven by seven metres, a third of which is occupied by the oven. The space in front of the oven functions as the shop, with a shelf that provides a home for a weighing scale and an 8cm pile of brown paper, a dresser for displaying the bread, and on top of it a Virgin Mary, her robe the richest of blues next to the white tiles, her palms open towards the loaves.

After nearly thirty years of scraping and sweeping the ashes daily from a cavernous brick oven fired by wood or almond shells, Rodolfo is finally clean. He appreciates the fact that, as he climbs the stairs between the ground-floor bakery and his house above it at the end of the day, he is no longer covered in ashes (he now heats the oven with a small cannon-like gas lighter that breathes a fierce flame into its mouth). He is clean but for a fine layer of flour that covers his whole body, making his dark skin a shade paler and resting on his eyelashes and the straps of his Scholl sandals. If he happens to put his hand on your shoulder, he leaves the faint, floury finger-mark of a baker.

Now in his late 50s, and handsome, Rodolfo has been working since he was seven. The second-youngest of ten children, his father, who worked as a clerk at the *comune* (local council), bought a house with a ground-floor bakery for his sons. Like most small family-run bakeries, which were essentially extensions of people's homes, the Placentis' was *per conto terzi*, which more or less translates as 'third-party oven': it was only licensed to bake bread, not to make or sell it – so instead they baked the bread made by local women. Larger bakeries in more prosperous towns had rooms in which the women could make the bread dough, but this one didn't, so every morning Rodolfo would be turned out of bed so that his mother could use it to prove their family's bread. He would then go out with one of his brothers to deliver a piece of *criscenti*, a small piece of dough rich with natural yeast, to each of his women. They would add this to their own flour, knead and shape their loaves – often enough for a whole week – incise each one with an initial to help identify it later, sprinkle them with sesame seeds, and then leave them, often in a bed, to prove. Now the extraordinary part, which I struggle to visualize even though he has drawn me a picture: Rodolfo would then go and collect the loaves, balancing them on wooden slats on his back, to bring them back to the oven to be baked. A couple of hours later, children (such as Vincenzo's uncle Liborio), would be sent to collect the hot bread, shoving it up their jumper to keep it, and themselves, warm in winter.

As time passed and as bread-making habits changed, the Placenti family changed their licence and became a *forno per conto proprio*, which is as proper as it sounds, and meant they could make, bake and sell their own bread. Soon almost everyone came to buy bread or had bread delivered, and only an ever-dwindling handful of families still brought their loaves to bake. These days, nobody brings bread to be baked, although the occasional lasagne, pot of beans or tray of pizza is brought in to be cooked in the residual heat.

The man-sized mixer is 25 years old, although Rodolfo can clearly remember the heavy labour of doing it by hand, and shows me the movement. One the dough is kneaded, he still cuts it by hand, dividing it into either a 250g ball for a *quartino* or 500g for a *mezzo*, and just a few 1kg loaves. For both *quartino* and *mezzo* the dough is shaped, or rather tucked, into a lozenge-shaped loaf, dusted with sesame seeds and left on planks under thick sheets to rise. Once the oven is hot enough, the trestles are brought in from the road to support the planks so that the loaves can be paddled into the oven. Roldolfo and Gisella work in the sort of harmony that comes from repetition, heel to toe and arm to loaf, with rocking movements like a dance. The paddling is repeated as Rodolfo pulls the loaves from the oven, the heat enough to make your cheeks burn. Baked loaves are upended into plastic crates, put into car boots and taken all over this part of the city, the delivery man shouting *u pani!* as he drives. His may be one of the last small bakeries in Gela, but for now Rodolfo survives, with one foot in the past and one in the present, because his bread is excellent.

Bread is everything in Gela. Even in this era of one-shop shopping, it is the one thing people do not want from a supermarket, and it is not unusual to buy bread twice a day for every meal. Everything else is the companion for the bread, which is where the word *companatico* (literally 'with bread'), comes from, and in turn gives us the words *compagno* (companion) and *compagnia* (companionship). Bread and butter; bread, butter and honey; bread, butter and anchovies; bread, olive oil and salt; bread and red wine; bread, olive oil and sugar; bread fried in a little butter or bacon fat; bread cut into cubes and dropped into warm milk with a spoonful of sugar; bread on to which you squash a very soft tomato; bread and caponata; bread to wipe the plate clean. Bread.

And then there is its eternal *compagno*: breadcrumbs. Sicilians use breadcrumbs all the time, a resourceful habit born of necessity and economy and the idea that you never, *ever* throw away bread, which is part of the fabric of their cooking.

There was never a shortage of crumbs in Vincenzo's family, with a farmer who grew wheat and a bread-making wife on one side and a grandma who ran a bakery on the other. Bread that wasn't eaten fresh wasn't seen as left over, but as an advantage that was made into softish crumbs or cut into slices and dried. These slices could be brought back to life with water, milk or oil and tomatoes, or ground into crumbs to be used as a stuffing, a coating, a topping or to stop things sticking. In Gela, fine dried breadcrumbs, which you can buy in every bakery, shop and supermarket, are called *pangrattato* or *muddica*, and they are used for everything. It was also a family habit to have a bowl of *muddica* toasted in a pan with oil on hand to serve with every sort of pasta, a habit I found quite odd until I got used to it. I don't do this often at home, but when I do Vincenzo is delighted.

The problem with breadcrumbs, of course, is that they are breadcrumbs. They gather in the rubber seal at the top of the fridge door and in between the tiles, crunching underfoot as you move around the kitchen. I sweep, but it often feels as if I am simply shunting them around our small, awkward kitchen the same way you put pennies in a coin pusher machine – hopelessly. But they are now at the scattered heart of my cooking, scattered too, through this book – you will find them in every chapter, in recipes from both kitchens, Rome and Gela. Crumbs call up English kitchens, too, and link everything: real nostalgia food, rose-tinted by time and thousands of miles. I am thinking of bread sauce made from Jane Grigson's recipe in *English Food* (in my copy there are breadcrumbs between the pages), stuffing and queen of puddings.

Sicilian hard wheat bread makes great crumbs, which isn't very helpful for those of us who don't live in Sicily. Coarse country-style loaves and sourdough do too, as does a white sliced loaf, whizzed in the food processor; use the bread you have. I make three sorts of crumbs. The first are not really crumbs, but the crustless interiors, the soft *mollica,* of a loaf, ideally a day old. These are best made by hand, tearing and crumbling the bread, or you could use a food processor. These are the crumbs I use for anchovy breadcrumbs, meatballs, *involtini,* the various vegetable patties I make each week (the method is more or less always the same: cooked vegetables mixed with crumbs, egg, some cheese, maybe a herb, moulded and then dipped in flour, egg and fine breadcrumbs, then fried). They are also the crumbs I use for bread sauce, *stracciatella* soup and queen of puddings. Any leftovers can be put in bags and stored in the freezer.

The second type is made from two-day-old bread (*pane*), both crust and crumb, which is grated (*grattato*). You could also use a processor. These crumbs are neither soft nor very dry, but somewhere in between *la mollica* and *pangrattato*. They can also be used in meatballs (although I prefer the softer type), or as a texture coating for fish or chicken *costolette*, or as a topping for baked pasta. I toast these in a little oil to sprinkle on top of pasta, but my family would prefer the much finer type for this. They can also be frozen, or baked to make the next type.

Finally there are the very fine dry crumbs, the texture of polenta or coarse sand, which you can make or buy all over the place in Sicily. They are made by leaving slices of half loaves in the sun until very dry and rock hard, then grinding them in what looks like a large coffee grinder. At home you can either toast *pangrattato* and then grind it until very fine, or toast a slice of bread and then smash it with a rolling pin. Very fine crumbs are good for a fine coating, such as for anchovies, and some people prefer a fine coating in general, so would use these where I would use coarser crumbs. These are also the crumbs to line things like cake tins, to prevent sticking. They will keep in a jar with a lid for a couple of weeks, but will stay in the rubber seal until you swish them out with a finger.

Polpette di melanzane
Aubergine patties

Serves 4

1kg (about 2 large) aubergines
100g soft breadcrumbs
50g Parmesan or salted ricotta, grated
1 tablespoon ricotta
2 tablespoons finely chopped flat-leaf parsley
50g currants (optional)
30 pine nuts (optional)
2 eggs, lightly beaten
flour, for dusting
olive oil, for frying
soft or fine dry breadcrumbs, for coating
salt and freshly ground black pepper

Roasting transforms aubergines from taut and spongy to silken, smoky and sweet. Not that the inside of a peeled roasted aubergine hints at this – it looks more like an old, rumpled dishcloth. You want to drain the unprepossessing flesh, which I do by sitting it in a colander over the sink and pressing very gently with the back of a spoon. It at this point that you might well be tempted to abandon the patties and blend the aubergine with garlic, olive oil and lemon juice to make a sort of babaganoush, all silky and incomparably rich, to spread on toast or stir through pasta. If I do make the patties I am never particularly fussy about measurements: just use a spoonful of this, a handful of that, tasting as you go. The breadcrumbs are important because they provide the substance that allows you to shape them, but you don't want the mixture to be too stout; it should feel soft and require floured or wet hands and a gentle touch. I pass the patties from hand to hand, like a ball, only gently.

Once shaped, there are three dips: flour, egg and breadcrumbs, fine ones for a crisp, consistent coating, or softer ones for a more ragged texture. Fry the patties on both sides until they are golden and crisp. They are good served with salad, or with some simple tomato sauce (see page 32 or 36).

Preheat the oven to 200°C/180°C fan/gas mark 6. Put the aubergines on a baking tray and bake them whole for 45 minutes, or until they have collapsed and are very soft inside. Remove from the oven. Once they are cool enough to handle, put them in a sieve and pull off the skin, which will leave you with soft rags. Pull the flesh apart into strips and leave it to sit for half an hour so that the liquid can drain away.

Chop the aubergine flesh roughly and put it in a bowl with the breadcrumbs, cheese, parsley, currants, pine nuts, one of the eggs, salt and plenty of black pepper. Use a spoon or, better still, your hands to mix everything into a uniform mixture.

Dust your hands lightly with flour, then shape the mixture into slightly flattened patties. Sit them on a surface lightly dusted with flour. Dip them first in the remaining egg, then in breadcrumbs. Heat 1cm olive oil in a frying pan, fry the patties on one side until a golden crust forms, then fry the other side. Drain on kitchen paper and serve hot or at room temperature.

Spaghetti ammuddicati
Spaghetti with breadcrumbs and anchovies

Serves 4

500g spaghetti
150ml extra-virgin olive oil
4 anchovies in salt or
    8 anchovies in oil, drained
100g breadcrumbs from the
    soft heart of a day-old loaf
3 tablespoons finely chopped
    flat-leaf parsley
freshly ground black pepper

Anchovy breadcrumbs are inspired. Breadcrumbs, soft or hard, as you wish (I like the soft ones), are tossed in olive oil into which you have melted anchovies. Now, you know how we are often reassured that the fishiness of anchovies will slip away like an obedient manservant, leaving just the wonderful seasoning? This is not the case here. The anchovy flavour remains indignant, its fishy saltiness producing golden crumbs that shout 'I am an anchovy breadcrumb!' Rest assured that if you hate anchovies, you will hate these breadcrumbs. If you like anchovies, I suggest that you make this for lunch tomorrow.

Bring a large pan of water to the boil, add salt and stir. Add the spaghetti and cook it until al dente.

Meanwhile, in a large frying pan over a low heat, warm the oil and anchovies for about 2 minutes, using a wooden spoon to nudge them until they dissolve into the oil. Add the breadcrumbs, increase the heat slightly and cook, continuing to nudge, until they are golden and crisp. If they are ready before the pasta, pull the pan from the heat and keep them warm.

Drain the spaghetti, mix it with the crumbs directly in the pan or – better still – in a serving bowl, toss, add the parsley and a grind of black pepper and toss again. Finish with the last few crumbs from the pan and serve.

Coniglio ripieno
Stuffed rabbit

Serves 4–6

1kg deboned rabbit
    (about 1.2kg unboned)
1 small red onion
1 tomato
3 tablespoons olive oil,
    plus extra for frying
1 tablespoon tomato purée
30g pine nuts
30g currants or sultanas
200ml white wine
about 100g soft breadcrumbs
10–12 slices streaky bacon
    or pancetta
salt and freshly ground
    black pepper

It is not just the the quality of the meat and skilled butchery that makes a visit to the Sartor butchers on Testaccio market a pleasure, but also the advice offered and the conversation passed back and forth across the glass counter. Early in the week is best, when the market is quiet and the pace slow, and cuts of meat, market and European politics can be discussed in a lively manner and advice doled out while lamb *costolette* are bashed out, or a rabbit skilfully boned.

I have always liked rabbit, the most delicate of game, and so appreciate the Italians' affection for it, and its ordinariness in butchers and on menus. If you don't eat rabbit, a boned-out chicken works well. I have watched my butcher Daniele bone a rabbit enough times to try doing it myself, but haven't. Most butchers will debone a rabbit if you ask in advance, creating a casing that begs for a stuffing, in this case is a typically Sicilian one of breadcrumbs, onion, raisins and pine nuts stained red with tomato, which works well with the sweetly savoury flesh. Once stuffed, you roll the rabbit up as you would a fat rug, cover it with bacon, which stops it drying out, and tie it tightly. It is a remarkable dish when cut into thick slices with an eye of stuffing. Well-buttered potatoes or lentils are good partners.

Spread the rabbit out on a work surface. Rub it with olive oil and season with salt and pepper.

Make the stuffing. Finely dice the onion and chop the tomato. Heat the olive oil in a pan, add the onion and cook until soft and translucent. Add the tomato, fry for 2 minutes, then add the tomato purée, pine nuts and currants and cook for 1 minute more. Add 100ml white wine and let most of it evaporate away. Now add the breadcrumbs little by little, until you have a stuffing that is neither too dry nor too damp (it should clump in your hands and stay together, but not feel too sticky).

You now have two options. Either you can spread the stuffing

over the whole of the rabbit, remembering to leave a generous empty margin near the edges. Or – my way – make a pile of stuffing, shaping it with your hands, about 7cm from the less fat end. Again, leave an empty margin, then roll the rabbit into a log shape, tucking the sides in as you go. Wrap the joint in bacon or pancetta, then tie it firmly widthways and lengthways with kitchen string.

Preheat the oven to 200°C/180°C fan/gas mark 6. Heat some more oil in a frying pan and brown the rabbit on all sides, then transfer it to a deepish roasting tin that is only a little larger than the rabbit. Put the empty frying pan back on the heat, add the remaining wine and scrape the meaty juices to dissolve them into the wine, then pour the lot over the rabbit in the roasting tin. Roast for 45 minutes; the outside should be nice and golden, but not too dark. Allow it to rest for at least 20 minutes before serving in thick slices.

Queen of puddings

Serves 6

150g soft white breadcrumbs
grated zest of 1 unwaxed lemon
    (or 2 if you really like lemon)
125g caster sugar, plus 2
    teaspoons for the crumbs
    and extra for sprinkling
550ml whole milk
40g butter
5 eggs
3–5 tablespoons raspberry jam

My enjoyment of my own culinary history has been enriched by moving away. I believe it was Sicilian breadcrumbs that helped me better appreciate English ones, one kitchen strengthening another, a ricotta, lemon and breadcrumb cake reminding me of queen of puddings. A bottom of lemony set custard, thickened with soft breadcrumbs, topped with a layer of raspberry jam and finished with a meringue hat, is quite simply one of the best puddings ever. It feels fitting then that we are finishing here, with an English pudding scented with lemon, so suggestive both of home and somewhere else, both here and there.

Preheat the oven to 160°C/140°C fan/gas mark 3 and grease a deep 25cm-diameter ovenproof dish with butter. Put the crumbs, lemon zest and 2 teaspoons sugar in a bowl and rub together with your fingertips so that the lemon zest really flavours the crumbs.

Warm the milk and butter over a low heat until the butter melts and the milk is hot but not boiling. Pour the milk over the crumbs and leave to steep for 10 minutes. Once the 10 minutes are up, separate the eggs and beat in the egg yolks (reserving the whites in a large, clean bowl).

Pour the custard mixture into the prepared baking dish. Bake for 20–30 minutes (depending on the depth of the dish), or until the custard is set on top but runny underneath. Remove it from the oven and let it sit for 5 minutes.

Meanwhile, warm the jam with 1 tablespoon water until runny, then pour or spread it over the surface of the custard. Beat the egg whites to stiff peaks, then fold in the sugar with a metal spoon. Cover the pudding with meringue, then bake for another 20 minutes, until the meringue is firm and the peaks are golden and crisp.

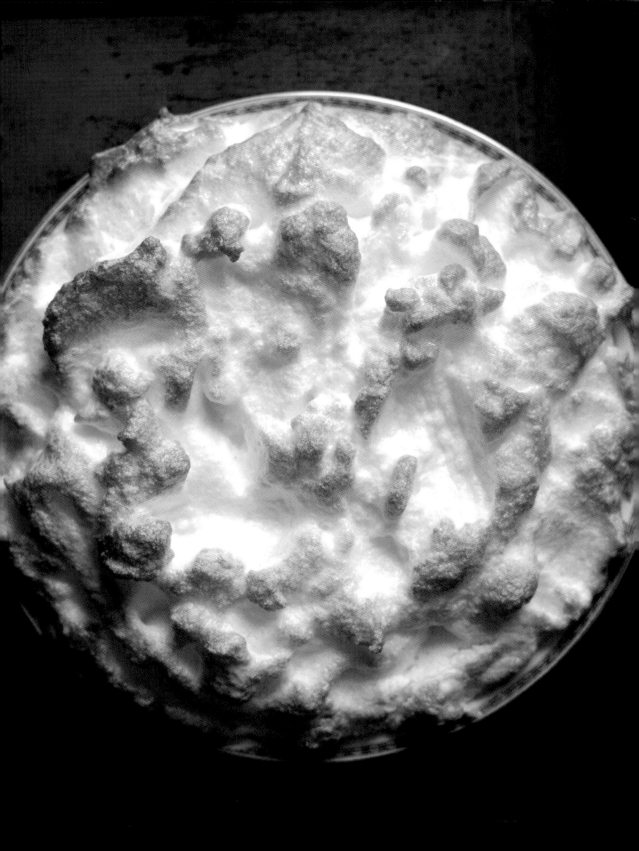

Index

Acknowledgements

This book is dedicated to Sara and Orazio D'Aleo and Lilla Venuti, whose spirits live on in recipes and stories. It is also dedicated to Vincenzo and Luca, who have eaten its contents, mostly with gusto, many times over.

Many people have shared recipes and stories with me, extended the hospitality of their homes with warmth and generosity, in particular Carla Tomasi, Cinzia Fioravanti, Bartolomeo Caristia and Carmela D'Aleo, Liborio D'Aleo and Fabrizia Lanza – thank you. Thank you.

In Sicily: Orazio, Fabio, Elio and Sara D'Aleo, Valeria Caristia, Rodolfo and Graziella Placenti, Giuseppe and Rosa, the Gagliano Family, Arianna Occhipinti, Nino Barraco, Filippo Rizzo, Rosa and Michael Malignaggi, everyone at the Anna Tasca Lanza Cooking School and the shopkeepers and stallholders of Gela. In Rome: Daniela del Balzo, Augusto and Andrea Alfonsi, Filippo, Antonio Farnella, Mauro Pierluigi, the Pucci family, the Sartor family, the stallholders of Testaccio market, Marco Morello, Sergio Esposito, the Fioravanti family, Jeremy Cherfas, Hande Leimer and Katie Parla. I would also like to thank the readers of my blog and column: I am grateful for the lively community and shared ideas.

To my publishing family: Elizabeth Hallett, Kate Miles, my tireless editor Laura Gladwin, designer Myfanwy Vernon-Hunt, thoughtful tester Linda Thompson and everyone at Headline, especially Lindsey Evans. I am grateful to work with such a creative and happy team. Thank you Nick Seaton for your pictures and friendship. To my editor at the *Guardian*, Mina Holland, and Molly Tait-Hyland at *OFM*, photographer Elena Heatherwick and the rest of the *Guardian* team. Also to my agent Jon Elek and Millie Hoskins.

Thank you too to those who advised and supported me: my family, Mum, Dad, Rosie, Ben, Paul, Kate; and my friends Alice Adams, Joanna Sutherland and Harriet Barsby. Thank you Giampiero Pelusi, Anna del Conte, Jill Norman, Felicity Cloake, Simon Hopkinson, Russell Norman, Shirley Booth, Luisa Weiss, Emiko Davies, Daniel Etherington, Leila Miller and Kitty Lindy Travers, Gillian Riley, Nancy Harmon Jenkins, Angela Frenda and finally Mary Taylor Simeti, whose book on Sicilian food has been a constant resource and inspiration.

First published in Great Britain in 2017 by HEADLINE HOME
An imprint of HEADLINE PUBLISHING GROUP

4

Cataloguing in Publication Data is available from the British Library

Hardback ISBN 978 1 4722 4841 1
eISBN 978 1 4722 4842 8

Book design by Myfanwy Vernon-Hunt, This Side
Typeset in Lettera and Lyon

Editor: Laura Gladwin
Project editor: Kate Miles
Proof reader: Annie Lee
Indexer: Caroline Wilding

Printed in Hong Kong

Headline's policy is to use papers that are natural, renewable and recyclable products and made from wood grown in sustainable forests. The logging and manufacturing processes are expected to conform to the environmental regulations of the country of origin.

HEADLINE PUBLISHING GROUP
An Hachette UK Company
Carmelite House
50 Victoria Embankment
London EC4Y 0DZ

www.headline.co.uk
www.hachette.co.uk